THE OLD
CHESTER CANAL

A history and guide

Published and edited by **Gordon Emery**
on behalf of the
CHESTER CANAL HERITAGE TRUST

Contributors

**Ray Buss, Gordon Emery, Terry Kavanagh,
Geoff Taylor, Stewart Shuttleworth and Roger Stephens** ©2005

Printed by

MASONS
PRINTGROUP
www.masonsgroup.com   tel: 01244 674433

**The printing of this book has been partially funded by the Local Heritage Initiative
supported by the Heritage Lottery Fund, Nationwide and The Countryside Agency.**

CREDITS

Thanks are due to the staff of Chester & Cheshire Archives; Chester History & Heritage Centre, especially Emma Stuart; the Grosvenor Museum, especially Simon Warburton and Hannah Crowdy; Waterways Trust Archive, especially Diane Backhouse; Chester Library; Shropshire Archives, and The National Archives at Kew.

Without the initial research of Edwin Shearing, Charles Hadfield and maps of Roger Dean, further research by Gordon Emery might not have begun.

Terry Kavanagh acknowledges the help and advice given by Jim McKeown, Boat and Engineering Manager, Waterways Trust, Boat Museum, Ellesmere Port, as well as Clive Guthrie, historian of shipbuilding on the River Weaver, with special reference to W J Yarwood & Sons Ltd, of Castle Dockyard, Northwich. He would also like to thank Joseph Boughey, canal historian, for his transcript of an audio tape sent to him by Gordon Davies of Australia in early November 1991. Also Stewart Ramsden for permission to publish the photo by T Pickthall, and Ed Walley for the photo of Waverton Mill.

Thanks are also due to Mike Penney for his photos, and Ric Turnock and Di Parker for the photo of Snowy. Geoff Taylor wishes to thank Tony Lewery for the use of his drawings and David Wain for his brochure.

Front Cover: *Chester Canal Jug* Grosvenor Museum
The Samuel Buttler named on the celebratory jug was a flour dealer who paid £10 for the freedom of the city (ie to join a guild and register his trade) on 19th October 1770. His will was registered in Chester in 1784.

Frontispiece (opposite): *Clayton boats ('Hamble', no 35 and 'Pinn', no 73) in Northgate Lock (Water Tower Lock), Chester 1937* Boat Museum Trust

CHESTER CANAL HERITAGE TRUST

The history of the Chester Canal has been curiously neglected, even though it forms the backbone of the Shropshire Union Canal. The Trust was started in 1997 by a group of people interested in the Chester Canal and heritage narrowboats. We wanted to find ways of enthusing others about them. We have five goals:

researching the history of the Chester Canal.
developing educational materials, and put on activities for all ages to explore and find out more about the canal.
supporting the use and preservation of heritage narrowboats, and the development of a floating classroom.
providing training in boat skills.
involving the community in achieving these goals through walks, talks and involvement in community events.

Funding from the Local Heritage Initiative has helped the Trust in pursuing some of these goals. It has enabled the production of this book as well as teaching materials for schools. Further information about the Trust's activities can be found on our website:; **www.chestercanalheritagetrust.co.uk**

If you would like to become a member, join in our activities or receive mailings,
e-mail: **info@chestercanalheritagetrust.co.uk**
or write to: The Membership Secretary, 26 Meadows Lane, CHESTER CH4 7BH

Charity registration number 1094394   Company number 04360134

'Towy' on the Chester Canal
Bunbury 2005
Tom Berridge steering.

(See also pages 184-6 & 299.)

Photo: Jeffrey Hall

CONTENTS

INTRODUCTION   Gordon Emery

A visitor to Chester today, standing by the quiet canal with people walking to the town, the occasional cyclist and a few painted steel boats of various lengths, could hardly imagine what a chequered history that this broad canal has had: how the project inspired the merchants and citizens of Chester over 200 years ago and then took some to the edge of bankruptcy; how it was cut through solid rock; carried pleasure trips to Beeston Castle, then fell into disrepair; how links with a major canal being cut by the famous William Jessop and Thomas Telford revived its fortunes; how it employed some of the populace, and was involved in five major company takeovers and amalgamations.

Its cutting resulted in accidents and death; thousands of tons of imports and exports travelled along it; and it gave birth to its own boatbuilding industries while supporting other major manufacturers and trades. It became a relatively fast, smooth method of travel and trade to Liverpool, a way of life for many boat families, and an early leisure enterprise before it declined with the invention of the steam railway and the diesel lorry, eventually becoming part of Britain's heritage tourism industry.

This book is about the old Chester Canal. Although references are made to the impact of the Ellesmere Canal, especially the Wirral Line to Ellesmere Port, the Birmingham and Liverpool Junction Canal (later the Shropshire Union main line), and the Manchester Ship Canal, we have merely touched on these important inland waterways except where they have influenced the immediate local scene. They are the subjects of other books. 'Canal to Llangollen' by Pellow and Bowen, 'The Shroppie' by Pellow and Bowen, and 'Canals of the West Midlands' by Charles Hadfield are recommended to readers interested in these histories and guides. Similar books to be found in the local library are listed in the SOURCES chapter, at the end of this book.

Nearly all measurements in the book are non-metric, mainly due to their historic origin, so the reader will find £ s d (pounds, shillings and pence) not £ p: likewise yards (nearly a metre each) feet or ft (30cm) and inches or in (about 2.5cm): pounds or lbs (454gm) a hundredweight or cwt (about 25 kilo) and a ton (nearly a tonne).

WHY BUILD A CANAL ANYWAY? Gordon Emery

By land ...

By the 18th century, land transport in England had improved little since Roman times. Goods had to be carried on the person (a Roman soldier had to be able to carry a hundredweight (25kg) for 20 miles a day), with barrow or handcart, on a packhorse or by waggon and horses. In 1618, King Charles I's proclamation, now at Chester Archives, against the destruction of highways would have been read in Chester by the bellman or cryer. In it, the *highways and bridges...growne into great decay'* were blamed on the practices of the *Common Carriers of this Realme, who for their singular, and private profit, doe now usually travel with cart and wagons with four wheels, drawne with Eight, Nine or Tenne horses, or more, and doe commonly therein carry, sixtie, and seventy hundredweight, at one Burden, at one time, which Burden and Weight is so great and excessive, as that the very foundations of Bridges are in many places thereby shaken and the High Wayes and causeys furrowed and ploughed up by the wheeles of the said Carts and wagons'.* Turnpike Acts and Toll Roads had improved matters but loads were still limited to a few tons although, by the mid-18th century, fly or express wagons carried loads to London in six days.

For people to travel around the kingdom the choices were to walk (often 40 miles a day), ride a horse (changing horses at inns on the way as a Mr Steele did when he visited Chester in 1818) or travel by coach. The journey from Chester to London in the early 18th century took four days, although by 1761 the first express coach or 'flying machine' to London ran from the White Lion in Northgate Street. The new coach, with

Proclamation of 1618
Cheshire RO, ZMP 1

¶ A Proclamation to reftraine the exceffiue Carriages in VVagons, and foure wheeled Carts, to the deftruction of High-wayes.

Here as Wee haue euer had fpeciall care that the Common High-wayes and Bridges, leading from place to place within this Realme, might be kept in due repaire for the eafe and good of Our louing Subiects; And obferuing of late(notwithftanding the good prouifion of Our Lawes in that behalfe made, and the conformitie and forwardneffe of Our Subiects in fo publique and neceffary a worke,) That Our High-wayes & Bridges are at this prefent growne into great decay, and very dangerous for paffage : Wee haue vpon due examination found, That the faid decaies are occafioned by the Common Carriers of this Realme, who for their fingular, and priuate profite, doe now vfually trauell with Carts and wagons with foure wheeles, drawne with Eight, Nine, or Tenne horfes, or more, and doe commonly therein carry, fixtie, and feuentie hundred weight, at one Burden at one time, which Burden and weight is fo great, and exceffiue, as that the very Foundations of Bridges are in many places thereby fhaken, and the High-wayes and caufeys furrowed and ploughed vp by the wheeles of the faid Carts and wagons, fo ouerladen, and made fo deepe, and full of dangerous flowes, and holes as neither can Paffengers trauell thereby in fafety, nor the Inhabitants or perfons by Law bound to repaire them, be able to vndergoe fo great a charge. where, heretofore all common Carriers vfually went with Carts of two wheeles onely, wherewith they could not well carry aboue twentie Hundred weight at once, or there abouts, which the Bridges, caufeys, and ordinary high-wayes did, and might well beare, without any great damage to the fame.

Wee therefore intending the reformation of the premiffes (and hauing herein taken the enormous front and rear steel springs, cut the same journey to two days. The post coach to Holyhead still took two days in the 1770's and charged £1/11/6 for inside passengers, with reductions for those willing to brave the weather on the top. Dean Jonathan Swift, author of 'Gulliver's Travels', still decried the journey to Chester:

When soon by every hillock, rut and stone,
In each other's faces by turns were thrown...
Sweet Company! next time I do protest, Sir,
I'd walk to Dublin ere I'd ride to Chester.

The end of the Journey
From 'Coaching Days
and Coaching Ways'

...and by sea

In fact, most heavy goods were transported by water wherever possible. Roman Chester had been purposely built on a river, and tiles for the roofs of the military buildings were made from clay beds ten miles upstream. Chester became a medieval port of renown: continental wine was only imported through four other English ports. It was famous for its fur trade: during 1543, one ship alone carried '1600 sheep fells, 68 dere, 69 fawne skins and 6,300 broke (badger) fells'. However the difficulties of shifting sandbanks and larger sea-going vessels meant that ships to the 'Port of Chester' anchored downstream along the Wirral shore at places such as Neston, Heswall and Parkgate. Although sailing ships had become larger and more navigable over the centuries they still succumbed to the problems of weather. They also had pirates and the press gang to worry about. In 1671 another proclamation, this time from Charles II, commanded *all masters and owners of ships to stay for their Convoy before they put to Sea.* A Chester merchant, Daniel Peck, had to send his cargo on ships of 150 tons. These were protected, in convoy, by the navy but he complained, in 1703, that *I cannot engage one Ship here for London the Masters cannot gett men to go about land because the men are certainly prest the first place they touch att.*

River travel too was subject to the vagaries of the weather. Although many rivers in England had been canalised with towpaths and locks, to carry goods on rivers with strong currents in winter was a dangerous business, while towpaths were regularly washed out. Thomas Steers (Mayor of Liverpool in 1739) had built Liverpool Dock in 1715 and canalised the Weaver, and the Mersey & Irwell. These took much of Chester's trade. The Dee was later canalised with good towpaths by Act of Parliament in 1732, but the new cut never reached its proposed depth of 16 feet (5 metres). It was claimed that the company cutting the canalised river were more interested in the sale of land at Sealand and along the river's former course than in river trade.

The first canals

Canals had been built in the ancient world. The Egyptians extended the navigable Nile. The Romans built canals, including Foss Dyke from Lincoln to the River Trent. They also cut canals to drain the fens, although drainage was not completed until (Sir) Cornelius Vermuyden cut a further series of dykes and channels in the 17th century. Locally, In Dyserth on the North Wales coast, the Romans cut a long channel to transport water to their lead mines. Around the time of the Battle of Chester, in the early seventh century, China was completing the Grand Canal, over a thousand miles long. Before William beat Harold and conquered England, the Dutch had put in a single lock on a canal and went on to build a double lock by 1373. With long inland rivers and lakes, medieval Europe sent 85% of its goods by water, even though the towns along the way charged heavy tolls. In England, a native of Denbigh and a master goldsmith, (Sir) Hugh Myddelton realised the value of canals for carrying water. At his own expense he pioneered London's water supply with 'the new river', a 38 mile waterway from springs in Hertfordshire to the city of London, completed in 1638. While the Fire of London was raging, Louis XIV of France was giving his royal ordinance to the Canal du Midi, a ship canal (nowadays too small to carry ships and used mainly as an inland waterway)150 miles long, ten metres wide and two deep, from the Atlantic to the Mediterranean across the south of the country.

An English cut

It was Henry Berry, a pupil of Thomas Steers, who built the first proper English canal by completing the Sankey Brook Navigation from St Helens in 1761 (with branches added later). However, it was the Duke of Bridgewater's canal from Worsley to Manchester, completed in 1762, and later extended, by his engineer James Brindley, that fired the imagination of the English and set in motion an outstanding era of canal building. This Bridgewater Canal halved the cost of coal for the textile industry in Manchester. Several canal plans followed: there were seven Acts of Parliament in 1772 alone. These early canals led to what has been called 'canal mania' with 42 Acts over the first five years of the 1790s. A nationwide system of canals, linking town, city and countryside was, it was believed, a sustainable and profitable new form of transport that would last for centuries. Furthermore, any person, town or city that did not catch on to the idea quickly would be left with little profit and even less trade. When the Trent and Mersey (the Grand Trunk) Canal was proposed there were many who wanted to get in on the act.

Georgian Chester

Chester in the mid-18th century had lost much of its sea trade to Liverpool, or rather its trade had not increased with the general increase in transatlantic or world trade, although a hundred ships a year still used the port of Chester. Each week the Adam's Weekly 'Courant' ran advertisements for cargo ships to London, Bristol, Dublin, the North Wales Coast and Liverpool.

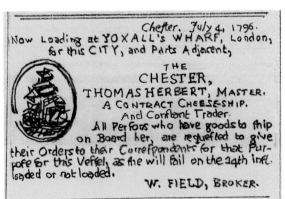

Shipping Advert
transcription
from the 'Courant'

As the county town of Cheshire, many merchants and craftsmen lived in the city. There were regular markets. An Improvement Act of 1761 forbade the dumping of *Ashes, Rubbish, Soil, Timber, Bricks, Stone, Slates, Coals, Dirt, Dung, Filth, Casks* and *Tubs* in the city streets.

The landed gentry from Cheshire, Shropshire and North Wales had town houses in the city and were building more. The winter season, and even the summer, had a series of balls, recitals, concerts, theatrical performances and lectures. A typical advert from the 'Courant' dated 27th April1772 proclaimed that:

It is proposed to have a
Masqu'd BALL and SUPPER
In the Great Room at the EXCHANGE
On one of the Evenings in the ORATORIA WEEK
Subscribers only to be admitted
Every Person subscribing one Guinea to be entitled
to one Gentlemen and two Ladies tickets

However, not everyone could afford a ticket. Compare the price of the evening's entertainment with some of the figures in the Council's treasurers' accounts in the years 1769 and 70 and the divide between rich, poor, homeless and criminal becomes evident:

City Waits, annual fee £2/-/-   [these official street singers would usually get tips as well]
Cryer £1/6/8   [his year's wages would be boosted by market tolls and cries for traders etc]
Beadle, in quarterly payments £8/-/-
   [The Beadle would regularly receive extra money such as:]
To the Beadle by Mr Mayor for Whiping a Vagrant £-/1/-
2 labourers 3 days £-/11/3
Sweeping 2 chimneys £-/-/8
Two labourers seven days each levelling the ditch through Cow Lane Gate £-/14/-
Joseph Taylor for repairing the gallows £-/10/6
Paid the Fee on transporting Appleton for Felony £5/-/-
   [a further fee had to be paid to get Appleton to Bristol before he took his enforced emigration.]

Visitors used the city of Chester as a destination and a stopover on their journeys, especially to Ireland. They perambulated the walls and went to the races. In 1741 Handel had stayed at the Golden Falcon in Northgate Street for three days while he waited for 'unfavourable winds' to subside, allowing him to complete his trip to Dublin. Whilst he waited he drank coffee at the Exchange Coffee House in the Town Hall square and practised his new work, The Messiah, in Chester Cathedral.

The Exchange: *Chester's town hall built in 1698 during the reign of King William and Queen Anne. In 1756 the west side gave way and Mr Turner, an architect, was called from Whitchurch to look at it. This was probably the Joseph Turner later associated with the Chester Canal. Canal meetings were sometimes held here.*

The Exchange was destroyed by fire in 1862 and was replaced by the current Town Hall, built at the side of the square, in 1869. The statue of Queen Anne was saved and placed on Bonewaldesthorne's Tower at the northwestern corner of the city walls, above the canal basin but later fell off and the pieces were carried away by council workmen.

Old engraving

12

THE GRAND PLAN Gordon Emery

Early beginnings

Thousands of years ago the course of the glacial River Dee once turned south where Chirk is now and joined the valley where the River Severn now runs, but after sedimentary deposits were laid it turned north to find a new exit into the Dee estuary. The present day Severn, meanwhile, is said to have its source south of Hanmer in Wrexham.

Little wonder then, that as early as 1674, Andrew Yarranton, in a survey of the River Dee, suggested that if the river were to be made navigable upstream (south) it could be used to convey goods via the Severn, Avon and Thames to London. To do this, canals would have had to link the rivers across land. Nearly a century later, in 1762, James Brindley, once he had built the Bridgewater Canal, *set out for Chester and Shropshire survey or a raconitering*, according to his diary. He had with him a sketch map of a continuation of the Dee southwards past Whitchurch. In the same year he attended the Pentice (Chester's medieval 'town hall' attached to St Peter's Church) but no records of his conversations with the council survive. Four years later, in 1766, the Bill for the Trent & Mersey Canal went to Parliament, and, the same year, John Chamberlaine, a Chester merchant from lower Watergate Street, realised that the Trent and Mersey Canal would divert traffic away from Chester to the Mersey. In 1768 a Richard Whitworth published a pamphlet at Chester entitled, 'A serious threat to the Citizens and Merchants of Chester' suggesting that the T&M Canal would take all the trade from the city. He too suggested a southward waterway but he suggested a canal via Pulford to Holt and then Whitchurch and eventually to Shrewsbury and the Severn.

The Pentice: Chester's medieval 'town hall' leaned on St Peter's Church. This drawing is based on a sketch by J Turner who rebuilt the Inner Pentice in 1794. Brindley visited it in 1762.
Sketch: Gordon Emery

The Proprietors

In all, council officials, merchants and the local aristocracy must have discussed a canal from Chester for several years, and at some time in 1768 decided to form a company to ensure Chester's inland waterway. The first shareholders of the Chester Canal were led by Lord Grosvenor, Thomas Grosvenor and William Egerton (of Tatton Hall, a cousin of the Duke of Bridgewater) who all signed up for the maximum 10% of the total share at £4000 each. Other shareholders included the Rev'd W Bootle for £3,000, B Lloyd Esq. for £1,000, Mr Partington and Mr Vigars for £1400 each. Dr Peploe, Chancellor of Chester Cathedral, let himself in for £2000 while James Folliot who owned six Chester ships and John Chamberlaine, mentioned earlier, the Hon Thomas Cotgreave of St John Street as well as doctors Denton, and Haygarth all signed up. On 27th September 1768, having already had surveys carried out from Chester to Middlewich, Mr Richardson, one of the shareholders who was a Chester banker, silversmith and ex-mayor together with Mr Brock, a lawyer and Town Clerk of Chester, travelled to Wolsley Bridge on behalf of the new Proprietors of the Chester Canal to meet the Proprietors of the T&M Canal, and asked their proprietors to help them extend the canal to Chester. Notices in the 'Courant' followed:

Navigation from the Trent to the Mersey
Fifteen proprietors or more appoint a Special Meeting of the said proprietors to be held in the old Roe-buck in Newcastle under Lyme in the County of Stafford on Thursday 27th October next at Eleven of the Clock in the Forenoon in order to consider the proposals for making a Navigable Cut from the city of Chester to join this Navigation when the Plans and drawings of the said intended Cut will be laid before proprietors.

It appears that no great opposition was put up at this meeting apart from the position at which the canals might join, so another Special Meeting followed attended by Richardson, Brock, Cotgreave and Latham, Surveyor for the Port of Chester, (for which they jointly received expenses of £10-14-3). No trace of the result has been found, but clearly the Chester Proprietors took the matter forward, for on 14th November another notice appeared in the 'Courant'.

The Canal Navigation
An Application to Parliament for an Act to make a Navigable Canal from this City to unite near Middlewich with the Canal now carrying on from the Trent to the Mersey, being speedily intended, and it being proposed that the same shall be the perpetual Property of those who subscribe in Shares not less than £200 nor more than £4000. Such persons as are inclinable an Undertaking to subscribe, and to promote so promising

to future Advantage, and to facilitate an interior Commerce within the kingdom, are desired by the Right Worshipful Mr Mayor, and by the right Honourable Lord Grosvenor, to meet at the Inner Pentice in this City on Friday the 25th Day of this Instant November, by Eleven in the Forenoon, when the Subscription is intended to be finally closed. W Hall Deputy Town Clerk.

The 1769 petition

The City Council Assembly minutes for 5th January 1769 show that the City affixed their seal to the petition to Parliament while an invoice from one Will Hebrew, dated 24th August 1769 for five guineas, shows that he sent petitions to Dublin, Wolverhampton, Birmingham, Burslem, Sheffield and the Counties of Flint, Denbigh and the Isle of Anglesey, as well as *getting the Petition to our members [MPs] signed by above 600 of the Citizens.*

Despite this, the application appears to have failed. No records of it or the *map engraved on a large copper plate* have been found (unless the same map was used at a later date), however a letter of 11th April 1769 from James Brindley to Mr Richardson sending an account for surveying he says that, *"I have not charged anything for myself, as your bill did not go forward..."*

The Chester Proprietors were not deterred.

A cunning plan

On the 19th and 26th June 1770 adverts appeared in the 'Courant':

Chester Canal Navigation
A general meeting of the present Subscribers, and all others willing to promote the Undertaking will be held at the Pentice, in Chester, on Monday the Second Day of July next at Eleven O'Clock, to consider of the proper Method of carrying the Plan into Execution.

The fourteen members present at the meeting resolved *to Proceed to Parliament ye next Sessions with ye most perfect Confidence that Ld Grosvenor + ye Members will be pleased to Continue their Subscriptions + give Ye Still Ye most effectual assistance...*

At another meeting a fortnight later, also at the Inner Pentice, it was noted *that Lord Grosvenor and the Members expressing their desire by Mr Vigars of continuing their Subscriptions and*

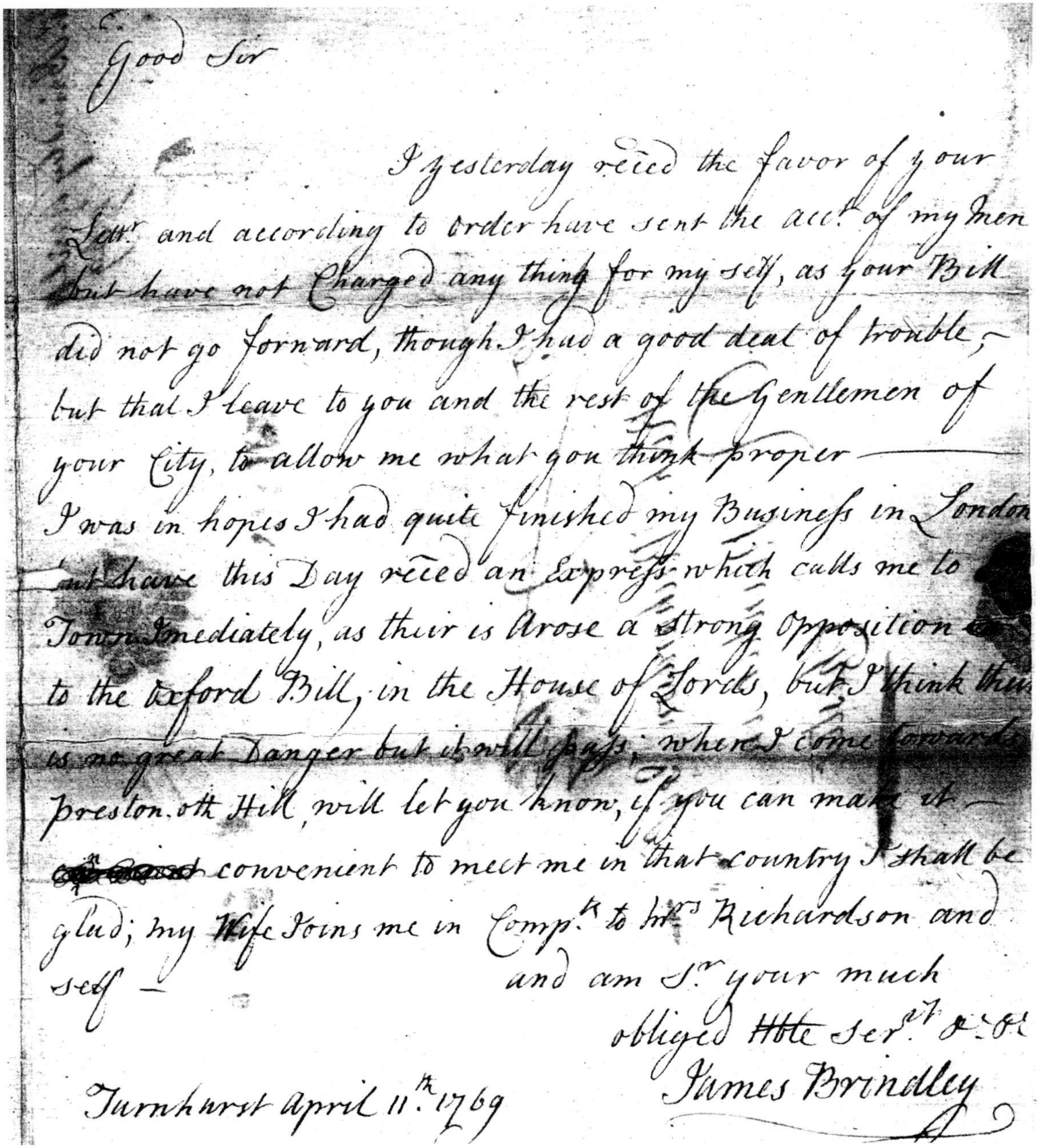

Good Sir

I yesterday rec'd the favor of your Lett'. and according to order have sent the acc't. of my men but have not Charged any thing for my self, as your Bill did not go forward, though I had a good deal of trouble, but that I leave to you and the rest of the Gentlemen of your City, to allow me what you think proper ———

I was in hopes I had quite finished my Business in London but have this Day rec'd an Express which calls me to Town Imediately, as their is Arose a strong Opposition to the Oxford Bill, in the House of Lords, but I think there is no great Danger but it will pass, where I come forwards preston. oth Hill, will let you know, if you can make it convenient to meet me in that country I shall be glad; my Wife Joins me in Comp't to M'rs Richardson and self ——

and am S'r your much obliged Hble ser't &c.

James Brindley

Turnhurst April 11th 1769

Brindley's letter to Richardson

Cheshire RO, Z/TAV/55

16

going into Parliament when the amount of Estimate be filled up. It is ordered that the Expences hitherto Incurred be defrayed... This sleight of hand ensured that new subscribers would pay for the previous failure to obtain an Act of Parliament.

The 1771 Petition

Another notice in the 'Courant' on 21st August 1770 advertised a meeting on the 31st *to open a Subscription* and *to appoint a Committee* to apply for an Act of Parliament. An *accurate Survey* and *an estimate* would be produced. A later advert stated that at this meeting *near TWENTY THOUSAND POUNDS were subscribed.*

Regular meetings followed with a committee of 13 members who had subscribed at least £500 each. On 11th September it was decided that Sam Weston should survey the intended course of the canal to Middlewich. In October, Walden and Potts decided not to continue as the Company's solicitors with William Turner taking over (Walden & Potts later became solicitors for the Ellesmere Canal Co.). At the meeting of 11th December it was agreed that Mr Latham was to go to London to promote the Bill, for which he was to be paid 30 guineas and a further 10 guineas expenses.

Despite initial plans in May 1770 to join the Dee a mile south of the city and later suggestions to join a mile north of the city at *Beach [Bache] Pool*, it was finally decided to take a course directly under the north wall of the city. At the City Assembly on 17th January 1771 *upon the Motion of John Chamberlaine on behalf of himself and certain Undertakers for Consent of this House to make a Navigable Cut or canal through Quarry croft under the Hospital Garden, the Northgate Garden, the House of Correction Garden near the North City Wall. It is Ordered that a Committee of the Whole House do meet at the Pentice on Thursday Morning next at ten o'Clock and Proceed from thence to View that part of the tract of the Intended Canal... and consider whether any of the Public Buildings, belonging to the Corporation is likely to be injured by such a Canal.* At the following council meeting Mr Golborne, for the city, reported that if the canal was kept four yards distant from the walls there was no probability of the Northgate or the City Wall receiving damage.

On the 31st January the Assembly *Ordered that the Common Seal of this City Be affixed to a Petition in Aid to Parliament for Promoting the design of the Subscribers to Obtain an Act of Parliament Impowering them to make a Navigable Cut or Canal from this in the County of Chester there to Communicate with the Canal now carrying on from the Trent to the Mersey, upon the said Subscribers entring into such a Bond ... as the Recorder shall approve of; to Indemnify this Incorporation...*

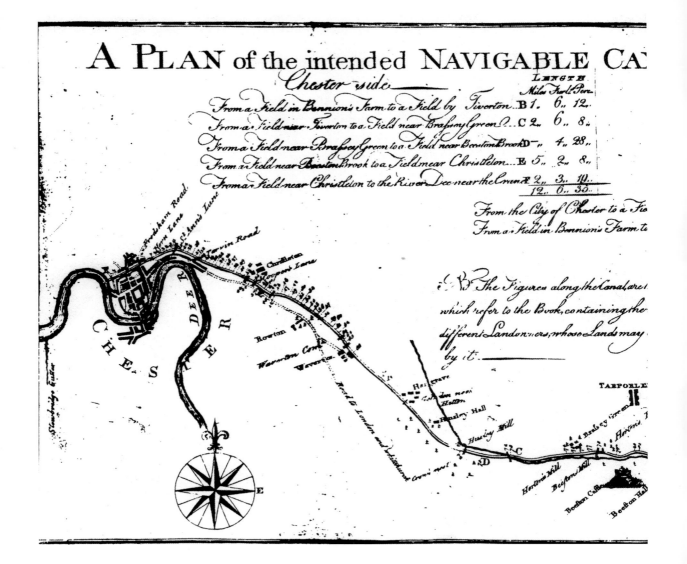

A PLAN of the intended NAVIGABLE CA[NAL]

Chester side ————

| | LENGTH |
| | Miles Fur. Perc. |
| From a Field in Bennion's Farm to a Field by Tiverton.. B 1. 6 .. 12 .. |
| From a Field near Tiverton to a Field near Brafsey Green.. C 2 .. 6 .. 8 .. |
| From a Field near Brafsey Green to a Field near Beeston Brook D .. 4 .. 28 .. |
| From a Field near Beeston Brook to a Field near Christleton.. E 5 .. 2 .. 8 .. |
| From a Field near Christleton to the River Dee near the Crane Æ 2 .. 3 .. 19 .. |
| 12 .. 6 .. 35 .. |

From the City of Chester to a Fie[ld]
From a Field in Bennion's Farm t[o]

N B The Figures along the Canal, are [those]
which refer to the Book, containing the
different Landowners, whose Lands may [...]
by it. ————

18

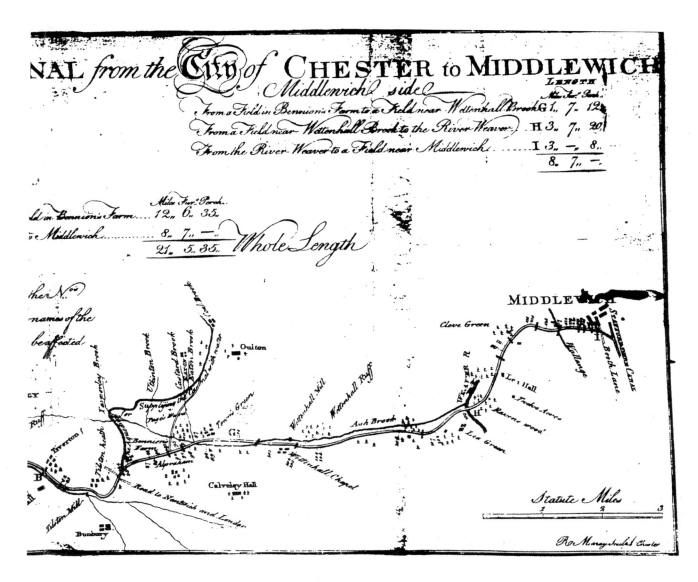

NAL *from the* City *of* CHESTER *to* MIDDLEWICH

Middlewich side

LENGTH

Mile. Fur: Perch.

From a Field in Bennion's Farm to a Field near Wettenhall Brook . . . . G 1 „ 7 „ 12

From a Field near Wettenhall Brook to the River Weaver . . . . H 3 „ 7 „ 20

From the River Weaver to a Field near Middlewich . . . . . . I 3 „ — „ 8

8 „ 7 „ —

Miles Fur: Perch.

...ld in Bennion's Farm . . . . 12 „ 6 „ 35

...e Middlewich . . . . 8 „ 7 „ —

21 „ 5 „ 35 *Whole Length*

The intended Canal to Middlewich

Cheshire RO Z/QRP/3

19

The application for *A navigable canal from the River Dee to Middlewich* took three months to pass through the House of Commons. A petition in favour from *merchants trading to Dublin* was read in February followed by the petition from Chester. A petition from the Proprietors of the T&M Canal was read against the bill, and battle commenced. Back in Chester it was decided to send Mr Chamberlaine and Mr Folliot to London to give evidence. Samuel Weston also appeared.

Although the Dee had been canalised to secure sea trade to Chester, a rather spurious argument was used in Parliament by Thomas Lane, Secretary to the Dee Navigation Improvement Committee: *That the said Navigation from the City of Chester to the sea, has been completed at an Expense of more than £80,000; but for want of an Inland Conveyance by Water, to and from the said City the Inhabitants therof, and the Interior Part of the Country cannot fully enjoy the Advantages of the said Navigation.*

Before the Commons committee, Weston stated that he had been an *Engineer Three Years* under James Brindley as a staffholder and in levelling. He *had Levelled for the Chester Gentlemen about Two Years ago*, and that he *had undertaken Twenty-six miles of Cutting upon the Leeds Canal.* Although he had *no experience of making locks,* he had made *arches of three, four and six feet.* He had *made nearly Four Miles of the Leeds Canal, set it out, and did the Whole.* He had never *Carried a Navigation over a River* although an aqueduct would be required *One hundred Yards long and Sixty Feet high from the Water* as well as *One hundred and Twenty Yards of tunnelling.* He had no experience of valuing land but *followed Farming. Mr Brindley's agents have acquainted him with the Expence of making Locks.* His estimate for the canal was £32,650.

John Lingard gave evidence that the landowners of 14 miles of the intended course had signed their consent and produced the map and field book of owners' names (now held at Chester Archives). James Folliot stated that a great trade went from Chester by sea and this trade could double with a canal. A thousand bales of cloth were sent annually from Gloucestershire via Shrewsbury at about 2/- per cwt (approx. 50 kg) and this could go by canal. Ships regularly plied the route to Dublin, 13 constantly, including six of his own. John Latham stated that without a canal the Dee navigation would only serve Chester. John Chamberlaine enjoyed great trade in Chester but if a canal (the T&M) were to go to Liverpool and none to Chester they would be ruined. Besides Chester paid £15,000 pa in customs to the King.

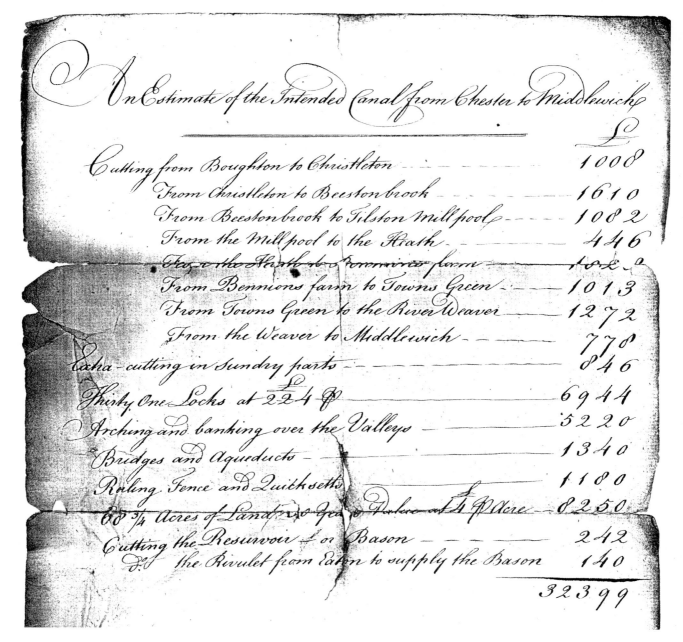

An Estimate of the Intended Canal from Chester to Middlewich

	£
Cutting from Boughton to Christleton	1008
From Christleton to Beestonbrook	1610
From Beestonbrook to Tilston Millpool	1082
From the Millpool to the Heath	446
From the Heath to ~~Bennions~~ farm	18??
From Bennions farm to Towns Green	1013
From Towns Green to the River Weaver	1272
From the Weaver to Middlewich	778
Extra cutting in sundry parts	846
Thirty One Locks at 224 ℔	6944
Arching and banking over the Valleys	5220
Bridges and Aqueducts	1340
Railing Fence and Quicksetts	1180
68 ¾ Acres of Land &c at £ ℔ Acre	8250
Cutting the Resurvoir or Bason	242
D.o the Rivulet from Eaton to supply the Bason	140
	32399

Samuel Weston's estimate of the canal to Middlewich

Cheshire RO, Z/TAV/55

21

In March 1771 a petition from Northwich to protect the Weaver Navigation was read against the bill. The Chester Canal minute book records that supporting petitions were to be collected from the potters and manufacturers in Burslem and the Cheshire towns of Nantwich, Middlewich and Winsford. These were presented to Parliament at the end of March, together with one from North Wales. The Bill moved through with a comfortable 46/29 majority at its Second Reading and was eventually passed to the Lords. There, after dispute about the Chester Canal joining the T&M Canal, it was ignominiously thrown out at its Second Reading.

The Proprietors were still not deterred.

Canal mania

In March and April a meeting was advertised for the 1st May at The Talbot, (now The Grosvenor) noting that subscriptions still remained open. The Proprietors (once again) agreed to adopt the existing subscriptions and formed a new committee. On the 19th August a further meeting in the Talbot was advertised for the 23rd; *in the meantime any Gentleman desirous of promoting this beneficial Scheme... may, by applying to Mr Walter Thomas or Mr John Chamberlaine, be informed of all Particulars relating thereto.* Sam Weston was to survey beyond Tilstone Heath. The canal was now to go to Nantwich and Middlewich.

CANAL NAVIGATION
Chester, Sept. 13th 1771

At a General Meeting of the Subscribers to this Undertaking, and others, held at the Exchange this Day, It was resolved to apply to Parliament in the ensuing Sessions, for an Act to make a Navigable Canal from this City to Middlewich, and there to join the Staffordshire Canal, and also to make A Branch from the Same, at or near Tilstone-Heath in Nantwich, in this County, and that a Survey of the said Branch be immediately taken.

Notice is hereby given, to all Noblemen, Gentlemen, Traders, and others, inclined to promote a Plan, so absolutely requisite to preserve the trade of this City and Neighbourhood, and that will be attended with the most general Advantages, that the Proposals and Subscription Paper now lie at Mr. Walter Thomas's.

The General Heads of the Bill that is intended to be brought into Parliament, are in the Hands of the Clerk of the Peace for the County, for the Inspection of any Gentleman, Landowners, and others, who may be interested in the Event.

'Courant' Sep 17 & Oct 1st

Estimates of cutting the canal had risen to £42,000, (although it eventually cost double that). As well as the early shareholders, the societies and guilds or companies of Chester subscribed another £2,000. According to one writer, *the good folks of Chester appear to have thought that their fortunes were about to be made... almost everyone that could by any means scrape together a hundred pounds was anxious to embark in this golden scheme by purchasing a share in it.* Actually cash was only to be called for in amounts of up to 10% at a time and the work was intended to take up to 4 years, with cash calls spread over the period.

In order to convince potential shareholders, and persuade landowners to give consent to the cut, some of the reasons for the canal appeared in a 'Courant' article on 17th September and another in the first October issue where they were set out in great detail, starting with a general polemic of the wealth of nations:

> *To the Printer of the CHESTER 'Courant'*
>
> *SIR*
>   *By giving the following a Place in your Paper you will much oblige*
>   *Yours, &c*

A WELL-WISHER TO NAVIGATIONS
General Advantages of Inland Navigations

WHEN Designs of great Expence and Importance are under consideration, the Advantages resulting from them to the Public in general, and to those who are more immediately concerned in their Success, should be first ascertained; and then impartially balanced against the Injuries and Inconveniences, if there be any, affecting the Properties and Pleasures of Individuals.

It is a maxim well-established by political Enquirers, that the Power of Nations, other Circumstances being alike, is always in proportion to the Number of their inhabitants, and the Abundance of their Wealth.

Those Nations that remain still in their first State of Nature, and subsist alone by Hunting, are of all others the most thinly peopled . Pasturage, by increasing the Sustenance of Mankind, increases their Numbers. Agriculture for the same Reason, still further, contributes to render a Country populous.

And lastly Trade, by bartering Manufactures for food, the Labour of the Hand for the fruits of the Earth, will to an inconceivable Degree further add population to a well-cultivated Country...

The article continued with a number of reasons why the canal should be cut:

That Inland Navigations have a tendency to facilitate and increase the commerce, and consequently to add to the Riches and Population of a Country, will evidently appear from a due Attention to the following Particulars.

The first and most obvious Effects of inland Navigation...they greatly diminish the Price of Carriage, and open east Communications between the distant Parts of the Country and from each of their Ports to the Sea...

... do not only greatly promote the Manufactures where they are already established... but occasion the Establishment of many new ones, in Places where the Lands before were of little Value ...

These Communications by Water, also greatly contribute to the Benefit of the Merchants, who reside at the Ports where they terminate , by enabling them to export greater Quantities of Goods from those Parts which lie at a Distance from the Sea; and to supply a much larger Space of Country with their Returns from Abroad.

An example of sea trade growth was given:

In the Reign of Queen Elizabeth, a Survey was taken...the largest Vessel at Liverpool was but of Forty Tons Burthen... and the whole amount but Two Hundred and Twenty-three tons. At present there are about Five Hundred Vessels belonging to it ; and each Vessel, on an Average, may be supposed to carry One Hundred and Fifty tons: so that the Quantity of Shipping in two centuries, has increased as two hundred and sixty-nine to one...

The long article continued with the advantages of not keeping so many horses and their food supply; advantages to merchants and landed gentry; the discovery and transport of minerals; the cultivation of waste lands; movement of manure; and support of villages and their inhabitants. The water itself, it was reasoned, was an obvious benefit to farmers in periods of drought while the low price of food would benefit the poor.

At the City Council on 24th October, John Chamberlaine's motion was accepted and it was ordered that the thanks of the Corporation be given to the Rt Hon Lord Grosvenor, Thomas Grosvenor and Richard Wilbraham Esqs for their service in favour of the late application for making a navigable canal. They were to be requested to endeavour to obtain an Act in the ensuing Parliamentary Session.

The argument to Landholders, against *some old Curmudgeon grumbling ... that so much good land should be spoiled* was put out in the 'Courant' on October 29th:

Let us suppose that the whole Extent in the intended Canal from Chester to Middlewich, and the Branch to Nantwich, to be 27 Miles, the land that would be covered with Water would not exceed two Cheshire Acres per Mile; but to reduce this into Statute Measure, and to include the Land occupied by Towing Paths, it amounts to altogether to six Statute Acres and a Half per Mile, which in the whole Course will require 175 Statute or 82 Cheshire Acres.

Upon a moderate Calculation of the Goods that will pass upon this intended canal, were they to be conveyed by Land Carriage, they would employ about 800 Horses per Year; now allowing one Horse to draw 20 Tons on the Canal, the same Distance, and in the same Time, was the Distance by the Canal and the Road equal, it would require no more than 20 horses to convey the same Quantity of Goods; but we will allow 25 horses. The Balance of Accounts in Favour of the Canal will stand as follows, viz,

Carriage at five Statute Acres per Horse ---	Acres 4000
Land to maintain 25 Horses, to convey the said Goods on the Canal--- Acres 125	
Land occupied by the Canal and its Banks, 27 Miles,	
at six Statute Acres and a Half per Mile Acres 175	
	300
Saving to the Public by the Canal,	Acres 3700

And if we allow three Statute Acres to keep a cow, this 3725[sic] Acres of Land would maintain 1241 cows yearly, or grow a very considerable Quantity of Corn for the Use of Man.

Another article about the proposed canal's advantages on November 26th provided comparison tables of fees that would operate if all the canals were linked:

	By the Road				By the Canal		
	Miles	Hours	£ s d		Miles	Hours	£ s d
Nantwich	20	11	1 0 0		18	8	0 3 0
Oxford	145	83	6 10 0		175	70	1 9 2

It also stated that the full cost (capital) would be £41,000 with an income from tonnage (toll or tax) of £3,800 yearly, deductions for repairs and salaries £650 pa leaving *the neat income of £3,150 which is Seven and a Half per Cent per Ann, upon the Capital.*

In another call for subscribers, on December 31st the 'Courant' advertised that:

...the Course of the Canal to Middlewich and to Nantwich having been lately accurately surveyed by Mr Thomas Yeoman, Engineer, of London... the said undertaking may be completed for the sum of £40,800.

Mr. Richard Richardson's Disbursements on Acct. of

1768		
Sept. 25	To Travelling Expences To Worsley Bridge in Compa: with Mr. Brock	12. 1. 1
Oct. 18	To Travelling Expences To Frodsham & Northwich To meet Mr. Brindley	3. 1. 7
26	To Travelling Expences To Newcastle in Company with Mr. Latham & Mr. Brock	13. 17. 1
Nov. 5	To Expences of a Journey To Whitton	5. 6
7	To Expences of a Journey To Whitton with Mr. Colgreave	5. 6
18	To a Messenger & his Expences To Fetch Mr. Brindley	1. 2.
26	To Expence of a Journey in Company with Mr. Brindley out 6 Nights	5. 1. 3
30	To paid for Wire To make a Chain	1. 7
Dec. 2	To paid Expence of a Journey To Trentham in Compy. with Mr. Brock. Mr. Colgreave & Mr. Latham	10. 1. 3
6	To paid Mr. John Varley a Bill of Expences upon The Survey from Oct. 13. To Dec. 5th	20. 11. 6
	To paid Mr. Saml. Weston a Bill for Surveying 18 days At 2/6 p day — 2.5.0 taking a plan 1.11.6	3. 16. 6
17	Paid Richard Hockrell for Attending ye Surveyors	9. —
27	Paid for Parchment for Petitions	3. 1
1769		
Jany 3	Paid a Messenger & his Expences To fetch Mr. Brindley	1. 3. —
4	Paid for Parchment & Postage	11. 3
14	Paid Postage of Petitions	3. 9
21	Paid Mr. Thomas Allen a Bill of Travelling Expences upon The Survey from Dec. 8 To Jany 21	16. 7. 2
	Paid Jas. Conway Assisting The Surveyors & Horse hire	3. 1. 6
Feby 10	Paid for mending a Theodolite	3. 6
Apl. 3	Paid for Postage of The Irish Petition	1. 6
	Continued —	103. 17. 1

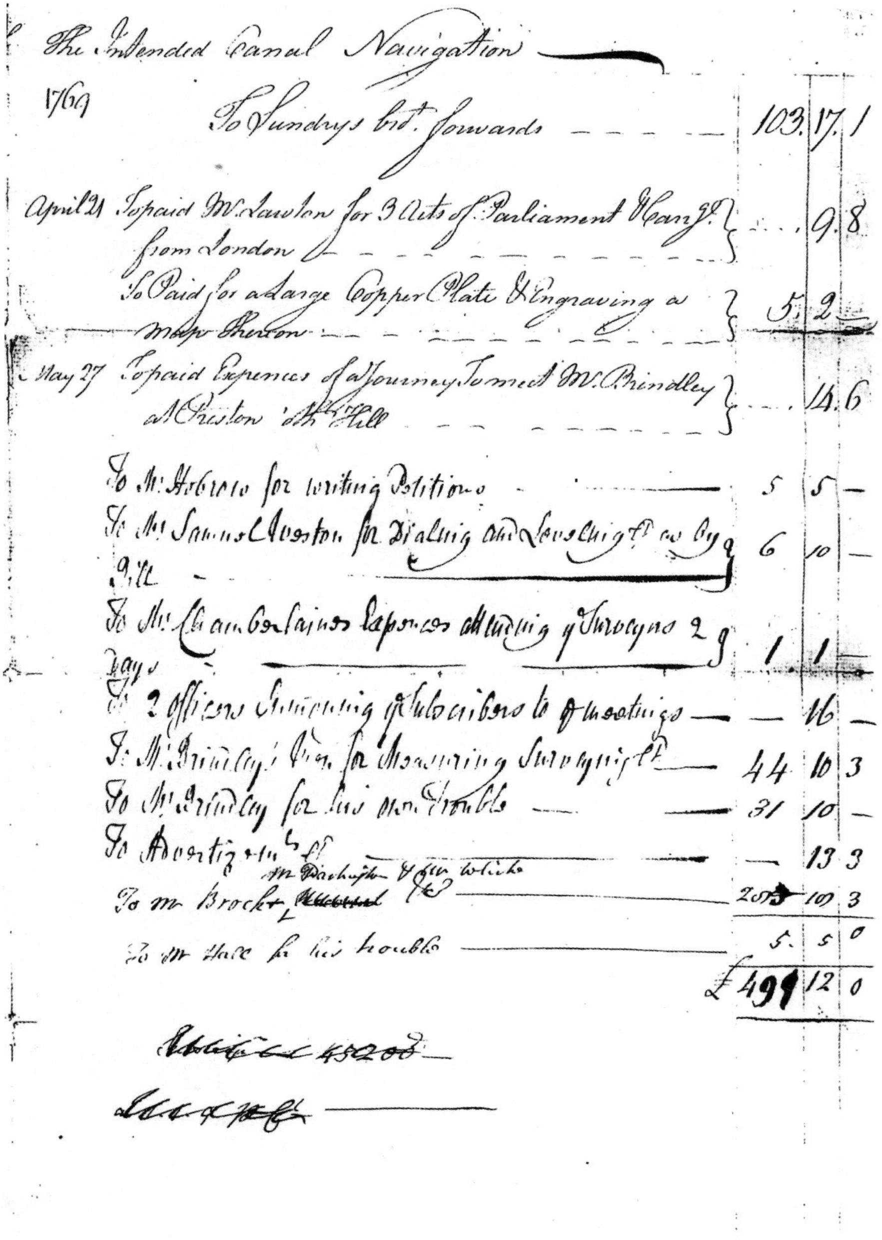

The Intended Canal Navigation ⸺

1769   To Sundrys bt. forwards ⸺   103. 17. 1

April 21   To paid Mr Lawton for 3 Acts of Parliament &c an[swer?]   . 9. 8
     from London

     To Paid for a Large Copper Plate & Engraving a   5. 2. —
     Map thereon ⸺

May 27   To paid Expences of a Journey To meet Mr. Brindley   . 14. 6
     at Preston dth Hill

     To Mr Holcroe for writing Petitions ⸺   5. 5. —

     To Mr Samuel Weston for Dealing and Leveling &c as by   6. 10. —
     a/n.

     To Mr Chamberlaines Expences Attending ye Surveyors 2   1. 1. —
     days

     To 2 Officers Summoning ye Subscribers to ye meetings ⸺   . 16. —

     To Mr Brindleys Men for Measuring Surveying &c   44. 10. 3

     To Mr Brindley for his own Trouble ⸺   31. 10. —

     To Advertizing &c   13. 3
       Mr Dachyfe & for white

     To Mr Brock &c   203. 10. 3

     To Mr Hare for his trouble ⸺   5. 5. 0

                            £ 499. 12. 0

Richardson's Accounts for the early surveys, completed after his death

Cheshire RO, Z/TAV/55

Plans could be seen and subscriptions were to be taken in Nantwich, Middlewich and Warrington. Meetings were to be held at the Exchange every Friday at 11 o'clock.

The 1772 Act

Sam Weston was again sent to London in January 1772 for the new session of Parliament together with some of the committee members. For the third time the City Council affixed their common seal to the petition but this time the Corporation subscribed £100 in case the Act was not obtained.

The sticking point for the Act was the junction to the T&M in Nantwich, but according to the minutes of 24th January this had now been resolved:

Mr Turner and Mr Chamberlaine having reported by letter to Walter Thomas Esq. that his Grace the Duke of Bridgewater had condescended to enter into a conference with them at which on the part of the Subscribers they had agreed to terminate the intended Canal at a field on the East side of Booth Lane near Middlewich thro' which the grand Staffordshire Trunk [the T&M] is intended to pass, & with no other seperation than the bank of the said Trunk and to recede from the part of the original Petition of Parliament ... on which condition his Grace was pleased to promise that he would not oppose our Bill. It is the unanimous decision that such agreement be confirmed & it is hereby confirmed accordingly.

Having given way to no canal connection but only the banks of the Trent & Mersey Canal in between, salt was now rubbed in the wound. For 'His Grace' or the Proprietors of the T&M had reneged on the deal and outflanked them. The minutes of 17th February show the sad end to dreams of a canal link at Middlewich:

Subscribers cannot help lamenting that their compromise hath not been literally adhered to... they consent (tho' reluctantly) to give no opposition to the Clause, offer'd by the Staffordshire [T&M] Proprietors, which gives a power to the Duke of Bridgewater & them, to restrain them from cutting their Canal beyond Booth Lane, or nearer the Staffordshire [T&M] Canal than 100 yards without their consent.

It was on this note that the Act was finally passed from the Lords in March 1772. It was given Royal Assent on 1st April 1772. Edwin A Shearing, who researched the Act in 1985 reflects that this was an *inauspicious date for a start*.

Behind the scenes

There was never just one surveyor for the Chester Canal. In 1768 James Brindley was employed. He used his men, Thomas Varley, Thomas Allen and Thomas Swinnerton who were paid by him at £23-12-6, £16-15-0, and £0-19-0 respectively. These sums together with expenses of £3-3-9 were invoiced to Mr Richardson, a total of £44-10-3.

Brindley wrote:
I have not charged anything for myself... but that I leave to you and the rest of the Gentlemen of your City.

But, by September 1769, when he asked Sam Weston to collect the fee, he knew he was being paid an extra £20 which was added to the original bill of £44-10-3 making a total £64-10-3.

This was received by Sam Weston from Will Hall (Weston was to carry it to James Brindley's brother Henshall).

In a small example of cooking the books this extra was changed to 30 guineas (possibly by Will Hall).

It appears from notes at the foot of an account

Brindley's Bill, with an additional sum added, then changed to 31.10. -
Cheshire RO, Z/TAV/55

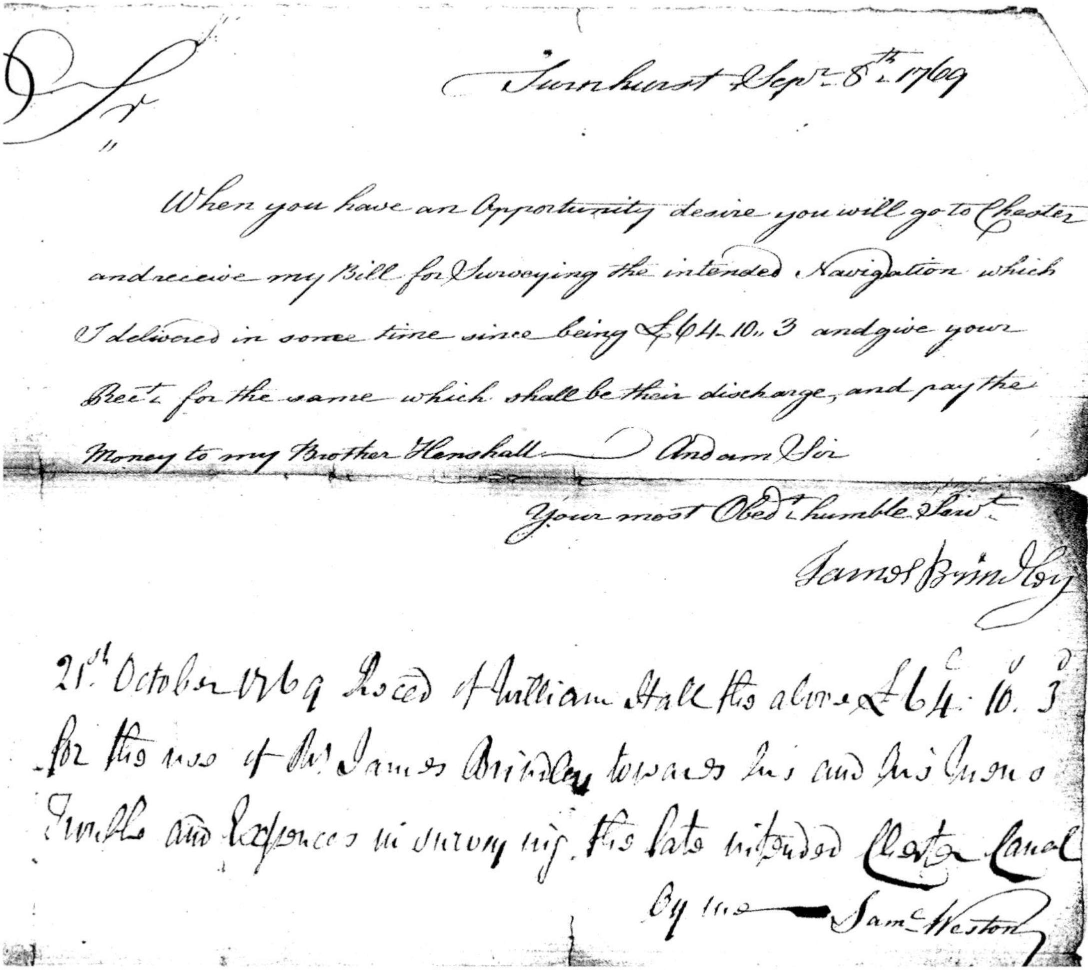

Tunhurst Sepr 8th 1769

When you have an Opportunity desire you will go to Chester and receive my Bill for Surveying the intended Navigation which I delivered in some time since being £64.10..3 and give your Recte for the same which shall be their discharge, and pay the Money to my Brother Henshall —— And am Sir

Your most Obedt humble Servt

James Brindley

21st October 1769 Recd of William Hall the above £64.10.3 for the use of Mr James Brindley towards his and his mens Trouble and Expences in surveying the late intended Chester Canal by me —— Saml Weston

Above: Brindley's letter (signed by him) to Sam Weston asking for his £64.10. 3 receipted by Weston.

Cheshire RO, Z/TAV/55

Below: the figures in the margin of Will Hall's account.

from Will Hall that the added £11-10-0 went to pay two sums of £6-10-6 and £4-7-0 with £0-12-6 left over. Whether this was to pay someone's subscription (in lots of £2-3-6 or £4-7-0) or just some other bills and a six month's supply of pints down the pub, we will never know.

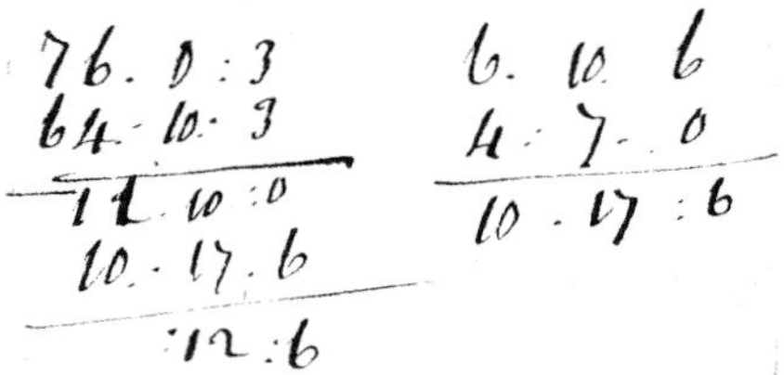

```
76. 0 : 3        6. 10. 6
64. 10. 3        4.  7. 0
——————           ——————
11. 10. 0       10. 17 : 6
10. 17. 6
——————
    12 : 6
```

Further expenses were paid to John Varley £29-11-6 and also to Sam Weston *a Bill for surveying 18 days at 2/6 per day 2-5-0 - taking a plan 1-11-6, £3-16-6.* A sum of *1-7* was also paid *for making a chain.* Samuel Weston sent in a bill dated May 28th 1769 for *Dialling [compass work] and Leveling £6-10-0*

In 1769 sums were paid *for mending a Theodolite 3-6, Postage of the Irish Petition 4-6, Mr Lawton for 3 Acts of Parliament... 9-8, a Large Copper Plate & Engraving a map thereon £5-2-0, Advertisements 13-3,* as well as travelling expenses for Mr Richardson, Mr Brindley, Mr Brock, Mr Chamberlaine and Mr Latham. Mr Brock, Mr Partington and Mr White were paid the grand sum of £288-18-3, probably for legal charges and drawing up the Parliamentary Bill.

Samuel Weston's bill for £46-5-6 in the spring of 1770 shows that he had begun to do far more for the Chester subscribers and was now employing men himself. He *Set out from Astmoor to Middlewich to take the Survey, paid 2 Men for telling the Landowners' names, paid Thomas Morris for staffholding 31 days at 2/6, paid Mr Poole for Vellum books and paper,* and charged £19-9-0 *For Myself Levelling and takeing the plan and finishing it* as well as all his *Victuals and Drink* at Northwich, Middlewich, Minshull and even the Black Bear in Chester. In July 1770 Thomas Morris and Sam Weston submitted a bill for surveying Eaton Brook (as a water supply) to the sum of £4-7-0

Although, at a canal meeting in December 1770, Hugh Oldham from Manchester was to be asked to survey the canal, it is clear, if only from the advert on 31st December 1771, that Thomas Yeoman had performed this duty and it was he who gave additional evidence to the Commons committee for the failed second petition. Even Yeoman's contribution was in name alone: he was a surveyor of some note with the Lee, the Aire & Calder and other navigations under his belt and became the first president of the Society of Civil Engineers in 1771. He stated in Parliament that he had *looked over the estimate* but *never saw the ground where the canal is to be carried.* In other words he just checked over Weston's plans and, at the age of 70, never did any actual surveying. Later surveyors included Thomas Morris, Josiah Clowes, and Mr Moon, originally the clerk. (See Postscript: Surveyors & Engineers.)

CELEBRATIONS Gordon Emery

The Bill is passed

As soon as the Post brought an account of the Chester Canal Bill having passed the House of Lords, the bells of all the churches in the City rang, and in the evening, illuminations were elegant and universal. The next day, the Proprietors of the Canal, with a great number of Gentlemen and the principal persons in trade, some in carriages and some on horseback went, in the afternoon , to the Glasshouse, about a mile from the City [at Boughton], to meet Messrs Chamberlaine and Griffiths on their return from soliciting the Bill. They were escorted amidst the joyful acclamations of some thousands of the inhabitants in the Exchange, where a proper entertainment was prepared for the reception of them and of such Gentlemen as pleased to honour it.

The Room was handsomely illuminated, a large bonfire lighted in the green Market Place, opposite to it, and every respectful compliment that could be thought of as the sincerest and highest marks of the public Approbation of their Conduct.

In the procession was a Boat fixed upon a carriage (the wheels of a post chaise) drawn by six horses...It was in truth expressive of the sincerest heartfelt joy, sympathetically communicated, to every well-wisher of the prosperity of this City ...as there is now a fair prospect of commerce flourishing, and of its becoming in due time a place of no small consequence in this part of the Kingdom

'Courant' 1772

We hear that the first Sod of the Canal from this City to Middlewich and Nantwich will be cut on Monday the 4th Day of May by the Right Worshipful Mayor of this City .

'Courant' Tuesday April 21st 1772

Yesterday at 11 o'clock in the Forenoon, the Mayor, Aldermen and Common Council of this City, with the Regalia, and the Militia Band of Musick, preceded by the Engineers of the Chester Canal, twenty-one Workmen, the Subscribers to the Undertaking, and the Companies of the City, with their Colours, went in Grand Procession from the Pentice, through the Watergate, to a Field in the Quarry near the Water Tower, and Here the Mayor cut the first Sod of the Canal, drank Success to the Undertaking, and was pleased to make a handsome Present to the Workmen; after which the Procession returned in the same Order, through the Northgate of the City. The Ceremony was attended with a very numerous Concourse of

People, assembled on the Walls, Towers and fields adjoining, who expressed their utmost Satisfaction on this Remarkable and interesting Occasion. Twenty-one Guns fired three rounds from the Cop, the Tower and the Walls, and the Bells of the City were rung, The Evening concluded with an Entertainment given by the Mayor and Corporation to Citizens on the joyful Event.
We hear that the Subscriptions to the Undertaking fills very fast.

'Courant' Tuesday May 5th 1772

The City Treasurers' Accounts show how much the workmen and the band were paid:

Paid for the Militia Band for playing before the Mayor 5-7-6
To a Gratuity by Mr Mayors Order on his cutting the first Sod of the Canal 5-5-0
(This sum of five shillings, a normal week's wages, for each workman must have ensured that some turned up with a hangover the next day.)

To wine as by Bill 0-7-0   (But perhaps their bosses didn't arrive too early either.)

Epitaph
December 1st 1772 saw another item in the 'Courant' occasioned by the interest in canals but this was an epitaph:

JAMES BRINDLEY lies amongst these Rocks,
He made Canals, Bridges, and Locks
To convey Water; he made Tunnels
for Barges, Boats, and Air-Vessels;
He erected several Banks,
Mills, pumps, Machines, with Wheels and Cranks;
He was famous t'invent Engines,
Calculated for working Mines;
He knew Water, its Weight and Strength,
Turn'd Brooks, made Soughs to a great Length;
While he used the Miners' Blast,
He stopp'd Currents from running too fast;
There ne'er was paid such Attention
As he did to Navigation.
But while busy with Pit or Well,
His Spirits sunk below Level;
And, when too late, his Doctor found
Water sent him to the Ground.

Brindley had died from a chill caught while surveying the Caldon.

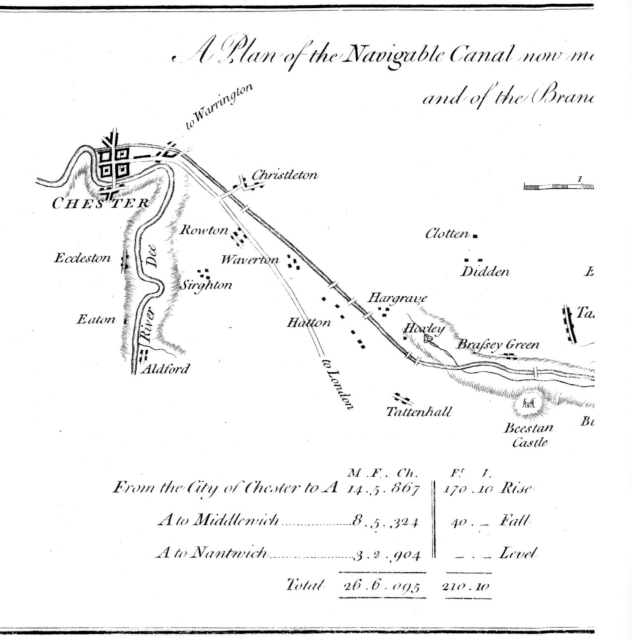

A Plan of the Navigable Canal now m...

and of the Bran...

to Warrington

CHESTER

Christleton

Clotten

Eccleston

Rowton

River Dee

Waverton

Didden

E...

Sirghton

Hargrave

Ta...

Eaton

Hatton

Hoxley

Brassey Green

to London

Aldford

Tattenhall

Beestan Castle

B...

	M . F . Ch.	F⁵. I.	
From the City of Chester to A	14 . 5 . 867	170 . 10	Rise
A to Middlewich	8 . 5 . 324	40 . —	Fall
A to Nantwich	3 . 2 . 904	— . —	Level
Total	26 . 6 . 095	210 . 10	

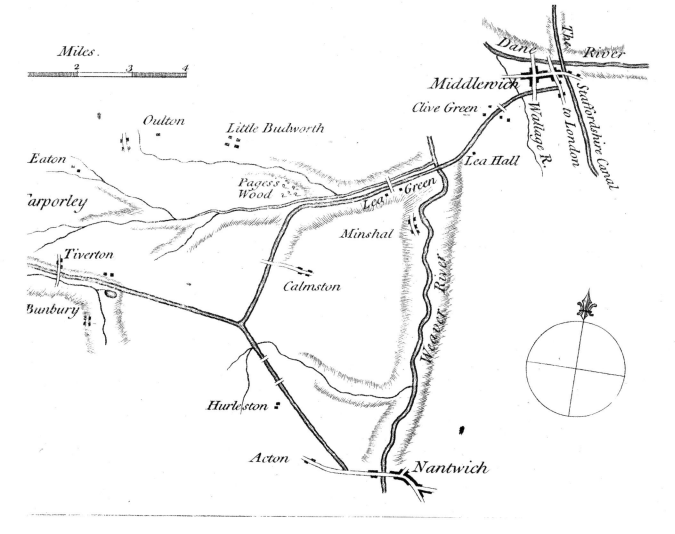

raking from the City of Chester to Middlewich,
ich from A to Nantwich.

Miles.

2   3   4

Oulton

Little Budworth

Dane

Middlewich

Clive Green

Eaton

Pages's Wood

Lea Hall

Wallage R.

to London

Staffordshire Canal

The   River

arporley

Lea   Green

Minshal

Tiverton

Calmston

Weaver River

Bunbury

Hurleston

Acton

Nantwich

Map of the Intended canal. *Note the inclusion of Nantwich.*   Gents magazine   Cheshire RO, PM11/1

CUTTING THE CANAL Gordon Emery

Hard Work

The April 1772 edition of the 'Courant' carried the following advertisement: *Proposals will be received from any Wheelwright, Carpenter or others, who chuse [sic] to make a Number of Wheelbarrows for the Use of the Undertaking, agreeable to a Model which may be seen at Mr Samuel Weston's in Crane Street.*

Vendors must have applied because, after an agreement to buy stone at Waverton Quarry for 2/6 per yard measured at the surface, canal minutes in May record that *Mr Weston to give orders to Mr Yoxall at Nantwich for Ten Wheelbarrows to be delivered at 8/6 and ten more by persons in the town at 8/6 and ten more in the country at 8/-.*

By this time Mr Weston had been employed as the Engineer for £150 per annum, his son as clerk for £20 pa, Mr Lawton to act as an assistant in cutting the canal, making locks and bridges at £100 pa, and Mr Philip Norbury as the bookkeeper for £60 pa and a house. On 19th March the committee ordered that: *Mr Weston begin to stake & set out the Canal under the orders & directions of Mr Thomas, Mr Chamberlaine & Mr Rogers,* committee members. Since the Chester Canal was intended to carry wide boats up to 14 feet beam, all locks and bridges had to be at least that width. This makes it a broad canal, unlike the T&M which, for cost reasons, was built as a narrow canal capable of carrying only 7ft narrowboats.

Weston started to buy land and *the Lime Kiln and make a Dock...on the inside of the Cop in the River Dee.* He bought stables, bricks and timber. Joseph Acton, a smith, was *to be given all common or plain work and a shop to work in.*

In July, Weston was sent on another mission: to survey *Brewers Hall [on the far bank of the Dee opposite Crane Street] to Gresford and Cae gidog [River Cegidog] Bridge* for access to the coalmines. The Committee was getting ahead of itself and little more is mentioned of this survey after Weston reported that a practical course was available. The Ellesmere Canal Company was later to survey a similar route from the south of the Dee to the west of Wrexham for its Western Canal.

In September 1772, Weston was to take on *as many men as he can employ in the Country* but not to exceed 150 cutters. In October the *Bridge at Northgate* was to be built. In November, Henry Bullock and Robert Mason, masons, were *to compleat the Bridge at the Northgate for the sum of Eighty Two Pounds Ten shillings.* Bricks were ordered in bulk lots of 800,000 at 9/6 per thousand and 600,000 from the Spittle Field at Boughton for 9/- the following January.

With work underway, Johnson & Co of London cut the Chester Canal Company's seal showing the proposed canal winding around Beeston Castle crag with a view of Chester City in the background. Until then Phil Norbury's seal of a *Dove with an Olive Branch* was used.

Chester Canal Company seal
Grosvenor Museum

As the surveying expenses show, the line was plotted using triangulation from a theodolite. Measurements were made using a chain (100 links to the 22 yard chain). Levels were taken with spirit levels and telescopes between staffs. Spirit levels are mentioned in the minutes, while the theodolite and chain bought, and the staffholders of Weston's employ are listed in Richardson's accounts. Levels would be benchmarked on rocks or trees and markers on the way. Pegs would then be set up for the top of the cut, and 'slope holes' cut to mark the intended water level. These were joined by a 'lock spit' ditch. In February 1774, Weston and Lawton proposed the first deviation on the line from the Golden Nook to Crow's Nest thus saving £500.

The enormous work of cutting the Chester Canal included tunnelling through rock north of the city walls, although local folklore says that, when the workmen started, they found that the canal ran along the line of the old Roman ditch which had filled up with rubbish over the centuries, saving expected labour and expense. The main labour-intensive job was cutting the canal for miles using just men and hand tools, wheelbarrows and planks, and horses and carts. Six horses and two carts were purchased in January 1773.

The cutting men would dig in lines ('reaching') of vertical cuts across the marked out sections from the lock spit. Top soil would be spread out over nearby farmland. Other spoil or waste could be used for banking, or spread out. In February 1773 three overlookers worked men in three sections: 40 men from the Golden Nook to Brockholes, 60 men at *Trooper's to Waverton Bridge* and 20 men *geting up the Rock and Rock Rubbish at Chester.*

Once a section of canal had been finished, waste could be taken away and materials could be brought by water. *Another boat, 50 feet long* was bought in March 1773. By December 1774 water filled the canal at Chester.

A report from the 'Chester Chronicle' in November 1775 details an unusual item found in the mud while cutting at Beeston: *A few days ago, a six pounder cannon ball was found, about 15 feet below the surface, by the workmen making the lock on the Chester Canal, at Beeston-Brook; where, it is supposed that the intrenched lines were formed during the siege of Beeston Castle by the Parliamentary army, about the year 1643. The ball is deposited at the General Printing-office for the inspection of the curious.*

Once the canal was cut, usually to about a yard below the final depth, it had to be made watertight. On clay beds this was no problem and much of the Chester Canal must have been relatively easy to make. However, where there was sand, gravel or peat the canal bed had to be puddled to retain water.

Puddle was made from the right consistency of earth, often loam, gravel, sand and clay (pure clay could shrink, crack and dry out) hand chopped and mixed with water into a gooey mess. This was then spread in layers, built up after partial drying, to a thickness of up to a yard on the canal floor and sides, and covered with poorer puddle or soil for protection before being filled with water to stop the whole mass drying out. The easiest section to dig on the Chester Canal was the hardest to maintain - shifting sands at Beeston Brook cause problems to this day. The later Ellesmere Canal cutters had enormous difficulty making solid banks through bogs southeast of Wrexham.

To avoid building too many locks and embankments, most early canals meandered around the contours of hills, keeping at the same level: one of the facets of English canals that nowadays appeals to the tourist boater. In fact later, straighter canals often meant that higher tolls had to be paid, making them less competitive against toll roads and, eventually, the railways. The first two lock bases on the canal were contracted to Lawrence, Laycock and Pritchley who were paid 1/9 a day. Richard Graham was appointed to overlook the men at the locks at the slightly lower rate of 1/8 a day. In August 1773, Henry Bullock was to lay the foundations for the third lock. In October 1774 an advert was to be placed in the Chester paper for *serving this company with fifteen or twenty pieces of timber suitable for the Long gates of the Locks.*

Bricking the canal banks in 1942, still using planks and barrows
Waterways Trust

Where there were highways, bridges had to be built across the canal's course: Cow Lane Bridge (Frodsham Street) was to be built with a 25 feet span, and a road on each side under the arch - three and a half feet in breadth; with a crown ten feet from the top water level. (This bridge was last replaced in the 1960s).

Towpaths were built along one side of the canal and the boundaries completed with fences in the town or planted with 'quickset' hedges in the countryside, to prevent trespass. Poplar rails were cut 3.5 inches by 1.5 inches by 8 feet at £2 per rood in March 1773. In 1775 the *Tails* beyond the Golden Nook were to be finished properly to protect the *Quicksetts* newly planted there. On the 20th November 1779 two men were *to plant Quicksetts to stop leakages in the*

Summitt Levell. Quickset and trees on a twelve mile section of the later Ellesmere Canal alone cost £321 in the early 19th century. In Chester, during 1789, an iceboat built in 1773 was broken up to make fencing along the side of Queen Street.

Where the towpath changed sides, turnover or roving bridges had to be built to ensure that the hauling horse did not have to have its towing rope removed while crossing the canal. Wharfs, wharf houses and stables had to be built at likely trading posts, such as *Crownest, Warton* and Beeston. Lockhouses also had to be built, such as the one at Bunbury, built in 1780.

Roving Bridge on the Wirral Line at Chester
Photo: Mike Penney

Accidents

Accidents were bound to happen but the first one recorded was a fatality: *One Day last Week as one of the men was working at the Canal near this City, he accidentally received a Blow with a Pick on his Head, from another of the men who was near him, which unfortunately fractur'd his Scull. He was carried to our Infirmary where he languished a few Days and then died.*

'Courant' 4th August 1774

Whether any action was taken to prevent further misfortunes is not known but the next reported accident was two years later: *Saturday last as one Samuel Jones, a Workman at the Chester Canal, was digging in that Cut, near the Water Tower, a Quantity of Rubbish , etc. unfortunately fell on him, which broke one of his Legs, and tore the other in so shocking a Manner, that he is rendered a truly pitiable Object.*

'Courant' 8th October 1776

The weather could prevent work from being carried out as reported in the 'Chronicle' of 5th February 1776 *In the course of last week, a number of workmen, belonging to the Chester Canal, being out of employ from the severity of the weather, drew a waggon loaded with coals, 38 hundred weight, from Madely in Staffordshire, to this city, about thirty miles distance, and after collecting money on the road, and round the city for two successive days, they unyoked at Mr Speed's, in Abbey-square, one of the proprietors of the Canal and presented the coals to him.*

The severe cold spell even prevented shipping on the Mersey, where a ferry boat was presumed lost in the ice.

Cash Flow

Only a couple of years after the project started, the company began to have problems collecting regular payments from subscribers: these were first penalised, then their shares forfeited as the Act required. The results of this cash shortage soon became apparent: money was borrowed at interest to pay the men, landowners were paid late or given bonds or promissory notes instead of payments, and nearly all orders from the committee included such statements as *at the Lowest terms possible*. This included new boats for the canal and the cutting from Beeston Mill to Beeston Brook.

Constant cost-cutting may have contributed to a series of inferior works and a loss of morale. When Mrs Lawton asked for the remainder of her late husband's salary and the price of his level, in January 1774, the latter was to be paid *at cost*. However, *Parts of the Aqueduct Bridge that have given way be immediately taken down and repaired in the best manner possible* may have been down to bad engineering, as Sam Weston left the Company shortly afterwards. In April 1774 John Chamberlaine tried to get some recompense for all the unpaid work he had been doing over the years. He was refused 100 guineas a year for his trouble but allowed 100 guineas in total, the company then declaring that *No allowance shall hereafter be made to any Subscriber for any extraordinary Business, but by the Order... of the Committee.* Canal workers were no longer supplied tools, they had to buy them from the company instead.

Everyone's expectation

Nevertheless, work pushed ahead and on 27th December 1774 *was launched into the New Canal, near Cow Lane Gate, in this City, a large Barge or Vessel 70 feet long, and 14 feet wide, and of the Burden of 70 tons; and immediately afterwards she proceeded full of People with French horns, etc, playing on board, under the Walls of the City, along by the Phoenix*

Tower, thro' the Rock which has been cut open at the Northgate, to the Dam at the End of the Canal now finished; being about 200 Yards to the Westward of the Northgate, where several Cannon were fired. From thence she was conducted thro' six Bridges and five Locks, now erected on the Canal between there and Christleton Quarry, and afterwards was reconducted to Cow-Lane Bridge. The Barge was named the Egerton and all the Works on the Canal answered every ones Expectation. A very numerous Concourse of People was assembled on the Banks of the Canal, and on the City Walls, whose Satisfaction cou'd not be better testified than by the very loud and general Acclamations shewn on the Occasion.

'Courant' 3rd January 1775

Some interesting particulars of the work in progress and the expenditure involved in cutting the canal between Chester, Middlewich and Nantwich are contained in this report from the 'Courant' of 2nd May 1775:

Canal navigation from Chester to Middlewich and Nantwich.
The committee having viewed the state of the canal and the works now carrying on between the river Dee at chester and nantwich and Middlewich; it appears that there are three locks built ion the rock near the Water Tower; that the canal is cut and completed through the rock at the Northgate and the Phoenix Tower to Cowlane Bridge in this city, being in depth about 30 feet and in length about 600 yards; that eleven miles are finished and completed from Chester to Beeston brook House, except a small part of the banking at Beeston Valley and a small quantity of brick-work betwixt that place and Beeston brook House; that three and a half miles and a half more towards Nantwich are already cut to complete to Nantwich; and about eight miles on the Nantwich line; that there are about 300 yards of the canal cut on the banks of the Weaver towards Middlewich; that there are five locks completed and one in use between Chester and christleton; and one other now nearly finished at Beeston Mill; sixteen cart bridges finished and four more in a very great state of readiness; nine culverts and one aqueduct bridge finished. [After] a careful examination into the state of the company's accounts, it appears that the following sums have been paid in carrying on the works from their commencement of the first day of March, 1772 until the first day of March, 1775. There follows a list of payments, from which it appears that a total net sum of £38,273. 12.6d had been expended on the works...

The first cargo of coal was taken to Beeston in 1775.

Jailhouse rock

When the canal was cut through rock at the Northgate it created several problems. The canal made it difficult to take prisoners from the Northgate Gaol on the south side of the canal to the *apartment made for prisoners* in the Bluecoat Hospital Chapel on the north side of the canal. The company first had to give bonds via Mr Chamberlaine to the sheriffs and gaoler covering the escape of prisoners while work took place. Part of the House of Correction on the north side of the canal was damaged (despite the earlier survey to say it would not be). In May '73 the Canal Company were asked by the City Council to consider compensation for taking down part of the House of Correction and the Pinfold nearby and to form a *communication from the same Gaol to the Chapel of St John*. By August that year the Corporation had taken a hard line stating that until Proprietors had built a sufficient arch over the canal and built rooms for the House of Correction and paid the City Treasurers the value of land taken, notice was to be given that the council would sue. In October 1773 an estimate of £65-9-0 was produced for an iron arch but this was just for labour and *Iron work of great value* was also needed. It is not known whether this arch was built.

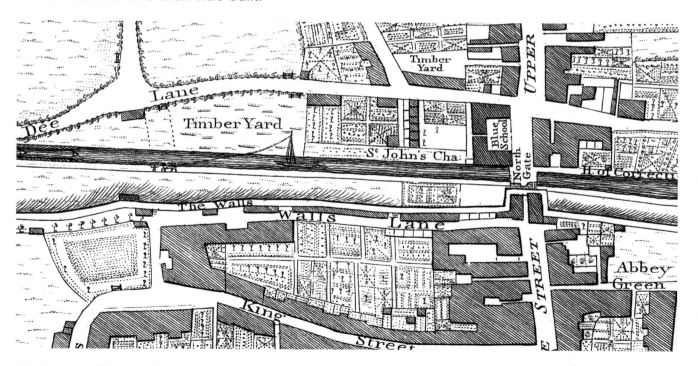

The House of Correction and Northgate (including the gaol) on a map of Chester surveyed by Sam Weston and published by Hunter in 1789 Cheshire RO, PM/4

Northgate Gaol (left) and House of Correction (right)
Grosvenor Museum, Moses Griffiths 1747-1819, pen, ink & watercolour

The prisoners were still resident as is evident by an order at the Assembly in May 1783 that *upon reading the Petition of the Debtors in the Northgate Gaol of this City Praying an allowance of Bread Weekly towards their support and maintenance. It is ordered that the matter of the said Petition be referred to the Sheriffs of this City and such allowance of Bread be made and to such of the Debtors confined in the said Gaol as Mr Sheriffs should think fit.* By this time a bridge must have been built between the chapel and the gaol because, seven years later in 1790, the City Council ordered that the *safety of the bridge leading from the Northgate gaol to the Chapel, over the Canal, be considered by the Treasurers of this City.*

Three years later, it was ordered that *Mr Turner be paid the sum of twenty pounds out of the City Treasury on his erecting a Stone Arch over the Canal from the northgate Garden to the Bluecoat Hospital, with an Iron railing thereon.* In 1801 the council paid the cost of erecting 'a drop' at the gaol for the execution of criminals. The use of the small arch for prisoners attending the chapel before public execution led to this arch being named the Bridge of Death or 'Bridge of Sighs'. In 1803 a new gaol was built beside the Infirmary, leading to the closure of the Northgate Gaol in 1808. An order was given for the bridge to be demolished on 16th July 1821 but this was never done, and, apart from the iron railings taken for munitions, the Bridge of Sighs remains there to this day.

Bridge of Sighs with iron railings
c1910 Waterways Trust

45

THE DEE LINK Gordon Emery

Locked Out

The apparent success of this short section of canal from Chester to Beeston now had to be translated into monetary terms and a passage boat was soon carrying passengers. But trade on the canal was needed and for the purposes of connecting the canal to the Dee a lock had to be made. As the canal had been built for boats of 14 feet wide, a lock of a similar size was needed. Imagine the consternation of the committee then, when *Mr Yeoman, Engineer having come from London to execute Canal & other works thro' the lands of the River Dee Company and having informed the Committee that he has orders from the Committee of the River Dee Company to execute the Canal Locks with a Lock of the dimensions of 7 feet...* The Company refused to pay for such a lock, and in November 1775 the Council Assembly Book stated that *The petition of the Company of Proprietors of the Chester Canal Navigation was read stating they had made considerable progress at great expense towards completing the Canal to widen it to admit vessels of fourteen feet, and complaining that the Proprietors of the Undertaking for recovering and preserving of the River Dee propose confining the branch of the canal which they are now cutting to the passage of boats seven feet in width, thus prejudicing the petitioners and restricting the City's trade. They prayed permission to continue their Canal either along the north side of the Water Tower or to tunnel under the City Walls into the field held by Mr Hart and across the old and new Crane Streets into the River Dee, terminating between the House of Industry and the Old Crane.*

Compromise

It appears that the narrow lock was built, the canal company still trying to get a wider entrance. Eighteen months later, the matter was decided at Chester Assizes: *by a Special Jury, a Cause wherein the River Dee Company were Plaintiffs, and the Canal Company defendants. It was an Issue by the High Court of Chancery, to try, whether the Plaintiffs had or had not complied with the Terms of the Canal Act of Parliament respecting that Part of the Canal and the lack, etc. which was made by them throughout their own Lands? When, after some Time spent on the Hearing a Compromise was agreed to, upon the following Terms: The Canal Company to pay to the River Dee Company the expence of making the present Flood-Gate and Works; to pay also a Halfpenny per Ton for all Boats, passing through the River Dee Company's Lands into the River except those laden with Stones, Gravel, Limestone, Potter's Clay, Slates, and Flint-Stones, which are to pass free of Tonnage. On these Conditions, the Canal Company are to have another Flood-Gate and Works erected (at their expense) so as to admit Boats to pass into the River of 14 Feet wide. Each Party to pay their own Costs.*

'Courant' 22nd April 1776

In June the City Assembly *ordered that the Forelands belonging to the Corporation lying between the old Crane and beyond the late Mr Champion's coal yard in Lease to Mr Chamberlaine be laid out and plan'd by Mr Turner as far and in such manner and Divisions as he shall think most suitable for the Purpose of making and erecting Wharfs, Keys, Yards and Warehouses and particularly a Graving Dock and that such Plan with an Estimate of the Expence of carrying the same into Execution be laid before this Incorporation...*

Joining the Dee

Eventually a new entrance from the River Dee was built with a single pair of gates 15ft apart, leading to a tidal basin. For *the first time one of the Canal barges, of the burden of about 60 tons, navigated out of the Canal, thro' the five-fold lock lately compleated at this city, into the river Dee, to proceed on her voyage to the colliery, to load coals for the use of the interior parts of the country.*

'Courant' 13th December 1776

At the end of December the Committee ordered *that Mr Moon agree with Wm Antrobus to attend the Locks at Water Tower... at a Salary of Ten Shillings a week.*

The Water Tower and the Dee Basin in the early 19th century Old engraving

RUIN Gordon Emery

Cost Cutting

While the city end of the canal appeared to be open for business, it was very different beyond Beeston. On 6th December 1776 it was ordered *that Mr Moon discharge all the Workmen upon the Canal beyond Beeston Brook.* A week later *that Mr Moon & Mr Morris fix whatever Workmen are absolutely necessary to be employed on the Canal in order only to preserve the Canal from Misfortune + Waste.* Morris had taken over as Engineer from Sam Weston. By January '77 the Committee was *finding it impossible to carry on the Works much longer without the further Aid of Parliament.* A few weeks later, Mr Clowes was asked to survey to Nantwich. He refused - perhaps he thought he would never be paid - so Moon and Morris got the job. By July *all workmen on the Canal* were to be discharged *except William Antrobus [the lock-keeper], the Ship Carpenter and one Carter.* In August, Mr Morris too was discharged with *Seventy Five pounds as full Compensation for his salary on his delivering up all the Books, Levell &c belonging to the Company. An inventory of the company's Barrows, Planks, Tools, Engines, Boats & other Materials* was to be taken by Chas Hill and Sam Weston. In December 1777 a few employees still remained: *William Antrobus attending the locks; Richard Johnson to attend the Banks and fences of the Canal + destroy the Moles; Three men at the Brockholes + about that Number cleans Horsley Moss Drain, both of which will be very soon discharged; Men occasionally employed about the Barges and Canals as they are wanted.* Edward Stone was employed as the wharfinger at Beeston in August 1779 and when he complained about his low wage it was recorded that *if Edward Stone be dissatisfied with the £26 a year + house directed to be allowed to him that he give the Company a Month's notice + resign.*

In August 1777, Mr Moon had been sent to survey from Wardle Green to Middlewich, and Bunbury Lock to Nantwich. It had been decided that the broad canal should be completed to Nantwich and the arm to Middlewich should now be a narrow canal, only seven feet wide, however all the share capital had been spent. A New Act of Parliament authorised a further call on shareholders of 60% as well as £30,000 by mortgage. An additional £6,000 was raised on calls and a Richard Reynolds lent £4,000. So, in May 1778, William Jessop and James Pinkerton were authorised to cut the canal from Beeston Brook to Nantwich for £3,764-13-0. By October 1778 it was ordered that the boats *Egerton, Bootle & Flatts bee put into Proper Repair fit to be stationed on the Nantwich Line as soon as finished.* Jessop and Pinkerton were paid a further £180 to build the Nantwich Basin.

In May 1779 money had run out so the Committee ordered *that the Canal shall rest at*

Nantwich for One Year. This meant that no more work was done on the Middlewich line. However, the rest of one year turned out to be nearly fifty years. The Chester Canal ran from the River Dee to Nantwich, a distance of 19.4 miles, with 18 locks (including three sets of staircase locks: five at Chester, two at Bunbury and another 'double lock' at Beeston).There was also the lock to the River Dee.

Negligence & wilful damage

Early on, in 1772, the Company had had to put up notices in Waverton, Hargrave and Christleton churches *offering a reward of Five Guineas to any Person or Persons, who will give information of anyone or more stealing Coal, Slack, Timber or other Materials, or damaging any of the Works belonging to the Proprietors of the Chester canal Navigation.*

However, greater damages were inflicted by boatmen who were probably not used to using locks:

WHEREAS I RICHARD JONES, of the city of Chester, did (in October last) by inattention in shutting the lower gates of the five-fold lock, on the Chester canal, did leave them in such a situation, that on the Lock filling, the pressure of water burst from its Proper situation one of the Gates, by which it was broke down and considerable expense and inconvenience brought on the Company of the said Chester Canal Navigation, and which expenses I am subject to and ought to pay, but the Committee of the said Chester Canal Navigation in compassion to me and my family, have forgave the said expenses on my begging pardon for this offence, and faithfully promising to be more careful for the future.

And as I RICHARD CROFTS, of Boughton, in the liberties of the said City, did by neglect leave open (on Saturday 3rd instant) one of the Cloughs of the Lock, at the West end of the Long Leave of the Chester Canal, whereby considerable damage was done to the works of the said Canal, for utter inability to pay the money, and asking pardon for the offence, promising to conduct myself with greater care in future, has induced the Committee to stop any proceeding against me.

For the great lenity shewn us as above, we sincerely return our thanks.
The mark of X RICHARD JONES, RICHARD CROFTS.
Signed by the said Richard Jones, and Richard Crofts in the presence of me, Charles Hill, Clerk of the said Company.

'Chester Chronicle' 14th March 1783

As in all property, straightforward vandalism was a problem:

Whereas some Person or Persons, have maliciously cut the Chains of the Locks from hence to Christleton: If anyone will inform of their Accomplice or Accomplices, or inform of any Person or Persons guilty of the same, shall on Conviction receive a Reward of 20 Guineas, from the Proprietors of the Chester Canal Navigation JOHN MOON, Canal Office, Chester
N.B. The public are to take Notice, if any Person or Persons, are found injuring the Works in any respect whatever, they will be punished with the utmost Severity of the Law.

'Courant' 24th January 1775

The long towpaths through the countryside must have appealed to many who thought they could use them as a right-of-way:

All persons riding on the Banks of the Canal (who have no Right to do so)
or otherwise damaging the Works, will be prosecuted as the Law directs.

'Courant' 21st November 1775

Vandalism continued, but when the offenders were caught, the penalty could be severe:

WHEREAS some evil-disposed of person or Persons did, on Saturday or Sunday night last, break and destroy several coping Stones in Christleton quarry, the property of the Company of Proprietors: Notice is hereby given, that any person who will discover the offender or offenders, so that he or they be convicted thereof shall receive a reward of Ten Guineas. Or any person, actually concerned in destroying the same, shall on his discovering and convicting his accomplice or accomplices, receive the like reward, and full pardon. And whoever shall inform against, and convict any person or persons guilty of damaging the works of the said Company in any part thereof, shall receive a reward of TEN GUINEAS for every such conviction, by applying to MR JOHN MOON, at the Canal-office, near the Eastgate, in this city.

'Chronicle' 20th June 1776

The 'Courant' of 23rd June 1778 reports that, at the Chester Quarter Sessions in June 1778, one Thomas Griffiths was *found guilty of maliciously breaking and throwing down a rail belonging to the Canal Company, and was ordered to be whipped from the Northgate to Cow-lane Bridge.*

Cul-de-sac

It is not known how the proprietors of the Chester Canal were hoping to deal with the hundred yard gap which would have remained between the T&M at Middlewich and the proposed canal to Middlewich. Perhaps they hoped that once they had cut the Chester Canal, the T&M

proprietors would give way and allow the canals to link.(That is what eventually happened, but 50 years later.) However, if this had been a vain hope it must have soon become evident that a canal between Nantwich and Chester, without a connection to the Grand Trunk (T&M), was doomed to failure. Canal transport relied on heavy loads over long distances. Nantwich's main exports were cheese and shoes, its salt-making industry having virtually died out at the end of the 17th century when rock salt was discovered at nearby Northwich. Most of the shoes went to local agriculture or Manchester. The small amount of exports in shoes and cheese to Chester could easily be carried on the reasonable toll road but, even if the canal was used, the books did not balance. The few heavy loads there were would not pay for canal maintenance while passage boats would hardly cover their own own costs. The company surveyed for rock salt at Nantwich but none could be found and boring ended in May 1780.

The Chester Company tried putting two boats on the Staffordshire Canal and reduced tolls so that *all Goods & Wares from the Staffordshire Potteries passing down the Chester Canal be charged at the same rate as by the Staffs Canal to Liverpool.* This meant they had to subsidise overland waggons. Meanwhile Jackson & Co were not to be charged tonnage on boats returning light if they had paid for over 20 tons on their outward journey. Goods which used the canal en route from Liverpool to Whitchurch, Drayton and Shrewsbury were to be charged the same as Chester trading vessels, with Joseph Bostock carrying goods overland.

Unfortunately, by 1780, *the Bootle, Peploe, Speed & Egerton Flatts* were to *be laid up in the Bason at the Phoenix Tower.* All unnecessary land belonging to the Canal Company, including the land opposite the walls at the Phoenix Tower, was sold wherever possible. Debts mounted, shareholders stopped paying their continued calls for cash, many shares had now been forfeited, while loans were taken but not repaid. In 1782 the Bunbury Reservoir was partly drained by John Fern of Brownhills in revenge for not being paid, and a lock gate at the Water Tower collapsed. Mr Moon resigned the same year.

In June 1783 the *North Side of Tilston Mill Lock having wholly fallen down... so as to obstruct the Navigation of the Canal + the expence of putting the same again into proper Condition ... to amount to £80... that the Flatt Peploe... to be sold to open the Navigation... as soon as possible.* The lock was repaired in March 1784. *Lock gates in Spitalfields* were *greatly damaged* in November 1783. In December the *Flat Bootle* was seized by Crown House officers for bringing *kernel (grain) from Liverpool* and not paying customs. On 5th November 1787 it was reported that *the Walls of Beeston Brook Lock... given way due to Sand being washed out. In 1794 Wardle Bridge was said to be dangerous* but the committee decided they had to save what little money they had to repair the lock at Beeston, but even this was beyond them. In 1790 a breach at Christleton cost £77-15-0 to repair. Although some trade continued with goods being unloaded to get past Beeston Lock an Act of Parliament in 1796 stated that *the said Canal Navigation is now, and has been for a very long Space of Time, in a very ruinous Condition.*

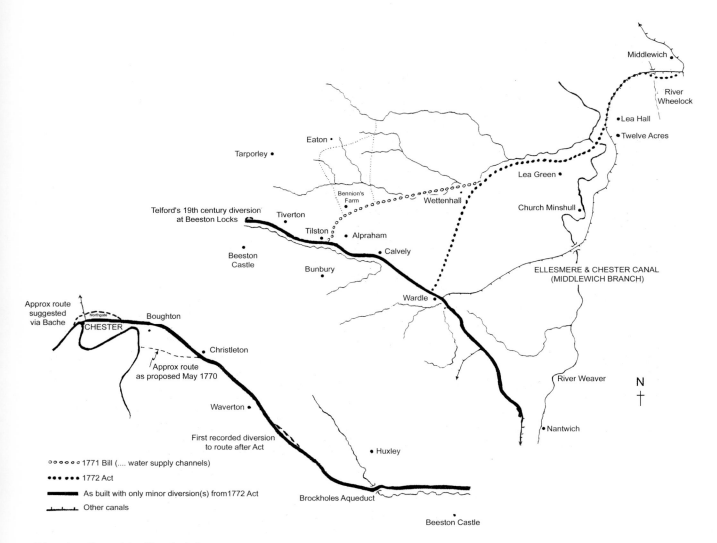

Chester Canal to Nantwich
Based on a map by Richard Dean

THE ELLESMERE CANAL Gordon Emery

New hope

Now running on a shoestring budget with worthless shares, the Committee was informed, on 17th April 1789, of a possible junction from the Ellesmere Canal near Nantwich. So it is not surprising that, in April 1791, the Committee voted not to oppose a Shrewsbury to Liverpool canal that would join the Chester Canal at both ends.

The Ellesmere Canal proprietors held their first meeting on 31st August 1791 at the Royal Oak in Ellesmere. Their committee included MPs from Shropshire and Montgomeryshire and the Mayors of Liverpool, Shrewsbury and Chester. The idea was to link the Rivers Mersey, Severn and Dee. Proposals were put forward for an Eastern Canal to link with the Chester Canal at Tattenhall and to go south cutting the 'Wich' Valley via Penley Green to Shrewsbury. This canal was to have a Coal Arm from Penley via Overton, Ruabon and Trevor to Valle Crucis, west of Llangollen and a branch to Bersham. The deposited map has four names normally linked with the Chester Canal inscribed: Jos Turner, Thomas Morris, John Chamberlaine and Wm Cawley; while the reference book names John Duncome, William Turner and Arthur Davies. There were also plans for a Western Canal via Wrexham and a long tunnel at Ruabon to the Dee at Chester. Another line of this canal was to go through the Wirral from Chester to the Mersey.

A year later, on 29th August, the Chester Canal Committee suggested that *if the Gentlemen now endeavouring to obtain an Act of Parliament from Shrewsbury to Chester find it necessary to join the Chester Canal that they be permitted...on paying the Rates and Duties agreeable to the Act of Parliament for making the Chester Canal.* By September a link at Tattenhall had been agreed. Chester Council agreed to petition Parliament for the two canals in January 1793 but held the petition up in March until the Ellesmere proprietors agreed to a clause protecting Chester's water supply. The Petition for a junction of the Eastern and Western Canals with Chester Canal was agreed by the Chester Canal Committee in March. The Ellesmere proprietors had, by now, made changes to their proposed canal system, opting for the Western Canal with a link to Tattenhall but a different route to Ellesmere and the omission of the Coal Arm. The Act was passed in April, however the Ellesmere proprietors prioritised the cutting of the broad Wirral Arm and, to the dismay of the Chester Canal Company, the narrow western route south of the Dee at Wrexham.

Cutting on the narrow canal was started in 1793 from Frankton, west of Ellesmere, to Trevor. An expensive stone aqueduct was built over the River Ceiriog by 1801 and a tunnel cut through solid rock under Richard Myddleton's Chirk Castle Estate, completed in 1802. This and the Whitehouses Tunnel led, another 3 miles, to the most expensive and impressive work: the iron aqueduct across the Dee at Cysyllte, near Trevor. The 8.7 mile section had four locks

Chirk Aqueduct and Railway Viaduct
Henry Robertson dwarfed the aqueduct with his viaduct built for the Great Western Railway, finished in 1848. The bridges are 21 metres and 30 metres above the river respectively.
Photo: Gordon Emery

at Frankton. Another section from the foot of the Frankton Locks to Carreghofa near Llanymynech (11 miles and 3 locks) joining the Montgomeryshire Canal, was opened in 1796. This meant that limestone could be brought onto the canal as it was built.

The same year a section was opened from Frankton to Weston Lullingfields, 15 miles northwest of Shrewsbury, where a wharf, four limekilns, a public house, stables and a house and weighing machine were installed selling large quantities of lime and slate. Completion of the line to Shrewsbury was then shelved because the Shrewsbury Canal had already reached the town. William Jessop was the Chief Engineer of the Ellesmere Canal with Thomas Telford, General Agent, Surveyor, Engineer, Architect and Overlooker of the Works, who took over Jessop's job in 1801.

All this canal cutting had been at the expense of the canal link at Nantwich. Initial hopes of restoring and revitalising the Chester Canal had, according to a meeting in July 1794, sent shares soaring *from no value to £20 or £25 but sank to £15 but may rise if the new canal is cut.*

Clearing the way

The whole Chester Canal had been mortgaged to Samuel Egerton for £20,000 and interest due by February 1794 stood at £15,176-19-7. A new Act of Parliament in 1796 enabled a series of Chester merchants and other shareholders (named as Thomas Lord Grey de Wilton, John Crewe, Joseph Turner architect, Reverend John Childaw, Thomas Griffiths, William Seller brewer, John Fletcher printer, Robert Bates, Paul Panton of Plas Gwynne Anglesea and John Bakewell druggist) to purchase the mortgage for £8000, from William Egerton, Samuel's heir.

In 1794 the City Assembly was petitioned for a lease on the land east of the Water Tower to build a dock. In April 1795 Weston & Son were asked to estimate repairs to the whole of the Chester Canal. However, in July Mr Fletcher was contracted to carry out all repairs except for Beeston Lock.

Tenders were invited for further work in the 'Chronicle' of 29th July 1796:

CHESTER CANAL NAVIGATION
TO CONTRACTORS &c.
PERSONS willing to contract for repairing Beeston Lock, on the Chester Canal, agreeably to

the Plan and Specifications left in the hands of Mr. Hill, the Clerk of the Company, are desired to deliver in their Proposals, sealed up, to the Chairman, at the Inner Pentice, in the City of Chester, on Monday the 1st August next, at Eleven o'Clock, when the same will be taken into Consideration.

At the same Time, WILL BE LET, the Widening and Cleansing the Canal to its original Dimensions from the Head of Beeston Lock to the Termination at Nantwich.

Also WILL BE LET, the Making and Filling up betwixt Barbridge and Nantwich, on the said Canal of Seven Swivel bridges of the same Dimensions as the present old ones.

One assumes John Fletcher must have won the tender because in 1797 he was paid sums of £150 and £197 for finishing these repairs to Nantwich.

Fletcher was also asked to register a passage boat at the Clerk of the Peace's office and this was soon running a regular service, first to Beeston in January 1797, then to Nantwich in May 1797, when Beeston Lock had been repaired by him. Sam Dutton was paid twelve shillings as Wharfinger and was to look after the Haughton Moss Drain and Burford Brook Water and to assist the passage boat through the swivel bridges. In November 1797 *a turning place* was to be made at the *head of the Water-Tower locks* but shortly afterwards the Passage Boat was ordered to descend the Water Tower Locks and unload at Tower Wharf on the Wirral Line. In September 1799 the Committee ordered *Mr Fletcher to immediately proceed to cut a Branch from the Canal across the Cowlane Wharf ...build a quay alongside* and *a swivel Bridge for carts be erected across the Branch.*

John Chamberlaine and William Cawley were busy importing pebble: on 20th October 1786 they were *permitted to carry Sea-Gravel up the Canal to Cow Lane Bridge ...to lay down on the Canal Company's land on the north of the canal on paying three halfpence per Ton for Tonnage + Wharfage + One shilling per cargo for a person to assist their Boat up + down the Locks...*

The Wirral Line of the Ellesmere Canal

Weston and Son were the contractors for this broad arm of the canal. Work began on the 8.6 mile branch in November 1794. A passage boat was working the line by 8th June 1795 and coal flats by February 1796. Three locks were built at Whitby Wharf (called Ellesmere Port after 1796) in 1796 and the Wirral Line joined the Chester Canal in January 1797. Two of the Water Tower staircase locks were removed and the rises incorporated in two new locks, one which later acted as a dry dock or graving dock, and another into the Lower Basin. By 1802 a new tidal lock was open to the Dee, upstream from the original entrance.

It was estimated that every time a boat went through a lock 60,000 gallons of water were lost through the levels and eventually into the Mersey or the Dee. Water had to be continually fed into the system. At one end of the Wirral Line it was supplied by the Chester Canal and, at the other, pumped up from the Mersey at Ellesmere Port by a Boulton and Watt steam engine erected by John Wilkinson. There were two locks to Ellesmere Port dock and another into the tidal basin to the Mersey.

Tower Wharf on the Wirral Line c1815
Batenham

New trade

Another steam engine was to be used at Chester, but for a different purpose. *A Letter from Messrs Boulton and Watt of Soho near Birmingham having been read at this Meeting stating the very inconsiderable loss that would arise by taking water for the purpose of supplying a Steam Engine in case the water was returned again to its original source and it being intended for Joseph Walker Esq. and company to erect [lead]works on the North side of the Chester Canal on the Cowlane Land and that a Steam Engine will be necessary for carrying on such works. This Committee do hereby give their consent to the said Joseph Walker and Company laying a pipe from the said Chester Canal to supply such Steam Engine.*
Chester Canal Minutes 3rd June 1799

These lead works beside the canal continued to grow with a tall leadshot tower, built in 1800, which supplied ammunition for the British forces in France who finally overcame Napoleon at Waterloo. Bryant's 1831 map of Cheshire shows the site as a *Shot Manufactory*. The 51 metre lead shot tower was still commercially viable up to the 1980s and it was only at the end of the 20th century that the lead mills closed.

Hurleston Junction

While the Napoleonic Wars helped a new lead trade in Chester, inflation put paid to the idea of completing the Ellesmere Canal from Pontcysyllte, even though a new route was passed by Act of Parliament in 1796, omitting the Ruabon tunnel but passing John Wilkinson's ironworks in Bersham, northwest Wrexham via 'Frood' and Hope to Chester. A feeder arm was planned with a ten acre reservoir at Ffrwd. Apart from the reservoir and about two miles from Summerhill to 'The Yord' at Ffrwd, set to work at a cost of £9135-1-4, the rest of the canal was never cut. Also, Kirk at Ffrwd Colliery was authorised to raise water to

Leadshot Tower of 1800. This, according to a 1783 patent, produced 'small shot perfectly globular in form without dimples, notches and imperfections'.
Photo: Mike Penney

the level of the 'Frood Canal'. The branch was abandoned in 1798 and, by 1813, according to the Cambrian Travellers' Guide, this section was dry. To this day, dog walkers use the towpath along the short section of empty canal and people come across Canal Cottage set out in the fields at Bersham. The reservoir is still visible in wet periods.

On 3rd January 1797 *A Plan, Book of Reference, and Estimate of the Whitchurch Branch of the Ellesmere Canal from New Mills near Whitchurch to the Chester Canal near Nantwich being delivered to this Meeting By John Fletcher (the Engineer appointed by this Company to survey the same) and signed by him and Mr John Duncombe (the Engineer appointed by the Ellesmere Canal company) agreeable to a clause in the Ellesmere act of Parliament: Ordered that the said Plan, Book of reference, and Estimate be approved of by this Company, as the most eligible line to be adopted for a Canal from the Ellesmere canal near Whitchurch to the Chester Canal near Nantwich.*

The empty Ffrwd Canal
Photo: Mike Penney

Although the Chester Canal Company now agreed to a new link at Nantwich rather than the link at Tattenhall, little was done while the works at Chirk were taking place. Chester Canal Committee meetings must have been forlorn affairs, many were cancelled because not enough members even bothered to turn up. Eventually the Chester proprietors threatened to cut off water supplies to the Wirral Line if the junction at Nantwich was not made. After an agreement was made in 1802 the Ellesmere Canal was cut by Samuel Betton from Frankton Junction to Tilstock Park near Whitchurch,12.1 miles on the level, open by 1804. After this it had to be cut, by Fletcher and Simpson, through *two morasses* (the difficult peat mosses of Fenns Moss and Whixall Moss at Bettisfield on the Welsh/English Border where banks had to be drained, filled and stabilised with birch trees) to reach Hurleston,16.9 miles with 19 locks, where it was open on 25th March 1805.

Boats loading limestone from Trevor Rocks, near the Sun Trevor Inn, c1855

Without the Ffrwd Branch as a water supply, another Act was passed in 1804 to take water from the River Dee. Water was taken from the Horseshoe Falls, an almost semi-circular weir built by Telford on the river, north of Llangollen at Llantysilio, down a navigable feeder arm (for half-laden boats only beyond Llangollen) 5.7 miles, finished by 1808. This feeder became an important waterway in the supply of Welsh slate at Llantysilio and limestone from Trevor Rocks (named after the Trevor men who worked the rock) on Eglwyseg Escarpment above Llangollen. Both eventually had inclined plane tramways built to supply the minerals direct to the canalside.

The completed Ellesmere Canal in 1811 then ran on the Wirral Arm from Chester and from near the other end of the Chester Canal at Hurleston to Frankton via Tilstock Park, with three branches: towards Prees but never completed past Quina Brook, 3.75 miles; Ellesmere town, 0.25 mile; and Whitchurch town, 1 mile (now mainly disused). From Frankton it ran northwest to Pontcysyllte and Llantysilio. (The open route today is usually known as the Llangollen Canal). A small private canal was later cut by Exuperius Pickering from Trevor towards Plas Kynaston collieries (now filled in). Pickering also built a coal wharf and chain bridge across the Dee at Lantysilio, as well as building an experimental machine to raise canal boats without losing water, somewhere near Ruabon, but this machine was not good enough and was never used.

Pontcysyllte Aqueduct. *The amazing iron aqueduct, 39 metres above the Dee on stone pillars, solid for only the first 21 metres of their height, was completed in 1805 by Henry Davidson under Thomas Telford, who had supplied plans and drawings to Jessop in 1794. The cost of this structure on the Ellesmere Canal, at £47,000, was more than the original estimate for the whole of the Chester Canal. Mortar between the stone of the aqueduct piers is said to have been mixed with bull's blood to strengthen it. (Nowadays builders use 'plasticiser' or the cheap version - washing up liquid.) The joints of the cast-iron segments, built at William Hazeldine's foundry, were caulked with lead and Welsh flannel boiled in sugar. The towpath is set over the water channel thus reducing the drag effect of the narrow channel on boats. A lever under the towpath controls a drain plug in the centre, used before maintenance with dramatic results. However, boatmen dropping water off the aqueduct could be fined ten shillings (see Regulation 12).*
Photo: Mike Penney

From the foot of the Frankton Locks the Ellesmere Canal ran southwest to Llanymynech where it joined the Montgomery Canal and also ran southeast to Weston (now disused).

Connection

In January 1805 a four page estimate of repairs by Thomas Morris junior totalled £2555-0-0. In April Morris proposed a series of side basins on the Water Tower Locks to save water. Jessop agreed, suggesting less basins but leaving it to Morris. It appears, however, that no basins were ever made. Trade was on the up, and a new warehouse and house were to be built at Nantwich. The Llangollen Canal was a narrow canal, so seven foot boats were authorised to navigate the Chester Canal in November 1806 although the first cargo had been carried in January that year when *six vessels heavy laden with oak timber from the Ellesmere Canal, having passed along the old Chester Canal, arrived at Tower Wharf.*

Some of the rules of the Ellesmere Canal were also brought in. In August 1808 the minutes show *Notice be given to the Several Carriers of Boats employed in the Canal Trade that their Boats will not be permitted to Navigate the Canal after the 29th day of September next unless they are propperly indexed.*

Each boat had to be taken to a company dock to be indexed. The gunwale when empty was marked. Weights of about 2.5 cwt (270 lbs) each were then put in, two at a time, by cranes, the distance from the first mark to the water level being measured, and recorded each time. These readings were entered into books issued to each toll-collector who, thereby, had the vital statistics of every boat moving on the waterway. To check or gauge the tonnage carried, he had only to measure with a gauging-rod from the gunwale mark to the water level, and consult that reading in his book. Some companies, instead of gauging the craft, compelled them to carry index plates, at bow and stern, which showed the tonnage carried at the depths marked. These readings were then averaged to give an acceptable figure. The Chester Canal Company evidently did not accept the latter method of indexing.

In another attempt to save water, in June 1811, it was ordered that *all narrow Boats going up the Canal thro' the Water Tower Locks + the double Locks at Bunbury, shall pass thro' the same in pairs until further notice.* Carriage had increased so that in June 1812 carriers had to pay tonnage quarterly, within one month under threat of non-payers' boats being stopped *without exception.* From 13th May 1811 the Ellesmere Canal Company had free tonnage on materials for building towpaths and roads.

The Chester Company had begun to clear old debts and, by 1812, it was clear that the Ellesmere Canal and Chester Canal relied on each other for trade and water. Amalgamation was a forgone conclusion. The Chester Company wanted 630 shares added to the 3080 shares of the Ellesmere Canal but were forced to accept 500. On 4th December 1812 the Chester Canal Company's seal was used for possibly the final time - on the petition to Parliament for uniting the Chester and Ellesmere Canals. What had started as a grand plan 40 years before, then had sunk to desolation, was now, once more, at the cutting edge of canal technology.

Chester Canal at King Charles' Tower
Old engraving

THE ELLESMERE & CHESTER CANAL Gordon Emery

Dividends

The fortunes of the proprietors had changed for the better. In 1814 a dividend of £2 a share was paid. By 1815 this had doubled. It was reduced to £3 in 1816 and £2 in 1817 but by 1819 was £4 again. Earnings in 1815 were £16,223, in 1816 they were £22,782, and by 1826 had reached £26,183. A regular trade of iron ore was sent to Trevor and boats returned with slate, limestone (44,592 tons in 1814), coal, slack or lime coal, timber and pig iron as well as agricultural cargo such as grain, malt and cheese. Frost & Sons, millers, opened alongside the canal in Steam Mill Street during 1819. Rebuilding of the North Piers and the tidal lock at Ellesmere Port soon took place.

Decanter of the Ellesmere & Chester Canal Co.
Waterways Trust
Photo: Mike Penney

Iron

The ready supply of pig iron from the edges of the Welsh coalfields where waterpower, limestone and coal were ready ingredients for the industry soon led to the use of iron on the canal. The construction of iron lock gates began in 1819. In 1820 a further £200 was spent trying to secure the staircase or double lock at Beeston, still suffering from running sand, and, in 1827, Telford rebuilt the whole Beeston canal section on a new course with two locks, the lower uniquely formed of iron plates to prevent further damage by the shifting sand, and the upper of stone. New cranes were ordered to be set up, in July 1826, at Tower Wharf, Cowlane and Pontcysyllte. Iron was also carried from W Hazledine's works near Shrewsbury to Chester, then by sea to Menai for the construction of Telford's Menai Bridge. After the later connections to the main canal system, over 70,000 tons of iron were carried to Liverpool and Manchester via the canal, half of it from Staffordshire and one sixth from North Wales. By the 1870's iron pipes were shipped out daily from Plas Kynaston.

Chirk Bank

There was one calamity, however. In 1826 the long puddled embankment at Chirk that had been built to divert the original Ellesmere Canal along the bank of the River Dee to its later course at the Cysylltau crossing collapsed and a mass of rubble dammed the river below. Water and rubble built up and totally destroyed the lower pits of Chirk Bank Colliery. Amazingly no men were down the pit for the first time in several years. Despite local history books that state the contrary the author is reliably informed that new pits were dug further up the bank in 1829 and the colliery continued to work until the 1840s. Another breach happened here in 1903. Finally, in the winter of 1989/90, the canal embankment was rebuilt with ferro-concrete.

Regulations

Rules were in force for boatmen on the canal:

1. No boat will be allowed to pass along the canal at any other times than between the hours of seven in the morning and five in the evening during the month of November, December January and February and between the hours of five in the morning and nine in the Evening during the months of May June July and August in any year.

2. Boatmen when they meet on the Towing Path of the Canal must drive their horses to the left side of the Towing Path, as is usual on Turnpike Roads and the Horse next to the hedge or furthest from the Canal, must drop the line, in order that the Horse near the Canal may pass over it.

3. When Boats meet at the bottom of locks they must go first one up then one down, till the whole are past through and any boats steering for an upper level and within sight of any boat steering for a lower level and not exceeding the distance of One Hundred Yards, from a Lock, the boat so steering for the upper level must pass up before the boat steering for the lower level passed down, so that one Lock full of water may serve both Boats.

4. Each Boatman must unhook his horse at the distance of at least one boat's length, from every Lock and haul the boat into the Lock by Hand.

5. No Articles are to be loaded or discharged while the Boat is in any Lock or Bridgeway. (Earlier minutes suggest that this rule did not apply to the wet dock.)

6. No Boatmen will be permitted to fish in the Canal or to have any Fishing Tackle on Board the Vessel.

7. No Boatman will be permitted to leave his horse loose upon the Towing Path of the Canal under penalty of Ten Shillings.

8. No Boatman will be permitted to make use of any Shaft, or Pole, for the guidance of his Boats, if there be any Spikes or Iron, at the end of such shaft, under a penalty of Ten Shillings.

9.Any Boatman or other person refusing to unload his Boat upon any of the Wharfs belonging to the Company in such manner and under such regulation, as the Wharfinger or other person to be appointed by the said Company shall for the proper convenience and accommodation of the Public direct shall for every offence forfeit the sum of Ten Shillings.

10. Any person or persons who have articles remaining upon any of the Company's Wharfs for a larger space than 24 hours and who shall refuse to give a proper account of such Articles to the Wharfinger or other person appointed to receive the same shall forfeit Ten Shillings - and if with

any intent to avoid the payment of Wharfage or other charges which may be payable upon the said articles or false account shall be given every person so offending shall forfeit and pay the Sum of Twenty shillings for every Ton of Goods or other things and so in proportion for any less quantity than a Ton which may be over and above the weight specified in such account - And if any difference of opinion shall arise between the Wharfinger or any other person appointed by the Company, and the owner or owners, concerning the Weight of any such articles, the same to be ascertained by weighing in the manner directed by Acts of Parliament relating to the said Canal, at the expence of the person giving the Account if such account shall prove to be false or otherwise at the expence of the said Wharfinger.

11. Any Boatman passing up or down any Lock who shall neglect to shut the whole of the Gates of such Lock before drawing either of the Paddles shall for every such offence forfeit and pay the sum of Ten shillings.

12. Any Boatman flushing Water through any of the locks after his boat is lowered to the level of the pound below shall for every such offence forfeit and pay the sum of Ten shillings.

13. Any Boatman throwing water out of or cleaning his Boat while passing over either Pontcysyllte or Chirk Aqueduct shall for every such offence, forfeit and pay the Sum of Ten Shillings.

Minutes show a rule about dogs from 1816: *that no Boatman or Servant of this Company be allowed to have any Dog with him whilst passing along the said Canal or Towing Path unless such dog be chained or tied to his Boat and that any person violating this order shall on proof thereof pay a penalty of ten Shillings and six pence for every such offence...*

In 1823, as the canal became busier and perishable goods were carried, the rule of daylight only travel was changed: *all Boats laden with Commercial goods and Grain be permitted to pass along the canal in the night.*

According to the 'Chester Chronicle' of 11th August 1826 a further regulation was added:
At a General Assembly of the Ellesmere and Chester Canal Proprietors, held at the Canal Office, Ellesmere, on Thursday the 27th day of July, 1826, LORD VISCOUNT CLIVE, in the Chair.
It was ordered, that the following be added to the Bye-Laws, of this Canal Company, and that the same be enforced from and after the 1st day of September. next.

THAT no BOATMAN be permitted to moor his BOAT for the night on any part or parts of the several lines of CANAL undermentioned, viz:-

...OLD CHESTER CANAL

Nor on any part of the old Chester Canal, betwixt Nantwich Wharf and Bar Bridge.

Nor on any part of the said Canal, betwixt Bar Bridge and Bunbury Locks.

Nor on any part of the said Canal, betwixt Bunbury Locks and Beeston Brook

Nor on any part of the said Canal, betwixt Beeston Brook and John Lyon's House.

Nor on any part of the said Canal, betwixt John Lyon's house and Christleton Bridge.

Nor on any part of the said Canal, betwixt Christleton bridge and Chester.

Under a penalty of Ten Shillings for the first offence, Twenty Shillings for the second offence, Forty Shillings for the third offence, Four Pounds for the fourth offence, Eight Pounds for the fifth offence, and Ten Pounds for every subsequent offence.

PROVIDED ALWAYS, that if any boat or vessel shall at the close of that time allowed by the Acts relating to the said canals for the day's voyage of such boat or vessel, happen to be between any of the stations hereafter appointed for mooring such vessels it shall be lawful for the boatman in charge thereof to prosecute his voyage to the next station.

EXEMPTIONS FROM THE ABOVE ORDER OR BYE-LAWS

Any boat loading, or discharging at any Wharf, or discharging place, between any of the above stations, may moor for the night at such Wharf, or discharge place only.

Lime Boats discharging Lime at any place between any of the above stations may moor for the night only, at such places as the cargo of Lime may be discharging at.

THOMAS STANTON
General Agent to the Company.

Canal Carriers

Carrying powers on the Mersey were granted to the Ellesmere & Chester Company in 1830. Two companies were hired to take cargo and hire warehouses at Ellesmere Port but in 1836, after complaints, the remaining company and its 25 flats and one lighter were bought out for £25,000.

At the first meeting of the carrying committee, held on 6th December 1836, it was decided *that Mr Thomas Balmer be appointed be appointed Principal Agent for the carrying department - That he do reside in Liverpool and have the entire direction of the establishment there, at Ellesmere Port, and at Chester. That he do personally inspect the books...every fortnight at Chester once a month (sic)...*

He was to receive £400pa with Edward Tilston, Principal Agent at Chester under Mr Balmer at a salary of £300, and Richard Kyftin at Ellesmere Port on a salary of £250. Samuel Salt assisted at Ellesmere Port for £150, John Whittle at Liverpool for £150. Eight other clerks were paid a total of £650. Six flats were to be built to carry across the Mersey at £250 each and the Steam Tug Company asked to tow them. At first, the Steam Tug Co wanted £1 per flat pulled but when they asked for another 50% the committee decided to build its own steam tug. By July 1838 a clear income of £3131.2.10 had been made for the previous year and a second tug was to be built, the first one being nearly completed. By 1839 the first tug was up and running with its two 20HP engines.

In 1842 the company was given permission to carry passengers and goods, or to haul boats of other carriers on their whole canal system (before the Canal Carriers Act of 1845 which authorised all canal companies to carry and the Canal Tolls Act which allowed companies to vary tolls). By the mid-19th century about 20,000 tons of coal were being shipped down the canal from the Welsh coal fields.

New Dock

Whitby Locks or Whitby Wharf was always referred to as Ellesmere Port by Telford. From a few locks, houses and wharfs the port expanded enormously over the years. In 1828 Telford was ordered to build a warehouse, and two years later the company bought out a private boatyard to expand further. In 1833 twelve houses were built for workers, and in the same year Telford reported that: *The extensive system of warehouses and basins will be ready in three months.* Fifteen more houses were built in by 1837 while a private tannery two cottages and a house were bought from a private investor, John Brint. The company required a further hectare of land for expansion in 1840. With the population growing, a church and school were built by the company the same year.

The late Thomas Telford's planned new works at Ellesmere Port were completed by W A Provis to William Cubitt's design. A new dock was built 435 feet long and 139 feet wide. The grand opening was to be marked by the steamer 'Earl Powis' sailing into the dock with bands playing. Whoops - the steamer was a few inches too wide for the new lock gates so the 'Bridget' schooner led the way followed by seven other vessels. The ceremony took its course with the band marching around the dock to a dinner being provided in a converted warehouse. The 480 workmen sat upstairs with their free dinner of roast beef, pork, goose, boiled beef, plum pudding, cheese and a pint of ale, while the wealthy were seated in a lower room.

Opening the new dock at Ellesmere Port
Illustrated London News

According to the 'Illustrated London News' there were now *upwards of seventy houses, some of neat aspect and commodious interior, a church, schools, two or three inns, two sets of locks; a splendid and most ample range of warehouses erected on arches over various branches of the canal, and which afford great convenience for the loading and unloading of vessels, besides the vast new dock.*

Middlewich Branch

In the early 19th century, the Ellesmere & Chester Canal was still not linked with the main English canal system but in 1824 the Birmingham and Liverpool Junction Canal Act was passed authorising a link from Nantwich southwards to Autherley, near Wolverhampton, where it would meet with the Staffordshire and Worcestershire Canal. With this connection to the main canal system, the Trent & Mersey Canal proprietors now had no reason to delay a junction of the Chester Canal at Middlewich. The original Chester Canal Act had already been passed so it was only necessary to cut the canal from Barbridge and arrange a route for the additional 100 yards through the town. The T&M Act of 1827 gave their company permission for the final link: the Wardle Green branch with one lock. However, it also gave them permission to charge an extortionate toll of 9d per ton on coal, limestone and salt and even more on other items. Nevertheless the 9.7 mile Middlewich Branch with 3 locks was opened in 1833, linking to the Wardle Green Branch.

Birmingham & Liverpool Junction Canal

Unlike some of the older winding canals, Telford planned the Birmingham & Liverpool Junction Canal as a straight route with embankments and aqueducts as the only hope for competition against the railways. It became England's most expensive canal. Lord Clive, the Chairman of the Ellesmere & Chester Canal took on the role of Chairman for the new canal. Work started on the Nantwich link in 1827, with John Wilson as contractor, and Andrew Easton as Resident Engineer. Wilson was hampered by the collapse of Nantwich Bank in a wet winter two years later. The next section south from High Offley to Church Eaton was contracted to William Provis (who later carried out works at Ellesmere Port). More problems occurred including subsidence of the Shelmore embankment and changing the proposed 690 yard tunnel at Cowley into a cutting apart from 81 yards. The most southerly section from Church Eaton was again contracted to John Wilson, and finished, on his death, by W Wilson, his son. The canal was completed in May 1835 to a length of 39.5 miles with 26 narrow locks and a stop lock at Autherley Junction. There was also the 10.3 mile long Newport branch with 23 locks, also cut by Provis, and the 0.25 mile Humber Arm to a wharf at Lubstree. Meanwhile Telford had died

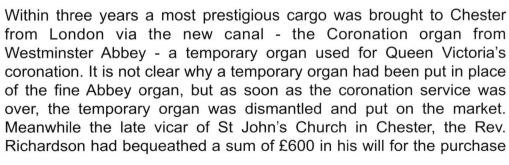

without seeing completion, blaming the problems at Shelmore on Lord Anson's required diversion around his pheasant shooting wood.

The canal cut nearly 20 miles and 30 locks off the journey to Liverpool using the Trent & Mersey. Around 5,000 boats used the canal in 1836 but tolls had to be reduced because of competition with the Grand Junction Railway from Birmingham to Warrington, which opened in 1837.

Within three years a most prestigious cargo was brought to Chester from London via the new canal - the Coronation organ from Westminster Abbey - a temporary organ used for Queen Victoria's coronation. It is not clear why a temporary organ had been put in place of the fine Abbey organ, but as soon as the coronation service was over, the temporary organ was dismantled and put on the market. Meanwhile the late vicar of St John's Church in Chester, the Rev. Richardson had bequeathed a sum of £600 in his will for the purchase

The wooden coffin at St John's Church: said to have been transported by canal from Nantwich by the Rev. Massey then set up in the ruins by the sexton for the Rev. Richardson.
Photo: Mike Penney

of an organ. His executors Thomas Dixon and the Rev. Lyon, Rector of Pulford, set out to buy the best organ they could. Needless to say, they snapped up the instrument, which was brought to Chester and, it is said, unloaded at Cow Lane then transported by cart along Frodsham Street and St John's Street to the Church. Rev. Lyon still had £19-15-0 left from the bequest and this was used to pay a portion of the cost incurred in altering the organ gallery. On 28th October 1838 the Lord Bishop of Chester presided at the inaugural ceremony.

The Birmingham & Liverpool Junction Canal Junction was amalgamated with the new 'Chester & Ellesmere Canal Company' name under an Act of Parliament in May 1845, but 'railway mania' had started.

Chester & Ellesmere Boats 'Dace' and 'Florence' at Cowlane Wharf Old engraving

71

SHROPSHIRE UNION Gordon Emery

The 'Shroppie'

Only a month after amalgamation, a committee was formed to look into the conversion or addition of railways on the canal system. William Provis, now the company engineer, informed them that converting the canals to railways was the cheapest way forward. Under Robert Stephenson's guidance three Acts were sought to combine railway and canal companies in the area, including the Chester & Ellesmere Canal, the 26 mile Montgomery Canal, the 17 mile Shrewsbury Canal and a lease on the 10.5 mile Shropshire Canal. The Shropshire Union Railways & Canal Company was born with a total length of 200.54 miles.

However, the Stafford to Shrewsbury Railway, started in 1846 and opened in 1849 was their only new railway because, in 1846, the London & North Western Railway Company took a lease on the Shropshire Union, prevented further competitive railway building, then operated their existing railway tracks. In 1849 the circle was completed by bringing the head office of the Shroppie back to Chester, where it had all begun.

Luckily for the Shroppie, the L&NWR could use their canal system to compete with the Great Western Railway: it was this that may have saved it from extinction. The fleet of carrying boats expanded from 213 in 1870 to 450 in 1902. However revenues dropped significantly in World War I. Canal subsidies during the latter part of the war, under the Canal Control Committee, kept the company afloat, although a breach closed the Weston line in 1917. Subsidies were withdrawn in1920. The SUR&CCo now decided to give up carrying completely.

Questions asked in Parliament were printed in the 'Chronicle' of 25 June 1921:

SHROPSHIRE UNION CANAL
MR NEVILLE CHAMBERLAIN'S QUESTIONS IN THE COMMONS
In the House of Commons, on Monday, Mr Neville Chamberlain asked the Minister of Transport whether he was aware that the Shropshire Union Railways and Canal Company had intimated that, on August 14th next, they would close their carrying business over their own system and any canals connected therewith, also over the River Mersey between Ellesmere Port, Liverpool, Birkenhead, or any upper Mersey ports, and also between their canal and the railway system via Calveley: that many of the places and districts served by the canal system were no accessible by rail, and the cessation of the service therefore amounted to a

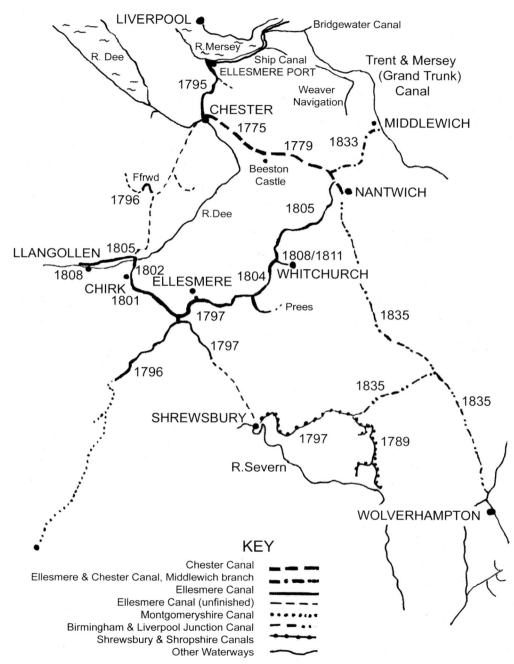

The canals of the Shropshire Union Based on a map by Roger Dean

Image labels:

LIVERPOOL
Bridgewater Canal
R. Mersey
R. Dee
Ship Canal
ELLESMERE PORT
1795
Weaver Navigation
Trent & Mersey (Grand Trunk) Canal
CHESTER
1775
MIDDLEWICH
1779   1833
Beeston Castle
Ffrwd
1796
R.Dee
1805
NANTWICH
LLANGOLLEN 1805
1808   1802
1808/1811
WHITCHURCH
CHIRK   ELLESMERE   1804
1801
1797
Prees
1797
1835
1796
1835
1835
SHREWSBURY
1797   1789
R.Severn
WOLVERHAMPTON

KEY
Chester Canal
Ellesmere & Chester Canal, Middlewich branch
Ellesmere Canal
Ellesmere Canal (unfinished)
Montgomeryshire Canal
Birmingham & Liverpool Junction Canal
Shrewsbury & Shropshire Canals
Other Waterways

withdrawal of reasonable facilities in accordance with Section 2 of The Railway and Canal Traffic Act, 1854; whether the Shropshire Union system was leased in perpetuity to the London and North-Western Railway Company, Limited; and whether he could take steps to provide that canals owned or controlled by railway companies should be transferred to bodies controlling waterways or groups of waterways only.

Sir E. Geddes: I am aware that the Shropshire Union Railways and Canal Co., whose undertaking is leased in perpetuity to L and N. W Rly., have intimated that they will close their canal carrying business after August 31st next. They state that they are incurring heavy loss in connection with the operation of their carrying business, and that they are advised that they are under no legal obligation to act as carriers. The canal itself will remain open for navigation by suitable boats, subject to the payment of tolls.

The carrying business closed. Boats, 136 canal boats and around 80 river barges, were sold to private companies or laid up.

Cheese

Narrowboat 'Peel' was used by Mr J G Fish, a cheese factor at Whitchurch. From 1892 it conveyed cheese in loads of up to 18 tons on the Shroppie, collecting from cheese warehouses at Ellesmere and loading at Whitchurch every Wednesday. The cheese collected was brought to Whitchurch where it was unloaded, examined and labelled before loading in the boat again and sending to Ellesmere Port and Liverpool for export. 'Peel' was fitted with three floors and bearers. Cheese was stacked only up to two high on the lower shelf and a single layer on the next. For air circulation the cratch was fitted with metal vents pierced with small holes. The top floor was packed with straw to protect the soft cheese which was only individually wrapped in cloth and not boxed. The cheese had to be carefully and cleanly handled. On the outside the boat had special sheets: top sheets and secondary sheets treated with a heat resistant substance. After delivery the boat returned on Friday, usually loaded with animal feed or agricultural goods. When Mr Fish died 'Peel' was transferred to the Manchester line until the Shropshire Union stopped carrying. The boat was finally broken up in 1949. 'Peel' was registered number 449 in Chester as a dwelling and had to bear a wheatsheaf mark. Like many other Shroppie boats its crew lived aboard. Registration was for three men, three women, or a man, his wife and up to two children under 12 years old.

THE CANAL BOATS ACT, 1877.

40 and 41 Vic., c. 60.

City and County of the City of Chester.

Certificate of Registration of Canal Boats.

THE CHESTER URBAN SANITARY REGISTRATION AUTHORITY

Registration Number
of Boat. } _449_

Whereas application has been made to us, the Town Council of the City and County of the City of Chester, acting as the Registration Authority under the Canal Boats Act, 1877, to register as a dwelling a canal boat, of which* the _Shropshire Union Railways and Canal Company of Chester_ ————— are the owners, and which is accustomed or intended to ply [as a fly boat worked by shifts†] on the canal whereon the said district abuts :

And Whereas we have ascertained that the said boat conforms to the conditions of registration provided by the regulations of the Local Government Board for the number of persons allowed by the said regulations to dwell therein ;

Now we, the said Town Council of the said City, acting as the Registration Authority, do hereby certify as follows, that is to say :—

1. That the Boat named‡ _Peel_ whereof the _Shropshire Union Railways and Canal Company of Chester_ are the owners, has been duly registered as a dwelling ;

2. That the place to which the said boat has been registered as belonging for the purposes of the Elementary Education Acts, is Chester ;

3. That the number with which, in pursuance of the statutory provision in that behalf, the said boat is required to be numbered is _449_

4. That the distinctive mark with which we require the said boat to be marked is a Wheat Sheaf ;

5. That in accordance with the provisions contained in the subjoined Article of an Order of the Local Government Board dated the Twentieth day of March One Thousand Eight Hundred and Seventy Eight the maximum number of persons for which the said boat is registered as a dwelling is as follows :—

Three Men or three Women, or a Man, Wife and two children under 12 years of age

Living aboard

It was the 1877 Canal Boats Act, strengthened by an Amendment Act in 1884, which ensured that all boats were registered for living accommodation. The Nantwich boat register records 78 boats with accommodation in the rear cabin (of which only 14 remained of the original in 1914). Out of these only one had a forecabin where a further two adults could live.

The 19th century census records boat crews living on board near the SU boat-building yard in Chester on the night it was taken. Examples include: 'Edward' Sally Boat No 32 Shropshire Union Co holding 25 tons, Head William Bruce, 45 years old from Lambeth in London with his wife Harriet, 30 years old from St Ives in Cornwall; 'Catherine', 50 tons Master William Catherall, 30 years old, born in Queensferry with his mate of 18 years old from Ellesmere Port.

The SUR&CCo minutes show the appointment of *a Lady Boat Inspector* to ensure that children went to school while, at the end of the 19th century, Christian evangelists saw the hundreds of, often illiterate, children and canal people living aboard as open to missionary work and charity. In Chester there was a floating mission run by the Independent Chapel in Queen Street on a Shroppie flat boat where Sunday services, Sunday school and temperance meetings were held. This was replaced at the turn of the century with a chapel at Tower Wharf which closed when the SUR&CCo stopped carrying.

There was a mission at Ellesmere Port provided free of charge by the SUR&CCo, operating by 1884 and run by the Incorporated Seamen and Boatmen's Friend Society and Mersey Mission to Seamen.

Another mission, at Nantwich, was held in a cheese shed by an Anglican curate until a mission room was built. This probably closed in 1906 but the Salvation Army was allowed to use a warehouse at Barbridge for services, while the SUR&CCo let a small cottage to the missionary *on easy terms*. When LTC Rolt and his partner cruised by in his narrowboat during 1939 they saw *a wooden mission room on the water's edge. We wondered whether the latter was intended for canal boatmen on the lines of a seaman's mission, as its site suggested, but when a service was held there next morning the canal folk were conspicuous by their absence, although several boats passed by.*

The Canal Boat Acts were amended in 1925 and became part of the Public Health Act in 1936. Current public health legislation ended the need to register in 1969. (See also Sally boats and Fly boats: Welfare and Worship, Education)

Found Drowned

Although the canals were private transport systems, children and adults were attracted to these still waterways passing through towns and cities. No doubt there were many unauthorised boats, swimmers and walkers using the canals after they were cut. Use of the canals often led to disaster both at work and play as reported in local papers:

A Boy Drowned in the Canal

Samuel Challinor, aged 7, son of Joseph Challinor, 49 Orchard Street, engineer on a canal steam tug. Deposition by Samuel Spilsbury, 10 Lyon Street, boatbuilder at SURCCo.

'Chronicle' 29th May 1886

Chester Boy Drowned

Harry Bellion, aged 14, of 46 Vernon Road, Chester. Deceased had been employed at the SURCCo boatyard in Chester, and had been apprenticed as a boatbuilder for a month. He could not swim.

Alfred Lowndes of 88, Garden Lane, boatbuilder, said the deceased was an apprentice working under him on Wednesday afternoon. He saw him last about ten minutes to five in the afternoon. Deceased had been carrying boards for him and had brought his last board to witness he had done with him. Witness had been working on the boat "Phoebe". Deceased was supposed to go back to the Shop to make 'plugs'. His proper way was to go round by bridge. He had no right to go over the boats, and witness cautioned him on this point, warning him that he would get into the canal. Witness could not say how deceased got into the water. William Reynolds, of 18 Station View, Captain of the SU flat 'Ann', deposed to grappling for the boy and recovering the body about ten o'clock on Thursday morning. Deceased was just outside the lock, near to the 'Phoebe', and other boats alongside. It would be possible for deceased to fall between the sterns of two boats.

The jury returned a verdict of "Found in the water and no evidence to show how he got there". Mr Owen, boatyard foreman, expressed the SU's regret etc. at this, the first fatality in the yard.

'Chronicle' 10th October 1914

Two Children Drowned at Chester
Danger of Playing by the canal

Mr E Brassey held an inquest at the Town Hall Chester, on Monday, respecting the death of John Speed, the six year old son of Thomas Charles Speed, 13 Charles street, Hoole. About 7pm, on Tuesday, deceased went to play with other children in the street, and shortly afterwards he was seen at the canal side, near the top of Hoole Lane locks, and must have accidentally slipped into the canal. No one actually saw him fall in, but a small boy, who was on the canal side, ran into Richmond terrace and said a boy was swimming in the canal, near the locks. Several people went to the spot but could see nothing but bubbles, and a piece of bread on the water. A youth named Fred Cooper, got a boat hook, and with assistance from a canal boatman, named William Rogers, they recovered the body.

Artificial respiration was applied by Commander Pearce, 6 Hoole Park. Doctor Woodruffe was sent for, and on arrival pronounced life extinct. The body was afterwards taken to the mortuary. Evidence was given by Sarah Ann Speed, mother of the deceased and Doctor H. L. Waren Woodruffe. The latter said he was sent for shortly after 8.30. He saw the deceased by the canal side. He said he was dead. Death was due to drowning.

The Coroner, in recording a verdict of "Found Drowned", and there being no evidence to show how he got into the canal, said in three days two young children, aged five and six years, not attended by anyone, had been drowned in the canal. It ought to be a warning to parents not to let their children go out into danger alone.

'Chronicle' 19th June 1920

However, drownings were not confined to children: *The Chester Coroner (Mr E Brassey), on Saturday conducted an inquest concerning the death through drowning in the river Dee of Geo. Evans (24), 5 Tower Wharf, Chester. It appears that the deceased was employed by the Shropshire Union Canal Co. as "tidal" lock keeper on Sealand-road locks. On Friday, about 8.50p.m., he left his home to go for a walk, and said he would call at the locks and put things right, as he came back to his supper, before the tide came in. About 10.15 he was talking to two men named Woodbine and Walker, and was heard to say, "There is a rat on the bank. I will get over the wall and try to get it, as they get into my cabin." He got over the wall, and a few minutes afterwards Woodbine followed him and saw his cap floating in the water, and Evans was not to be seen.*

The police were at once informed and the body was recovered by Inspector Williams and conveyed to the mortuary,

Dr W. H. Griffith said he examined the body on Saturday, and saw no marks of violence. In his opinion death was due to drowning.

Annie Elizabeth Barrett, 5 Tower Wharf, Chester, sister of the deceased, said that deceased was unmarried and living with his mother.

Thos. Woodbine, 46 Gladstone-avenue, Chester, stated that about 10.15 on the day in question he and a friend of his named Benjamin Walker, met deceased, whom they did not know before, on the canal bridge, and got into conversation with him. Deceased got over the

wall with the intention of going after a rat. Witness did not see him afterwards.
The coroner said he would adjourn the inquest for one week and order a post mortem
examination of the body.

'Courant' 23rd June 1920

A narrow escape

On Wednesday night an elderly woman named Mrs Jonas, residing at 14, Churton Road, Boughton, had a narrow escape of being drowned in the Shropshire Union Canal near the City Road Bridge. A canal boatman named William Reynolds, residing at Ellesmere Port, reported to the police that he heard a noise in the canal between Russell Street and City Road Bridge, and running to the edge of the towpath saw a shawl floating on top of the water. He succeeded in getting hold of Mrs Jonas and rescuing her. She was assisted to a house in Russell Street, where she was attended to, and subsequently removed in a cab to her home. Mrs Jonas is the mother of thirty-three children, and some time ago gained prominence by being the recipient of a special prize in a competition offered in regard to large families by a London journal. She is suffering from the shock caused by the immersion, but it is not known how she got into the water. Since last January no fewer than five persons have been drowned in the canal within the city boundary, and the Chief Constable pointed out in his last annual report that the canal from Hoole Lane to Frodsham Street was open to the streets and during darkness was a very effective death trap. During the last 15 years it had claimed no fewer than 31 victims, and he suggested that for the protection of life, it ought to be fenced off.

'Chester Chronicle' 21st December 1895

Manchester Ship Canal

In 1883 proposals were made in Parliament to build a ship canal from the Mersey at Ellesmere Port to Manchester. Objections were made in the Commons by the Shropshire Union and later, in the Lords, by L&NWR. The Bill failed because of access to the Ellesmere Port Dock. A new Bill in 1885 included new fixed depths of water and free access to the dock. The Act was passed and construction started from Eastham to Ellesmere Port. After tides washed out new embankments on two occasions a new one was finally stabilised. The steam packet 'Earl Powis' was the first vessel to enter the new canal on July 16th 1891. Ellesmere Port expanded considerably and, in 1902, the new Urban District of Ellesmere Port and Whitby came into being.

Ellesmere Port

Within the last few years it has become a place of immense traffic. It commands a considerable trade in iron ore, and has become the principal depot for the ore brought from Whitehaven, Ulverston, etc. which is there forwarded to the large manufacturers in Staffordshire. It is brought to this place by coasting vessels, whence it is forwarded by the canals to its destination. Goods arriving by the canals from London, Birmingham, Wolverhampton, all parts of Staffordshire, and Wales, are here transhipped into barges, and towed by steamers to Liverpool. The steamers arrive every tide, and convey passengers as well as merchandise. The Docks, Wharfs, Piers, and Warehouses are spacious, and mostly of recent construction; they are of the most substantial workmanship, and the large dock will hold upwards of fifty coasting vessels. The Bridgewater Trust occupy the premises under the SURCCo, and are the river carriers between Liverpool and Ellesmere Port.

'Bagshaw's Cheshire Directory', 1850.

Slater's Directory of 1848 says: *Extensive carrying companies have resident agents established here, and goods are forwarded by them to all parts of the kingdom.*

Animation and bustle are likewise imparted to it, by the arrival and departure of coasting vessels and flats, and the discharge or reception of their several cargoes, which has of late considerably increased since the SURCCo have had the port and warehouses under their sole management.

'Slater's Commercial Directory', 1856.

Before the opening of the Manchester Ship Canal no vessel larger than 500 tons ever went to Ellesmere Port, but after the opening of the waterway from Eastham vessels of between 3,000 and 4,000 tons have gone up and discharged and received cargo. A very great improvement has in consequence taken place in the trade. From America the importation of pig-iron has recently increased to an enormous extent, thousands of tons being constantly passing through Ellesmere Port for distribution all over Staffordshire. Although the English trade has decreased, it has not been crushed out, for coasting steamers still arrive with the iron from the iron ports.

A visit to the wharves, where the flats are moored, revealed the fact that a great trade is being done with bog ore and other materials used in the manufacture and working of iron, great quantities of which are brought from Iceland and Spain. The trade in manufactured iron of all description from America has of late shown a very great increase, large consignments being frequently sent down the centre of England.

Ellesmere Port Docks
Early 20th century

With regard to the grain trade, it may be pointed out that this now forms a very important feature of the place. The SURCCo started at Ellesmere Port with one warehouse. A second was afterwards erected, which would accommodate 4,000 tons of grain. The company again had to extend its operations, and to build a new set of warehouses near the dock entrance. These were found to be insufficient to cope with the trade, and a few weeks ago a large and commodious warehouse was opened on the bank of the Manchester Ship Canal, fitted with all modern appliances for the rapid discharging and loading of grain, compared with the old days, when grain had to be dealt with by hand, the modern facilities now in operation cannot fail to cheapen the cost of transit.

During the last six or seven years the overside delivery of grain from the huge steamers in the Liverpool docks has greatly developed, and Ellesmere Port is reaping some of the advantages. The saving of time to the shipowners by overside delivery is considerable. The advantage is very great when the quay space is limited. There is a great saving also in the cost per ton of discharged overside as compared with being placed on the quay and handled. The SUCo receive grain into their barges from the modern steamers in the Liverpool docks, and distribute it from Ellesmere Port all over the Kingdom at the Liverpool through rates. Having regard to the enormous cargoes that the American liners now bring into Liverpool, it is considered that it must be a decided advantage to the shipowners to get such cargoes as grain delivered overside, thus leaving the quay space for general cargo. Steamers constantly arrive in Liverpool with from 5,000 to 6,000 tons of grain, not including general cargo on board, and it can, therefore, easily be seen what a difficulty there would be in storing an entire cargo of 10,000 to 12,000 tons on any particular portion of the quay. In the near future it is believed that overside delivery will still further develop, and thus satisfactory terms with regard to it will be arranged between the Mersey Docks and Harbour Board and the steamship owners.

The trade in bone ash and pottery is also of an extensive nature.

'Courant' 14 June 1899

Keeping the waterways

When the Shropshire Union Carrying Company closed in 1921, many of the boats were bought up by independent traders who became 'Number Ones' or owner/masters. Others were sold to companies who took over carriage (see later chapters.) Amazingly tonnage on the Birmingham line only declined by a fifth over the next eight years.

In 1922 the L&NWR took over the Shropshire Union completely. Shortly afterwards the L&NWR was itself taken over by the London, Midland & Scottish Railway. Maintenance was now kept to a minimum. By the mid-1930's canal carrying on the Llangollen Canal was under considerable pressure from road transport: carrying by canal was at the end of the line. Another breach, in 1936, closed the Montgomery Canal. (It is currently undergoing restoration.) World War II saw control of the railway-owned canals under committees of the Ministry of Transport but by 1940 canal carrying on the Llangollen Canal had virtually ceased and it was only kept open as a water feeder. In 1948 the waterways were nationalised and run by British Transport Waterways. Since 1963 they have been run by British Waterways (Board). At Ellesmere Port much of the local canal heritage is preserved at the Boat Museum.

Boatbuilding Tools Tony Lewery
Top shelf: caulking mallet & irons, augers, pole plane, braces.
Bottom shelf: gouges, chisels, adze, draw knife, planes, shearing hammer, broad axe, mattock, bevel, mattock, maul, rove bunter, punches, bevel, game block (in which planks were wedged for boring.)

BOATBUILDING Geoff Taylor

Early boatbuilding in Chester

Shipbuilding was taking place on the Dee Estuary before 1066. Kelsterton, near Connah's Quay, was a small shipbuilding hamlet. Kel - from the Danish - *kjoll* = a keel or small ship; *ster*, an Anglo-Saxon suffix denoting employment. In Chester there were well-established shipbuilders and boatbuilders operating on the Dee since the Middle Ages. Lyson's Magna Britannia, in 1810 noted that: *Shipbuilding has been carried out at Chester for many centuries - there are now more ships built at Chester than at Liverpool, they being great in estimation amongst the merchants of that and other principal sea-ports of England and Scotland as particularly well founded, and in the mariner's phrase "sea-worthy".*

Some of the shipbuilders and boatbuilders who were based in the vicinity of Chester and the Dee Basin during the time of canal construction were:

Roodee
John Troughton 1783 - c1818
John Wilson & Sons 1828
William Beshton c1855 - c1865

River Dee Company Yard
William Courtney c1800 - 1820
William Mulvey 1820 - 1852

Chester and Cheshire Directories also list
Peter Jackson, shipbuilder, Old Crane Street 1781   Michael Cooper, Boatbuilder, Old Crane 1789

The early yards, often referred to as Boat Docks, were family owned and consisted of a stretch of land alongside the canal with a timber slipway, some covered workspace and storage, a saw pit and a steam box. The frontage would be 75 ft to 150 ft to accommodate one or two boats to be 'slipped' (launched sideways).

Dee Basin slipway c1913
Beached river launch with steam engine powering band saw and steambox
Geoff Taylor Collection

As the early yards were family concerns, there would be a complement of just a handful of men, sometimes only two - the owner and an employee, as the 1881 Census extract for my great grandfather, Joseph Taylor, illustrates:

Dwelling: Barnes Meadow, Darlaston
Census Place: Sedgley, Stafford, England

	Married	*Age*	*Sex*	*Birthplace*
Joseph TAYLOR:	Married	38	Male	Tipton, Stafford
Relationship: Head	Occupation: Boat Builder Employing One Man			
Mary TAYLOR	Married	37	Female	Rowley Regis, Stafford
Relationship: Wife				

Whilst operating in Darlaston, Joseph and his family lived in an upturned narrowboat. It must have been terribly cramped!

Construction and materials

Although iron boats were introduced in the late 18th century, wood continued to be the favoured material for construction. The timber used for boatbuilding was oak and green (unseasoned) elm. This green elm was used for the bottoms of the boats as, in this form, and immersed in water all the time, it was not subject to rot and decay to the same extent as seasoned timber. The elm planks were about 3in thick, 18in wide and 7ft long for narrowboats; they were at least 14ft long for flats. These were fixed to the keelson using long iron spikes.

Wolverhampton Corrugated Iron Co Float under construction in Taylor's Yard c1930; Frank Taylor on crossbraces.
Geoff Taylor Collection

Oak was used for the frame and timbers. Oak planks, called strakes, were riveted to wooden, and later iron, knees. The oak planks had to be joined and this was achieved by using a scarf joint. These were very long joints for strength. The planks had to be bent into rather tight curves where they joined the stem and stern posts of the boat and, as they were about 2in thick, they required steaming for several hours to enable them to bend and follow the shape of the boat. They had to be removed from the steambox with haste and clamped in position before they cooled.

The inside of the hull was waterproofed with chalico. This was a mixture of dried horse dung, and tar, sometimes with cow or horsehair added for even greater strength.

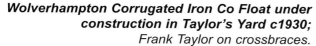

Oak narrowboat construction
Tony Lewery

One of the less enviable jobs was the need to rub up the dry dung to produce a powder. (My father would often regale me with this detail as it was one of his jobs when he started in the yard - he usually managed to tell the tale when I was tucking in to my tea!)

Rolling oakum
Tony Lewery

This chalico was then 'parged' (plastered) onto the inside of the hull, thus rendering it waterproof. Oak shearing, thin boards set vertically, finished off the inside of the hull. This protected the chalico seal and made a barrier for the later caulking.

The seams between the planks outside had to be sealed by caulking them with oakum and then coating with tar. Oakum is teased out, used hemp rope treated with tar and linseed oil which is then rolled into a crude rope and then forced into the seams with a caulking iron, hit with a caulking mall of lignum vitae. (Picking oakum was a regular workhouse chore and was also used as a punishment in prison. A year or so of picking oakum played havoc with the prisoner's fingers - especially pickpockets! Oakum was also used a stuffing for mattresses and so was a good example of recycling - hence the expression "money for old rope".)

Caulking and tarring,
Dee Basin slipway, c1920
Geoff Taylor Collection

Launching (slipping) the 'Ellesmanor',
Wolverhampton Corrugated Iron Company float c1930
Geoff Taylor Collection

Once fitted out, the boat would be ready for launch. In most cases the launch would be broadside to the canal. The boat would be placed on wooden skids and then allowed to slide into the water.

Midlands' carriers

The Wolverhampton Corrugated Iron Company established their rolling mills in Ellesmere Port in 1905. Several other Midlands' based businesses relied on the Shropshire Union Canal to carry their goods. The Midland and Coast Canal carriers had four composite canal boats built at Crichtons & Co. in the late 1920s.

Crichtons had established their yard on the Dee at Saltney in 1913. The four boats that were constructed for Midland and Coast were: 'Apollo', 'Diamond', 'Spade' and 'Star', fitted with bow cabins and intended for horse-drawn working. 'Apollo' is still in service as a pleasure cruiser based at Shipley in West Yorkshire. She now bears little resemblance to her original form, having been converted to a motor boat and shortened to 56ft, as well as having a steel bottom.

The cabin of Diamond is a static exhibit at the Black Country Museum in Dudley.

Early canal boats on the Chester Canal

The Duke's boats on the Bridgewater were clearly used as exemplars in the first days of the Chester Canal. As early as July 1772, Sam Weston was sent to view them and, in June 1773, it was ordered *that Michael Cooper [a Chester boatbuilder] be sent to View the Duke of Bridgewater's Passage Boat and take Dimensions of the same, and that he deliver in an Estimate to the Committee for building one of the same sort.*

Several other boats were ordered: *another boat 50ft long be constructed for £9.* The 'Chester Courant', carried an advertisement for boatbuilders and a little later the minutes show quotations: *Henry Hilton to build boats 36ft x 6ft x 3ft deep at a cost of 4 shillings per foot ... Joseph Fryer to build boats 50 feet and under at 3/6d per foot and 50-70 feet at 3/4d per foot at 7ft beam.*

Towards the end of the 18th century, Europe was emerging from the effects of a mini Ice Age, so it is no surprise to see another minute on the 26th November 1773: *Henry Hilton to build Ice Boat on the lowest possible terms.*

On 4th February 1774 the Chester Canal Minute Book records: *Proposals for boatbuilding at £48 - £60, 60 foot x 7 foot x 4 foot: Mr Moon to treat [negotiate terms] with persons for building 6 Boats on the Lowest terms he can.* Within five months a further two boats were ordered: *Two boats be immediately constructed for such as are generally built at Bangor for his Grace the Duke of Bridgewater.* There is no record to show which boatbuilders fulfilled these contracts.

The February 1774 proposal was for 7ft boats - narrowboats, but by 27 December 1774 a wide boat had been constructed near Cow Lane Gate. It is recorded that: *A 50 ton boat passed through the Northgate Lock.* The Canal Proprietors must have shared the same satisfaction as the crowds who witnessed the passage of boats alongside the City Walls because by 3rd February 1775 there was a requirement *that a Barge to be built to the same dimensions as the Egerton - on the lowest terms, to be carvel built.* It is likely that this was the vessel Bootle.

Details from the Minute Book reveal an increasing demand for boats that could not be satisfied locally: On the 3rd June 1775 it was ordered: *that 2 of the boats at the Twelve Acres near the Weaver, be cut into two pieces, each boat to be conveyed to the Barbridge Valley as soon as possible.* It was specified on 28 July 1775 *that the boats at Barbridge be finished with square sterns agreeable to the plan produced by Mr Powell!* A further two boats of the same construction were ordered by August in the same year.

Notwithstanding the pool of local boatbuilding expertise on the river Dee, there was need to recruit more craftsmen. It has been suggested that the need to search elsewhere for boatbuilders was not so much due to the lack of local talent on the Dee, but that many of the men were indentured (contracted) to their employers.

It was minuted on 5th August 1774: *that an Advertisement be put in the Birmingham Paper for four journeymen boatbuilders.* In the space of a few years, existing boats were in need of repair and modification: on the 26th October 1778 minutes stated:*that the Egerton and Bootle and Flatts bee put into proper Repair fit to be stationed on the Nantwich Line as soon as finished,* while in February 1779 it was ordered: *that the seven feet boats be broke up and converted into a Boat similar to Powell as soon as Edward Bird can.* By April 1780 it is recorded: *that Bootle, Peploe, Speed and Egerton be laid up in the Basin at the Phoenix Tower.*

Boatbuilding continued apace. Four more boats were ordered from Johnson & Co in 1780, while repairs and also de-commissioning took place. The Company required that the Ice Boat be broken up at Cow Lane in 1778. Cow Lane had become a centre for Chester Canal boatbuilding: it should be remembered that the Wirral Line had not been cut and what we consider today to be the centre of boatbuilding, the SU Yard, did not exist. Thirty years on at Cow Lane: *On Saturday last, two flats, built by Mr John O'Kell, were launched from his building yard, near the King's Wharf, on the banks of the Ellesmere and Chester Canal, in this city. They are named the Chapman and Parkins and are intended to trade between Northwich and Liverpool.*
                                          'Chester Chronicle' 9 December 1813

A sad sequel to this report is this 'Chronicle' advertisement:

To Shipwrights, Wheelwrights, Timber Dealers and Others.
To be Sold by Auction
At the premises, the Wharf, nearly adjoining Cow Lane Bridge
The whole of the very extensive STOCK-IN-TRADE
Late property of Mr John O'Kell deceased.

Much later on, in the 19th century, Musgraves established a timber yard at Cow Lane and Charles Seddon of Middlewich established a warehouse nearby.

Cow Lane timber yard, early 19th century. *The painting shows a stylised narrowboat with an unnaturally small boatwoman and a straight rudder bar, whereas they are usually curved down in motion or up when standing. The Cathedral was later refaced and altered in a Victorian 'Gothic restoration'.*
Grosvenor Museum (Unknown artist)

Canal boatbuilding on the Chester Canal used the same techniques and materials as those on the Dee. In the early years the construction was entirely of wood. The canal was cut during a period of rapid growth in canal construction, and nationally there was insufficient skilled labour to meet the demands for new canal boats. The Napoleonic Wars did not help as the navy did not bother to advertise for boatbuilders, they just helped themselves. The minutes of December 1779 show that Mr Hamilton of the company was ordered to *take proper steps for Liberating Edward Turby boatbuilder impressed by Captain Price.* Whether Turby was released or sailed off to distant lands aboard a man-of-war is not known.

It has been suggested that the rapid demand for new canal boats led John Wilkinson the Ironmaster of Bersham and Bradley Forge to have what was considered to be the first iron boat constructed in 1787. Wilkinson launched this boat named the 'Trial', with great ceremony, as many pundits had declared that an iron vessel would sink. They had not recognised Archimedes' Principle or the evidence before their own eyes that iron cooking pots floated!

'The Gentleman's Magazine' of 1787 gives an interesting account of the launch of the 'Trial':

Birmingham July 28

A few days ago a boat built with English iron by J Wilkinson Esq. of Bradley Forge, came up to our canal town, loaded with 22 tons and 1500 weight of its own metal, &c. It is nearly of equal dimensions with other canal boats employed upon the canal, being 70 feet long, 6 feet 8 1/2 inches wide. The thickness of the plates with which it is made is about 5-16ths of an inch, and is put together with rivets, like copper, or fire-engine boilers; but the stern posts are wood, and the gunwale is lined with, and the beams are made of, elm planks. Her weight is about 8 tons; she will carry in deep water upwards of 32 tons, and when light she draws about the same as a common boat, viz. eight or nine inches of water.

The development of iron boats saw the canal boatbuilding methods slowly change from all wooden construction through composite build with iron sides and elm bottoms, then eventually all iron construction. Concrete, steel and fibreglass hulls did not come along until later on.

The first canal boats could be described as simply floating boxes. They had little hydro-dynamic shape and were made to hold maximum cargo. The mine boats of Francis Egerton, Duke of Bridgewater, used in his underground system were the forerunners of the narrowboat.

Narrowboats did not have their own means of propulsion: a horse towed them. Passage or Packet boats required a finer shape in order to offer less resistance in the water. Much later, it was the use of the propeller that required boats to have a refined hull and a modified stern to enable the propeller to work efficiently.

Mine boat, also called a 'starvationer' because its ribs showed.
Geoff Taylor Collection

The propeller developed from the screw-like irrigation devices used by the Egyptians, but it was Archimedes who is credited with the invention of the screw that was used as a pump. Later, Leonardo da Vinci produced drawings of a helicopter that resembled a propeller screw. However, it was not until 1835, when engineers Smith and Eriksson acquired patents for screw propellers, that this became a method of boat propulsion.

Smith and Eriksson had different designs. Smith had a double-pitch wooden propeller fitted to his boat. Whilst on the Paddington Canal, he suffered an accident. Half of his propeller broke off and, to what must have been his amazement, his boat surged forward at a higher speed - this chance accident had produced a much more efficient propeller.

Steam engines and the propeller signalled the decline of horse-drawn boats, although horses continued to be used well into the 20th century.

The Shropshire Union yard and graving dock
The opening up of the Wirral Line and the subsequent formation of the Shropshire Union Railway & Canal Co (SUR&CCo) increased the demand for boats. The yard at Tower Wharf developed into a fully integrated boatyard. Everything necessary for the construction of narrow boats and, particularly, flats was carried out at the yard.

Yard facilities included: workshops, a steam sawmill, two covered slipways, a flat building shed and a graving dock. The account books reveal the employment of shipwrights, blacksmiths, sawyers, painters, and firemen (stokers for the steam plant), not to mention office clerks and a timekeeper.

The 1881 Census lists the following occupations of men living in the vicinity of the SU Yard. It is likely that most of these listed were employed there.

Boatbuilders 21
Sailmakers 4
Ship's Carpenters 18
Shipwrights 22
Timekeeper 1

Mention of a timekeeper in the census is a reminder that the men at the yard had to clock in and clock out. They did not have a clock card as such, but each man had a tally that was placed on a hook on a tally board in the Timekeeper's Office to register his attendance. A bell was rung to remind them that it was time to start work. The lintel over the office still shows the wear from the bell rope. The bell gantry has long since disappeared.

The men picked up their weekly wages in a tin that was retained at the Yard.

The Tally Board in the office had 200 hooks - the yard was a significant employer in Chester. Boatbuilding and repair kept all these men in employment until August 1921 when the SU closed down their carrying business.

Wages were clearly an issue in a dispute, recorded in the 'Chronicle' on the 18th April 1914:

Chester Boatyard, SUR&CCo strike

We understand that a number of the boatbuilders at the Chester and Ellesmere Port boatyards of the SURC&Co ceased work this morning, without giving notice of their intention to do so. The men had applied through their Union secretary for an advance in their wages, though it is only about 12 months since they received a substantial increase. The manager saw a deputation of the men on Thursday and undertook to submit their application to the directors next week, but the men had a meeting afterwards, and, as above stated, decided to cease work at once.

Bell Gantry
Geoff Taylor Collection

Tallies and wages tin
Geoff Taylor Collection

This statement brought a reply from the men the following week:

Letter to the Editor

Chester Boatyard, SUR&CCo.

Sir, On behalf of boatbuilders employed by the SUR&CCo at Chester and Ellesmere Port, we wish to contradict part of the statement which appeared in Friday night's issue of The Chronicle. Our society tendered one month's notice for improved conditions to come into operation. This being the usual custom of our trade, we fail to see how we have left work without notice, especially considering the interview was only granted two hours before the expiration of that notice, and the result of the meeting held afterwards was conveyed to our superintendent. We admit it is only twelve months since we received an advance of two shillings per week in our wages, bringing them to 31s. per week for 54 hours (winter and summer) which is less than 7d. per hour. The first increase which has taken place for forty years or more.

Yours faithfully, EMPLOYEES.

Chester's other weekly paper, the 'Cheshire Observer', also reported the proceedings:

Cheshire Observer, 25 April 1914.
A Chester Strike. Boatbuilders and their Wages. Shropshire Union Men's Grievances.

The carpenters and boatbuilders employed by the SURCCo in their boatbuilding yards at Chester and Ellesmere Port came out on strike on Thursday last and so far the dispute has not been settled, and the men are still out, in all about 40 men are affected, and they are claiming an increase of wages and recognition of their union. It is understood that they want their earnings increased so as to bring them up to the level of other boatbuilding yards in the district, and that their demand is for 1d per hour more than they now receive. All the boatbuilders employed by the company are members of the union, and as they have all joined in the strike, boatbuilding and repair work in the Chester and Ellesmere Port yards are practically at a standstill.

The grievances of the men were brought to the notice of the manager of the company some week ago, when, it is said, notices were tendered by the me in accordance with the usual custom. The general manager promised to submit the matter to a meeting of the directors, but without waiting further the men left work on Thursday. The chief thing the employees want is recognition of their union, and if any increase of pay is granted without this concession, it is believed that the strike will have to continue. It may be mentioned that only twelve months ago the company gave the men an increase of wages.

The strike was settled eventually in August of that year:

Chester Boatbuilders' Strike Ends. Settlement After 17 Weeks.

The boatbuilders of the Chester and Ellesmere Port boatyards of the SUR&CCo, who have been on strike since April 17th, returned to work today (Friday), and others are expected to return on Monday. We are informed that a deputation saw the manager, and he agreed that they should be reinstated.

'Chester Chronicle', 15 Aug. 1914.

An indication of the volume of work undertaken at the yard is given by some extracts from the Boatyard Timber Measure Ledgers. One that covers the two-year period 1878 to 1879 lists the purchase of the following quantities of timber:

350 Crooks English Oak Log
148 Planking Logs English Oak
56 Logs American Oak
97 Logs Ash
50 Logs Red Pine
22 Logs Pitch Pine
49 Logs Yellow Pine

7

English Oak. Crooks.

Date.		No. of Log.	Size.	Description.	Ledger Folio.	Feet.	Rate.	Amount.	Total.
1878 Aug.	28	66	3½	do. Planks	22	5	1/7	7 11	7 11
	29	67	Cube	Eng: Oak. Log.	3	3	2/2	6 6	
				Labour			1/	3 8	10 2
			3½	do. Planks.	22	8	1/6	10 6	10 6
		68	Cube	Eng. Oak. Log.	3	27	2/2	2 18 6	
				Labour			1/	4 3	
				Coal.				2	3 4 9
			5	do. Planks.	30	28	1/10½	2 12 6	
			3½	do. do.	22	11	1/3¾	14 5	3 6 11
		69	Cube	Eng: Oak Log.	3	27	2/2	2 18 6	
				Labour Coal.			1/	6 3	3 4 9
			5	do. Planks.	30	41	1/7	3 4 11	3 4 11
	30	70	Cube	Eng: Oak Log.	3	34	2/2	3 13 8	
				Labour Coal.			1/	9 6	4 3 2
			5	do. Planks	30	66	1/3½	4 3 11	4 3 11
Sep.	2	71	Cube	Eng: Oak. Log.	3	22	2/2	2 7 8	
				Labour Coal.			1/	6 3	2 13 11
			5	do. Planks.	30	33	1/5½	2 6 8	
			3½	do. do.	22	6	1/½	6 3	2 12 11
	3	72	Cube	Eng. Oak. Log.	3	39	2/2	4 4 6	
				Labour Coal.			1/	15 8	5 0 2
			5	do. Planks	30	27	1/4½	1 17 2	
			6	do. do.	32	38	1/8	3 3 4	5 0 6

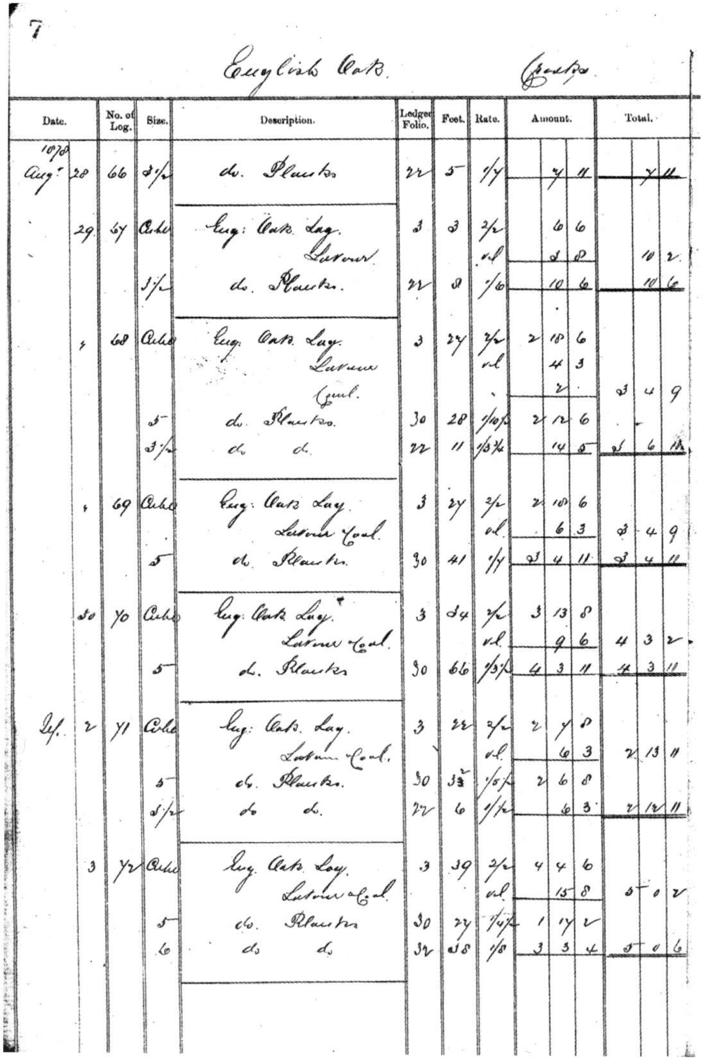

A page of the 1878 ledger
Oak at 2/2 per running foot
Geoff Taylor Collection

The SU Account Books also listed the cost of construction of narrowboats and flats. One such was *Colonel Bourne at a cost of £478/15/4.* The 'Chronicle' of 25th April 1874 gives an account of a launch ceremony of the same vessel:

The ceremony of launching a new flat took place at the boatbuilding yard of the SUR&CCo on Wednesday. The flat was named Colonel Bourne in honour of one of the directors. Colonel Bourne himself christened it in the presence of Lord Powis, Mr Moon and several of the directors. The vessel will carry 110 tons when crossing the Mersey, but the ordinary burden on the canal will be 48 tons. Two new boats were lowered from the stocks the previous day, showing that the work of building has been going on briskly of late.

There were also some interesting purchases recorded in the Account Books:

For repairs to the Flat 'Arthur':
Frying Pan 2/5d
Saucepan 4/10d
Bucket 1/3d
Blanket 9/3d

The accounts also carried many references to the purchase of brimstone (sulphur). My father used to tell me how "lousy" some of the boat cabins were when the boats were at the yard for repair. To fumigate the cabins they would put some brimstone onto a tin lid, light it; push it into the cabin and leave quickly, firmly closing the door behind. This was a sure way of killing off the bugs that remained inside. Dad always cautioned that it was a most unpleasant experience to go into the cabin before the fumes had cleared. The burning brimstone produced sulphur dioxide that would cause much coughing and spluttering as the acrid, acid vapours stung the eyes, attacked the lungs and eliminated the vermin. My mother always insisted that Dad remove his overalls in our back yard when he came home, just in case any insects had survived.

The 1881 Census mentions 29 sawyers and, while these worked throughout the city at various mills, several were employed at the SU yard. The yard had saw pits for reducing the large logs into planks and also band-saws for cutting the finer shapes of timber. Sawyers were vital members of the boatbuilding team. Until the logs were cut into suitable planks, the boatbuilders, shipwrights and ships' carpenters could not start to fashion a boat.

In 1884 a rather nasty accident occurred:

On Thursday morning an accident happened to two men named James Randles of Orchard Street and William Huxley of St Anne's Street who were employed at the Shropshire Union Boatyard Chester. It appears that these two men, who are sailmakers by trade, had been called into a shed where a band saw was in motion, for the purpose of repairing the sawdust bags. Whilst thus engaged, the wheels of the same, which is driven by steam, suddenly broke, and the pieces flew about the shed in every direction. One of them caught Randles in the mouth, and three or four of his front teeth were knocked out, and his face otherwise injured. The man, Huxley was also hurt, but not as severely as to hinder him from working. Randles was immediately removed to the Infirmary where his injuries were attended to.

'Chester Chronicle', 8th March 1884

Fred Evans, SU Sawyer
at the saw bed
Courtesy of the late Mrs James

1921 saw the SU leave the yard. This was the opportunity for my grandfather, Joseph Harry, to lease the yard along with the Graving Dock. Until the mid-1930s, Taylor's only occupied the lower part of the yard; a Mr Horne used the other half. Chester street directories list Horne as *a Canal Carrier of Cambrian Road.* When Horne finished, the family business expanded into the whole of the yard. The Flat Shed fell into disuse and was used, many years later as a fish store for Woods of Fleetwood. The section nearest Cambrian Road became the workshops of J Owens, Car Body Repairs.

Wilf Taylor died in 1961 and Taylor's then became a limited company. Under the guidance of Roger Brown, a director and former apprentice, the yard continued to operate until 1972 when it was sold to Bithell's Boats. Bithell's carried on the business for a further two years before David Jones took over in 1974.

Taylor's Boatyard, memories of the post war years

I have fond memories of the boatyard and boatbuilding in the 1940s and 50s. My playground was the yard - J H Taylor & Sons - formerly the Shropshire Union Railway and Canal Company yard on Cambrian View. Running the business in the late 40s were Wilf Taylor, assisted by his brother Horace (my father) and brother-in-law, Arthur Howard.

My childhood was filled with the experience of wonderful sights, sounds and smells: when planks and timbers were being steamed, the yard was filled with the vinegary, damp odour of steaming oak. The wood smoke from the improvised boiler stung my eyes. Men bawled at me to get out of the way as I stood transfixed, watching as the sacking was snatched away from the end of the steam box and the timber was withdrawn accompanied by several profanities as the heat of the timber conducted through the protective gloves. With incredible speed, the timbers or planks were offered up to the boat, clamped, and all was well. Occasionally, the wood split and cracked; this would release even more choice language, as new timber had to be prepared, soaked and steamed.

The steambox in the post-war period was fixed to the outside of the blacksmith's shop and the steam generated in a large oil drum set on bricks above a fire. Steam was then fed into the box via a pipe. Oak timbers for the launches were pre-soaked in the canal by tying them to some iron ballast and left within arm's reach in the water.

Shaping timber with an adze, especially the stem-posts, was amazingly skilful. The adze is similar to an axe, but the arched blade is set at right angles to that of an axe. No boatbuilding yard could be without an adze. Examples of the adze have been found in prehistoric excavations and it was the main wood-shaping tool for boatbuilders.

I well remember my uncle, Arthur Howard, using the adze at the yard. He was a talented and skilled boatbuilder and his manipulation of the

Adze in use with steambox to rear
Tony Lewery

98

adze was the height of skill and precision. He would rest the end of the haft on his stomach and then present the blade to the timber. With delicate and deft swings, he would remove just the right amount of wood, slowly developing the desired shape. On occasions, Arthur would shape a piece whilst it was lying horizontally on the ground. This would see him standing astride the piece and swing the adze between his legs to chip away at the wood. This was another amazing and seemingly dangerous feat, but his technique allowed the adze to swing with the regularity of a clock's pendulum with no obvious effort. The chippings he produced were often as fine the shavings that most of us could produce with a plane. Needless to say I had great pleasure in collecting the shavings and playing stoker with the coke stove and the furnace under the steam box.

Canal cruisers

There was always a buzz of excitement when told that a keel was to be laid down for a new boat. It offered me a unique opportunity to watch it take shape over the next few months - for the family it meant work and wages.

In the SU days, all timber was brought to the yard by canal, but by now all materials came by road. Large articulated wagons somehow managed to squeeze up the narrow road outside the yard and deliver a load of ready cut oak planks and African mahogany. The final cutting was done by hand, or on the band saw. Before long the shape of the boat could be recognised.

Templates and timbers were marked off a full size drawing on a massive screeve board that was a good 10ft x 10ft square. When not in use the screeve board was fixed vertically, like a big windbreak, between two pillars of the sheds. Carvel boats have the timbers fitted before planking up while clinker boats have the timbers fitted after planking.

Arthur Howard marking out the keel of a salmon fishing boat, c1980
Geoff Taylor Collection

99

*Carvel hull ready
for planking in
Taylor's yard*
Geoff Taylor Collection

Riveting the planks to the timbers always enthralled me. One man sat outside the boat, holding on with a lump hammer and punch, whilst inside the hull another finished off the rivet. The clenched ends of the copper nails were collected for selling as scrap copper. Day after day, the yard would be filled with the rat-a-tat-tat of the riveting under way. Uncle Arthur springs to mind again, as he would reprimand the apprentices for "choking the hammer". He would wrest the hammer from them and demonstrate how to hold it and to move it from the elbow, not the wrist - poetry in motion!

Whilst I only saw this process on launches, using copper nails and roves (small conical rings of copper placed over boat nails before clenching), very much similar work was done with iron rivets in previous years.

Once a carvel boat was planked up, the seams were caulked. Cotton caulk was used in the form of a rope that was wound on site from strands of caulking cotton. Three lengths of about 20ft were all tied to a nail at one end of a workbench and the other ends were attached to a nail bent into a hook and fixed in a wheel-brace. I was allowed to turn the wheel-brace and so twist the strands into a rope. It was a similar, on a small scale, to a process that was used in the rope-walk, owned by John Pemberton, a former Mayor of the city in the 18th century, along City Walls Road (and probably Whipcord Lane) that runs parallel to the canal at Northgate.

As the yard was on my way home from school, I popped in every evening to watch the men at work and listen to their yarns. These visits in lieu of homework, coupled with long school holidays, ensured that I was able to see most processes under way. One that took ages was drilling the propeller shaft. This was another work of art that used the most rudimentary methods. Lengths of string and wooden jigs set the line of the prop shaft. 10ft augers were then rested in the jigs and turned for hour after hour by hand to drill the shaft hole through the keel. Despite their best efforts to keep the line perfect, the auger would sometimes tend to follow the grain. However, small deviations were ironed out by filing the shaft with a homemade rasp that consisted of a 12ft mild steel tube, about 2in diameter, being passed backwards and forwards through the shaft hole. The steel tube had been roughened by chipping at it with a cold chisel. All this hard work called for regular tea breaks and a Woodbine.

The engine was installed quite early on after the prop shaft was prepared. Preparing the exhaust was another job that provided vivid memories. Copper tube, about 2 1/2in diameter, was used for this purpose. It usually had to take on a contorted shape to get from the silencer to the skin of the boat. Uncle Wilf always took charge of bending that was done in the blacksmith's shop. Any attempt to bend copper tubing without internal packing usually results in disaster as any DIY plumber will know. Producing a shape that was a bit like contorted intestine called for drastic measures.

A fire was started in the hearth and I was allowed to operate the bellows. These grunted and groaned in an asthmatic manner as I pumped the shiny handle up and down. I always marvelled at the wonderful patina and shine on the bellows, handle - the result of many years of use by gnarled blacksmith's hands.

There was a 28lb weight resting on top of the bellows, diaphragm. By pumping frantically I could fully inflate the bellows and then take a brief rest whilst the weight descended majestically, forcing the air into the hearth. The reward for all this effort and wheezing was a glowing, white-hot fire.

Meanwhile, Wilf had plugged one end of the tube with a bung of wood and clamped it vertically in a vice. Next, and this was the exciting part, I was allowed to put lumps of pitch into a large iron pot and melt it down on the fire.

The molten pitch was poured into the tube using a ladle and allowed to cool. Then Wilf would bend it seemingly effortlessly into the required shape. He would use old wooden pulley blocks as formers. The copper would become very difficult to bend as it was being worked on (this is called work-hardening). To soften it again, I was allowed to place the tube in the fire, melt the pitch and pour it back into the pot. The bellows were operated again to heat up the tube even more. When Wilf deemed it hot enough, it was brought out of the fire, belching flames and great plumes of black smoke from the vapourised pitch. In seconds, it was plunged into a bath of water nearby with the accompaniment of enormous sizzles and bangs as the water erupted like a volcano, and started to boil. Once the copper was softened, the procedure started all over again until the precise shape was achieved.

Pitch is an unusual material. It is a dilatant substance (opposite to thixotropic which is like non-drip paint) and becomes more viscous when a sharp force is applied to it. In layman's language, pitch appears brittle and can be smashed into pieces when struck with a hammer but when a steady force is applied, it becomes elastic, bends and flows. The drum of pitch outside the blacksmith's shop would give me hours of pleasure as I thwacked it with a hammer to test these principles.

The fitting of the exhaust heralded the removal of the launch from the workshop to the slipway. Almost miraculously the boat would be shoehorned out of the shop on a truck and by deft use of simple levers, to guide the truck and move the wheels, the boat would be moved to the slipway ready for launch.

Relatively affluent businessmen usually commissioned these cabin cruisers. The cost of such a boat was beyond the reach of most people. By the late 50s and early 60s, the introduction of glass fibre hulls brought the cost

Launch 'Marbeth III' being moved from workshop to slipway in Taylor's Yard c1960
Geoff Taylor Collection

Launch Party
Geoff Taylor Collection

of canal cruisers down and put them within the pocket of the general public. Owning a canal cruiser was then no longer the "sport of kings". The use of plastics also heralded the death knell of J H Taylor & Sons as the family stuck relentlessly to using traditional materials and could not compete in terms of cost and productivity with manufacturers of these "modern" boats that Uncle Arthur described as being "like floating bladders of lard!"

The day of the launch was always an occasion for celebration. The owner and his family and guests would arrive, usually with a picnic hamper full of goodies such as cold chicken drumsticks and similar delicacies. We only had chicken at Christmas, so I always felt that it was the height of decadence to have several dozen chicken drumsticks for a picnic. Bottles of brown ale were provided for the men and champagne for the honoured guests.

Once everyone was assembled, the launch began. The boat was shackled by heavy wire cable to a winch. To lots of grunts and the clink, clink, clink of the winch ratchet, the boat slowly entered the canal.

Winch at Taylor's Yard,
said to have been on the 'Great Eastern'
Geoff Taylor Collection

Strangely, maybe because there were ladies present, there was an absence of expletives. All that could be heard were shouts of "Whoa" and "Slacken the rope" while minor adjustments were made to the truck carrying the boat into the water.

As a youngster, I would watch all this with fascination as the cable wound round the capstan of the winch and changed direction round pulleys attached to the strong cast-iron uprights of the shed. My dad would sometimes shout to me to get clear "in case the wire cable snaps". He would frighten me with tales of cables snapping and whip-lashing like a snake only to remove a man's limbs or, at worst, decapitate him!

As the boat entered the water, there would be an anxious moment or two as she started to take in water through the seams. Usually they 'took up' in a very short time and all was well. Once fitted out, the boat was ready for its sea-trial prior to handing over to the owner. This was a rare treat for our family as the trial would be conducted on a Sunday and we used this as an opportunity for a picnic.

We set off towards Ellesmere Port and usually stopped at Stoak for our sandwiches. The return trip was the occasion for a time-trial. As we went under a bridge, Arthur would jump off and pace the boat. One memorable trip saw him jump off at Stone Bridge and miss the bank. He landed unceremoniously among the weeds in the shallows alongside. He cut an amusing figure as he stood, waist high, in the muddy water with his Trilby hat slightly askew, cigarette still alight and, to his obvious delight, his Dr Craig's Snuff safe and sound in its sealed tin!

Winter time
Winter was a particularly nostalgic time when the men, augmented by boatmen from Bithell's Boats would sit round the coke stove that glowed cherry red in the gloom of the workshop. Bithell's river boats including the 'Prince Charles', 'May Queen' and 'Raglan', always came to the yard for winter maintenance.

The men would take much-extended tea breaks and yarn unceasingly about the old days on the cut and river. One notable character was Boatie Smith. He had an earring, which I found curious in those days. Boatie had once sheltered under a canal bridge during a thunderstorm. He described, in vivid detail, how a fireball had rolled under the bridge and he had suffered a rather bad shock. A result of this trauma was that, whenever there was a thunderstorm, Boatie would lose his voice for several days. All these stories were punctuated by lulls whilst they lit up another Woodbine or took a lusty pinch of Doctor Craig's snuff!

Other winter visitors to the yard were the men from Pettit's, the local undertakers. The proud owner of a cruiser was Sandy Pettit. His funeral business was, and still is, located in Delamere Street. At that time they manufactured their own coffins so had several carpenters in their employ. When there was a lull in the undertaking business the men were detailed to go to the yard and rub down and paint Mr Pettit's boat. These carpenters would always turn up immaculately dressed, sometimes in pin-stripe trousers, as they would only have an hour or two before doubling up in helping with a funeral. They wore fine white cotton aprons and were rather too well-dressed for work in a boatyard.

Watermen's Regatta

Quite a few of the men at the yard were accomplished rowers. As they were employed as professional boatmen, albeit on the canal, they were not allowed to row in the Chester Regatta - this was strictly for amateurs. However, anyone who earned a living on either the river or canal could take part in the Watermen's Regatta.

Our mantelpiece at home carried two winner's trophies from the 1920 Watermen's Regatta. The awards were for my father, Horace, who was in the winning teams of both the Fours and Eights. This regatta was certainly a great visitor attraction and the banks of the Dee were lined with locals who were out for enjoyable, free entertainment. Here is a 1920's account:

Chester Watermen's Regatta - Keen Competition AND PLENTY OF FUN

On Wednesday, the Chester Watermen's Regatta took place. Though instituted only three years ago to encourage competition amongst the Chester boatmen, the regatta has become a most popular event. Valuable prizes were offered and entries numbered 242. It was found impossible to row off all the entries in one day, the preliminary heats were decided prior to Wednesday ... The attendance of the public was exceptionally large... HUMOROUS EVENTS; The humorous events created great amusement. The "duck" hunt was a new feature and caused much fun. The "ducks" succeeded in upsetting their opponents and winning the prizes given by Mr F Sturges... The blindfold race attracted a large number of competitors. Many competitors succeeded in bumping into each other or the banks with considerable force to their own discomfiture. Messrs W Hodgeson and F Weaton offered prizes in the tug of war competition ... the obstacle race was won after an exciting race by Shaw. W D Humphreys was second. Wilcox who led over the greater part of the course became firmly wedged at the last obstacle and had to watch the rest of the competitors go by.

The Regatta was rounded off with a dinner at The Bars Hotel, attended by civic dignitaries including the Sheriff and the Chief Constable, Mr J H Laybourne who is reported as saying:

He had always had the interests of those fond of the river at heart. There was no better place in England with better boats than Chester, and there was no place that took the same interest in boating. Other Corporations came to Chester to buy the boats which the Chester inspector would not pass. Certain people had talked for many years about the "dangerous Dee". In his opinion, anybody could spend a more pleasant day on the Dee, provided due care was exercised, than they could enjoy on any rivers in the country.

'Chester Chronicle', 1st October 1921

Professional boatmen and others at 1920 Waterman's Regatta with their trophies.
Horace Taylor at 2nd row to top, far right.
Geoff Taylor Collection

THE OLD
CHESTER CANAL
errata and update

page 6 & 7 1 cwt should be 50Kg

page 41 The first stockholder to forfeit all his shares for non-payment on calls seems to have been J Dixon on 11th October 1772

page 102 illustration is Marbeth II not III

page 142, line 14 should be 27th November 1799

page 218, para 2 Rick should be Ric

page 194 illustration of boat: Moreton should be Morton

page 219 line 1 should read birds, insects and other animals

page 247 line 13 The inscription reads J Mowle & Co. (Their iron foundry was in Leadworks Lane.)

page 137 Kernel (grain) should be Kennel (coal). This mistake was confirmed by the following newspaper article.

Smuggling   Terry Kavanagh

It seems that there was more to this than just bringing in a cargo without paying toll or custom on coal. In December 1783 the Chester customs seized the flat "Bootle" after apparently finding dutiable goods cocealed under her official cargo of cannel coal brought in from Liverpool. Accordingly the vessel and her cargo were forfeited, as evidenced by the following sale notice in the 'Chester Courant', 16th March 1784:

CHESTER

To be Sold by Auction, in the Long Room at the Custom-house, on Saturday 27th of March inst. at twelve o'Clock,

Brandy,	Irish painted Paper,
Rum,	Gum Senega,
Whiskey,	Hair Powder.

Also the Flat BOOTLE, with her Materials, Tackle, Apparel, and Furniture.

The Hull may be viewed on the Graving Bank, and the Materials, etc. at the Custom House Yard.

By Order of the Commissioners of His Majesty's Customs

N. IKIN, Collector

Cestria in graving dock, *c1920 (see pages 198, 203)* Geof Taylor collection

The Chemical Connection Edwin A Shearing

Chemistry Lock at Boughton near Chester was originally called Spittle or Spital Field Lock, since it was built in land known as the Spittalfields that formerly belonged to the Hospital of St. John, a medieval foundation nearby. This name was certainly used until 1810.

In 1807, Thomas Jones was given permission to take cooling water for a steam engine in his *works at Boughton,* provided he returned the water to the canal, used the cinders from the engine for the repair of the adjacent towing path and paid an annual rental of two guineas. We learn a minute of August 1810 that *Mr Jones of the Chemistry was to lay more soil... on the towing path in future and to remove any rubbish* w thereon.

Two years later the minutes record that *Mr Jones, proprietor of the Gallic Acid Works near the Spitalfields* had encroached on the towing path etc. Finally, the Tithe Map for Great Boughton (1849) shows *house, chymistry etc*, owner Robert Lewis Jones, on a site some 80 yards east of the lock, on the south side of the canal. So we have it established that here was a small chemical works or *Chemistry* as early nineteenth century Cheshire and environs would have it, making gallic acid (doubtless from oak galls and bark used locally in considerable quantities for tanning).

he name 'Chemistry' had become officially associated with the arby lock by 1856, when a list of Company servants includes imuel Dunning, lock keeper, Hoole Lane and Chemistry Locks. ole Lane had changed its name too, but that's another story.

booklet published for the Chester Canal Bicentenary Rally in 1972 iks the name 'Chemistry' with a firm called Major and Turner about 850. Major & Co seems to have been first listed as manufacturing chemists in a Directory of 1855 and as Major and Turner in 1860; Jones' works may well have been taken over by this firm, but I have not established this.

Two other places on the Shropshire Union system acquired the name Chemistry, presumably for similar reasons - the embankment on the Wirral Line just north of Stonebridge, Chester (now Balmoral Park), and the hamlet, now suburb of Whitchurch, on the abandoned Whitchurch Arm off the Llangollen Canal.

Yacht outside Roberts' Dee yard (see p227) 1913   *Geoff Taylor Collection*
J H Taylor with trilby and white shirt

page 281 The first mention of **Sam Weston** working directly for the proprietors is on 13th September 1771: *that Mr Sam Weston do take a Survey of the Country beyond Tilstone heath, as soon as conveniently can be and that Dr Denton, Mr Rogers and Mr Chamberlaine be requested to attend to inspect the Country & give their assistance in the said Survey & that they be paid all their expenses attending the Survey.* Later, on 13th December: *Sam Weston to make field plan to take to Parliament.*

Who built the bridges similar to Brindley's design? Bridge building was the sole responsibility of **John Lawton** until his death before January 1774. Minutes of 11th October 1772 show *That John Lawton shall have the sole direction of management of the Locks, Bridges and other works...*

PASSENGER CARRYING Terry Kavanagh

The Duke of Bridgewater's passage boats

The early British canals, like the old river navigations, carried passenger as well as goods traffic. Some canal companies had market boats, picking up people and light freight early in the morning, taking them to the local market towns, and bringing them back again in the evening. Others followed the Duke of Bridgewater's example and introduced longer distance services. In 1773, the great potter, Josiah Wedgwood, wrote: *From Warrington to Manchester the Duke has set up two passage boats, one carries [120] passengers at a shilling each. The other [carrying 80] is divided into three rooms, & the rates are 2/6 per head for the best room, 1/6, and 12d, and it is the pleasantest and cheapest mode of travelling you can conceive…*

A German engineer who visited the Bridgewater Canal after it was extended to Runcorn, described the packet boats, as they came to be called, in these words: *One cannot travel more pleasantly, in more comfort or more cheaply than in these boats; their length is 56 feet, width 8 feet and the height inside at the centre is 7 feet.* They were towed by two or three horses, and a speed of about 4 mph. was achieved.

The Duke's canal packets proved so successful that regular services were established on a number of inland waterways, often with coaching connections - and the Chester and Ellesmere Port lines were among them. Gore's 'Liverpool Directory' of 1796 states that, on the Bridgewater Canal *an elegant passage boat, for passengers and their luggage only* leaves Manchester for Liverpool daily at 8 am, and arrives at Preston Brook, near Frodsham at 2.30 pm, *where the Chester Coach meets it.*

Chester passage boats

Back in June 1773, the Chester Canal Committee ordered that local boatbuilder *Michael Cooper be sent to view the Duke of Bridgewater's Passage Boat and take Dimensions of the same, and that he deliver in an Estimate to the Committee for building one of the same sort.* But the boat they decided to build 18 months later was less refined in design than the Duke's packet boats, and measured only *40 feet long x 12 feet Beam x 4 Foot deep including the Keel…* I suspect it was modelled on his new passenger boat then under construction, and intended for the Manchester-Worsley route.

Be that as it may, the 'Courant' of 19th June announced: *On Wednesday last... a new Passage Boat sailed up the Canal, with several of the Proprietors on board, as far as Beeston-Brook-*

House where they dined, and returned in the evening. A few days later this passenger boat started running between the Northgate in this city and Beeston, the fares being as follows:

Chester to Christleton or Rowton Bridge	*2d}*
Waverton Common or Waverton Town	*3d} Common*
Golden Nook + Crownest	*4d} Cabin*
Brockholes Huxley	*5d}*
Beeston Lock or Beeston road	*6d}*

Passengers returning in the same Boat the same day to pay one half of the above Fares, for the Return Voyage. Passengers in the Grand Cabin, to pay double the above Rates. The cabin could be hired by private parties for 10s 6d. It was also possible to hire the whole boat for business or pleasure trips when out of service, for 21s a day. The captain of the boat, William Nasey, was paid 5s 6d a week and 2s 6d per day each day it went up the canal.

The service got off to a good start apparently, for in August 1775 a second passenger boat 45 feet in length was placed on order. Accordingly, the Committee resolved that Roger Woodfine, a Chester boatbuilder, *be agreed with to finish the Cabin work & all other Extra work necessary to fit up the 2nd boat in a Genteel manner, fit to accommodate Passengers agreeable to his present Proposals of £70 - to finish the same completely, and Glazing, Painting & all other work included, he finding Staff, and doing everything according to his Plan of proposals & he agrees to give this Committee the option of paying for it by Daywages, or as above when finished (the Pump excepted).*

The old boat was laid up during the winter months but, at the end of March 1776, it was ordered *that William Nasey be agreed with on the lowest Terms as to go as Master of the Passage Boat + that he take Charge of her Immediately.* By the end of April, this and the new boat were running to a regular timetable, with additional excursions to the Chester Races, for which cheap day return tickets were issued. It was ordered *that One Boat sett out from Beeston Brook each of the Race days at Ten O'Clock in the forenoon and another Boat at Eleven O'Clock, and both return from Chester to Beeston Brook half an Hour after the Races is over.*

Then, in the 'Chester Chronicle' of 20th June 1776, the Canal Company gave notice *that a passage boat will set out from Chester to Beeston Brook, every Sunday, Tuesday, and Thursday morning at eight o'clock, and return the same days at five o'clock in the evening; and* will set out from Beeston Brook to Chester every Monday, Wednesday. And Saturday morning at six o'clock, and return the same days at four o'clock in the evening. Hitherto, it seems both boats were drawn by the Chester Co's own haulage stock. But now it was decided *that Mr Moon agree with a person or Two to navigate the Passage Boats on the lowest terms he can by the trip to find their own Horses.*

The Nantwich run

When the canal was extended to Nantwich in 1779, the timetable was altered once again. During that and the following year the Company intensified their efforts to get trade for Chester and even Liverpool by transhipping goods from the Trent & Mersey Canal into road waggons at Wheelock, to be freighted from Nantwich in large *stage boats* to Chester and, if required, thence by sailing barges or 'flats' to Liverpool. They also put on a boat for dealers and traders frequenting the local fairs and markets. It was ordered *that a Boat for carrying Merchants Goods & Passengers do sett out from Chester to Nantwich every Tuesday Morning at Seven O'Clock and that a Boat will sett out from Nantwich with Merchants Goods & Passengers for Chester every Friday morning at 7 O'Clock.* Then the other boat was put on the Nantwich run. A local directory of 1781 states that *The Chester Canal Boat which goes to Nantwich, sets out from Cow Lane Bridge every Tuesday and Friday Mornings at Eight O'Clock, and a Boat sets out at the same time from Nantwich to Chester. Fare, 2s 6d. There is likewise a Market Boat goes every Saturday…[from and] to Beeston Brook, 6d.*

Unfortunately, the Company failed to attract enough trade to the canal, so the Nantwich market boats, called the 'Crewe' and the 'Spurstow', were sold at the end of September 1783. But these vessels continued to ply the canal under new ownership. And, in May 1786, the Chester Canal Minute Book states: *Richard Lloyd to Hire to this Company Two Boats viz The Spurstow and the Crewe for Two Pounds a month.* How long this arrangement lasted is not known, but all traffic to Nantwich stopped in November 1787, when Beeston Lock collapsed for the second time; and was not repaired for ten years owing to lack of funds. The Beeston service was probably stopped as well, but it seems to have started again in October 1790, as John Hockenhull, a horse contractor, was paid 9/- a trip to haul the boat. He was replaced in March 1792, when the Committee ordered that *Wm Bradshaws proposal to work the Passage Boat between Chester & Beeston Brook at 9/- per Trip be agreed to.* It stopped for good in August 1794 though, when the cash-strapped Company converted it into a maintenance boat *to repair the Locks, Bridges, and other Works to Beeston Brook.*

New business

Things began to improve, however, once the eight-mile long Wirral Line of the Ellesmere Canal had given the Company a direct link to the Mersey at Whitby in the 1790s. Thanks to the prevailing 'canal mania' enough money was raised to put the Chester Canal into some sort of navigable order again and, in May 1796 a new passenger boat costing £186 was ordered from Robert Littler, a Chester shipwright. This was a typical, if fairly beamy, packet boat with a long raised cabin amidships, divided into two classes with a galley amidships, and some open deck space fore and aft. According to the plan and specification supplied by John Fletcher, it measured 50 feet in length by 9 feet 6 inches extreme breadth; the best cabin, which was 4 feet 6 inches from the bow, measured 10 feet 6 inches in length, and aft of it there was a refreshment bar 6 feet long, the rest of the boat being for light goods and *inferior passengers!*

It was named the 'Chester' and launched on 29th October 1796, the builders and workmen being allowed £4 4s to celebrate the event. John Griffiths of Stoak was appointed master at 12/- a week, and six weeks later, *The Different Proposals for Hawling the Passage Boat being laid before this Meeting; Ordered That William Bradshaw's Proposals be agreed to viz. 18/- per Trip to Nantwich and back to Chester, 9/- per Trip to Beeston Brook & back to Chester. He to find Ropes + other Materials necessary for Hawling the said Boats.*

A twice-weekly service started on 17th January 1797 between Cow Lane Wharf, Chester and Beeston only, until the canal was open to Nantwich. The packet boat sailed regularly every Tuesday and Friday morning to Beeston and returned from Beeston every Tuesday at 2pm, the fares being 1/6 for the best apartment, and 1/- for the second apartment. The boat also ran on Saturdays from Beeston at 6 am. and returned in the evening, with cheap 6d fares for market folk *in the common Cabin.* On Sundays it left Beeston and reached Chester in time for religious services.

Then, in May 1797, it was ordered that the Chester Canal packet *will set off from the Wharf at Cowlane Bridge, Chester, every Tuesday and Thursday Mornings, at Eight O'Clock exactly, and arrive at Nantwich about two the same Day. The same Boat will also set off from Nantwich every Wednesday Morning at Eight O'Clock, and arrive at Chester about two the same Day and will also leave Nantwich every Friday at Eight O'Clock, and arrive at Beeston-Brook about Eleven the same Day; and will leave Beeston-Brook every Saturday Morning at Six, and arrive at Chester at Ten; and will return from Chester the same Afternoon at Four, be at Beeston-Brook at Seven; and leave Beeston-Brook every Sunday Morning at Six, and arrive at Chester the same Day at Ten.* The fares to Nantwich were set at 2/6 best apartment and 1/6 second apartment; *Children on the Lap pay Nothing.* The packet could be hired on intermediate days for £2 2s a day.

Chester Canal Navigation

The Public are respectfully informed, that the said Canal from Beeston Brook to the Wirral Branch of the Ellesmere Canal, near Chester, and from thence to Liverpool, being completely open fot the Conveyance of Passengers, Goods and Merchandise,

The New Boat

for the Accommodation of Passengers, Persons frequenting Chester Market, and for the Reception of Goods, will sail from the Cowlane Wharf at Chester, to Beeston Brook, for the first Time, on Tuesday next, at Eight O'Clock in the Morning, and continue to sail regularly every Tuesday and Friday Mornings, at Eight O'Clock, and set off regularly from Beeston Brook every Tuesday, at Two O'Clock in the Afternoon.

S. D

Fare in the best Apartment - 1. 6
Ditto in the second Apartment - 1. 0

Freight and Tonnage of heavy Goods and Merchandise 3^d. per hundred Weight; light Goods 4^d. per Hundred; and small Parcels in Proportion to their Bulk.

The same Boat

will likewise sail from Beeston Brook, on Saturday the 4th Day of February next; at Six O'Clock in the Morning, and set off from Chester the same Afternoon, at Four O'Clock, and continue to go regularly every Saturday, at these Times; and the Boat will also sail from Beeston Brook for Chester, every Sunday Morning at Eight O'Clock.

Persons going to, or coming from, Beeston Brook to Chester Market, in the common Cabin, to pay 6^d. each; and to or from Golden Nook Bridge and Waverton-Coal-Wharf, 4^d. each; at which Places only the Boat will stop, to take in Passengers.

All Passengers, except the Persons coming to, or returning from, Market to pay the same Fares as on other Days.

Chester Canal Company Minute Book
24th January 1797
The National Archives RAIL 816/6 transcript

What about operating costs? Well, a Company minute dated 7 April 1797 informs us that: *The Company finding the Expences attending the Boats so enormous, are of the Opinion + do order, That the Captain of the Passage Boat have notice to provide himself with another Place, and that he be paid a Gratuity of One Guinea [£1-1s] for the inconvenience of leaving the Company with such short Notice.*

His place was taken by William Bradshaw, the horse contractor, who doubled as skipper, *his wife taking care to keep the Boat clean, for which she is to be allowed according to the Discretion of the Committee.* In other words, she received no guaranteed wage; but at least Bradshaw himself would now be paid 10/- per trip to Beeston and 20/- per trip to Nantwich, *for Hawling the Passage Boat.*

The cost of repairs, planned or otherwise, had also to be taken into consideration. In November 1797, for example, we find that Committee member John Fletcher - in whose the name the packet had been registered - was *requested to agree with a Carpenter &c to repair Inside of the Passage Boat lately burnt by the Fire accidentally while lying at Nantwich Wharf.* And the bill for £5 13s 0d from Thomas & Sam. Barnes, Plumbers, of Crane Street *for Lead Work had for the New Passage Boat* may well have been connected with this fire. (Here it is worth mentioning that bilge pumps were made of lead in those days.)

The wharfinger at Nantwich Wharf at the time of the fire was one Sam Dutton, who was paid 12/- a week wages. He also assisted the packet boat through the swivel bridges at Haughton Moss Drain and Burford Brook Water. These duties earned him *the Priveledge of delivering the Goods from the Boat at Nantwich into the Town and collecting Goods for the Boat for which he is to charge customary Cartage.*

Inevitably, some goods sustained damage while in transit. On 23rd December 1798, for instance, the Committee ordered *That the Sugar belonging to Messrs Bowman & Kelly (which was damaged in the Canal Packet) be sold by Auction, at the Canal-yard [Cow Lane Wharf], on Saturday next in small parcels; and that the Notice of such Sale be given by the Bellman through this City.*

Not all packet-boat freight in Chester was handled at the Cow Lane Wharf of course. On 28 November 1797, it was decided *that the Passage Boat in future do go down the [Northgate] Locks into the Ellesmere Canal to take in the Goods for Nantwich &c in order to save the Expences of Cartage now incurred upon the Goods; and that the Goods be left at the Ellesmere-Canal-Warehouse [Tower Wharf] in future with that Intent.*

Chester Canal Navigation

The Chester and Ellesmere Canals being connected together at Chester, and the Chester Canal being now put into Repair, and navigable to Nantwich, convenient Passage Boats sail regularly between Liiverpool and Chester, and Chester and Nantwich; Likewise Goods are forwarded by the Canals between Liverpool, Manchester, Chester, Nantwich, and all parts of Staffordshire, Shropshire &c.

The Chester Canal Passage Boat

will set off from the Wharf at Cowlane Bridge, Chester, every Tuesday and Thursday Mornings, at Eight O'Clock exactly, and arrive at Nantwich about two the same Day.

The same Boat will also set off from Nantwich every Wednesday Morning at Eight O'Clock, and arrive at Chester about two the same Day; and will also leave Nantwich every Friday Morning at Eight O'Clock, and arrive at Beeston Brook about Eleven the same Day; and will leave Beeston-Brook every Saturday Morning at Six, and arrive at Chester at Ten; and will return from Chester the same Afternoon at Four, be at Beeston-Brook at Seven; and leave Beeston-Brook every Sunday Morning at Six, and arrive at Chester the same Day at Ten.

Fare in the best Apartment,

S. D.

From Chester to Nantwich, 2. 6 each Passenger.

Ditto, to Beeston- Brook -- 1. 6

Fare in the second Apartment

S. D.

From Chester to Nantwich, 1. 6 each Passenger.

Ditto, to Beeston-Brook, -   1. 0

N.B. Children on the Lap pay Nothing.

Freight and Tonnage of heavy Goods and Merchandizes from Chester to Nantwich 5ᵈ. per Cwt. -Light Goods and small Parcels in Proportion to their Bulk.

N.B. Iron in Bars and Pigs, Lime and Free-stone, and other Goods not perishable, will be carried at a lower Rate.

Canal-Office, Chester, May 11th 1797.

Chester Canal Company Minute Book
11th May 1797
The National Archives RAIL 816/6 transcript

To Ellesmere Port and Liverpool

Two years earlier, the Ellesmere Canal Company put on a packet boat from Chester to Whitby Wharf (Ellesmere Port) for the conveyance of passengers, parcels and luggage to Liverpool. Some of the passengers would have travelled by canal all the way from Nantwich, though they had to change at Chester. But after 1806, when the Chester Canal packet was sold and apparently stopped running, some intending passengers probably travelled by coach from Nantwich to Chester. In 1809 there was certainly a daily "Boat Coach" running between Wrexham and this city, where it met the Ellesmere Canal packet.

The Ellesmere Canal Packet Boat at the Canal Tavern and 'Telford's Warehouse' *(right).*
Hunter, copied by Chester Photographic Survey

This packet was built by Peter Jackson, a Chester shipbuilder, and launched into the Wirral branch of the Ellesmere Canal early in June 1795. The Chester Chronicle of 12 June 1795, reported that *no expense has been spared in the construction of the canal passage boat, as well as of the [two sailing] packets that are built to navigate the Mersey between the canal and Liverpool; which, in point of elegance, convenience, and swiftness (added to the experience and civility of the Captains) [Pat. Coffield; and Hinde and Whitby] cannot but obtain an extensive share of the public patronage, not only from the mercantile and trading part, but also from people of leisure and fashion… to promote which, the house of reception at the Mersey end will combine every advantage that salubrity of air, beauty of prospect, and internal accommodations can bestow, so as to render it a desirable and fashionable resort, as well for the sea bather as for the less stationary traveller.*

The canal packet was pulled by two horses, at an average speed of around 4 mph. There was one trip each way per day, with extra journeys on Race days and other occasions. It entered service at Tower Wharf on 1st July 1795, and proved so popular that, on 10th August, the Ellesmere Canal Committee ordered *that Mr Thomas Telford give directions for a Boat to be fitted up for the purpose of carrying Luggage and other articles belonging to the passengers using the packet Boat from Chester to the River Mersey.*

In the meantime the 'Chronicle' of 3rd July reported that *Wednesday the new canal passage-boat made her maiden trip from this city to the Mersey, with upwards of one hundred passengers; all of whom expressed the highest satisfaction at the comfortable accommodation, the cheapness, and pleasantness, of the passage... The boat made two trips the same day.* Indeed 1,700 passengers were carried in the first month, according to the 'Chronicle' of 31st July 1795. In the same newspaper we find the following advertisement giving fares, luggage charges and freight rates on the canal and river packet boats:

Chester and Liverpool Packets by Ellesmere Canal and River Mersey.

The above packets began to convey passengers and parcels between Chester and Liverpool on Wednesday, 1st July. Time each day 2 1/2 hours before High Water at Liverpool and 3 1/2 before High Water from Chester, as stated in the Liverpool Tide Table.

Fares:	*s. d.*	*s. d.*
Along the canal in the best apartments	1.6.	
From the canal to Liverpool	1.0.	2.6.
By the canal in the other apartments	1.0.	
From the canal to Liverpool	6.	1.6.
Luggage included, not being articles of traffic:		
Each basket, parcel, etc., by canal	2.	
to Liverpool	1.	3.
Each small basket or pannier from		
Whitby Wharf to Liverpool	1/2.	
Every sack, Whitby Wharf to Liverpool	2.	

Tipping was strictly forbidden: *the Ellesmere Canal Committee… will not suffer their servants to take any money or other gratuities from passengers.* Intending passengers were also informed that the time taken for the whole passage was about three hours.

Such a speedy time is doubtful, however, given that the Ellesmere Company took out the following advertisement in the 'Chronicle' of 12th August 1796: *To prevent the Irregularity and Delay which have arisen by reason of the two Packets from Liverpool not arriving at the Whitby End of the Canal at the same Time, that the Company have agreed with Pat. Coffield, of Liverpool, to convey the Passengers daily, and this with some other Regulations which have been adopted, it is hoped will greatly expedite the Passage, and give general satisfaction…*

To that end, the Canal Company leased their *stout-decked* sailing packet and luggage boat to Captain Pat (and later, Mrs) Coffield. In the Ellesmere Canal Company's Minutes for 26th November 1800 we are informed that Mrs Coffield proposed paying them £300 pa. as rent for navigating the vessel used between Ellesmere Port and Liverpool, the Company insisting *that a room or apartment be made as a resting room for ladies, and that the packet boat be always immediately cleaned as soon as the passengers are discharged; and this Committee insist upon Elizabeth Coffield always keeping three sober, steady and able men at least, on board the packet to navigate the same.*

Three years earlier, on 27th June 1797, the 'Courant' announced that the Ellesmere Canal Committee, *for the accommodation of parties of pleasure, and those ladies and gentlemen who visit the Mersey for the purposes of bathing, have built an elegant and commodious Packet Boat, which will sail daily during the bathing season, from the Tower Wharf, Chester, precisely three hours before high water, wait if desired, three hours for their convenience, and return in the evening. On any of the intermediate days, select parties may have the use of the packet to any part of the canal and back, from eight o'clock in the morning till eight o'clock in the evening.*

Fare for parties for the whole day, free of every other expense...£1 11s 6d
For passengers during the bathing season to the Mersey and back
Best apartment.....2s 6d
Second apartment...1s 6d

N. B. Any further information may be had from Capt Ackerley, King's Street, Chester.

Advertisement 1823   Cheshire RO Z60/4/13

In 1801 both the bathing boat and the canal packet were leased to Samuel Ackerley, who was also tenant of the Ellesmere Tavern at Tower Wharf, he paying £1,000 pa. for the franchise. The following year he was paid £7 7s for overseeing the construction of a new canal packet costing £229 11s, which was built by Robert Littler, a Chester shipwright. This in turn probably accounts for an entry in the Ellesmere Canal Company minute book, dated 4th November 1802: *On the recommendations of the super-intending committee for the Wirrall Line, that heavy Bales of Goods which have been carried in the Packet Boats and have had the effect of damaging and delaying the same shall in future be carried on the Flats only and no such Goods admitted in the packet Boats.*

ELLESMERE CANAL TAVERN.

CHESTER.

S. Ackerley Captain of the Canal Packet.
Respectfully informs the Ladies & Gentlemen travelling betwixt
Liverpool & Chester that Breakfast, Dinner & Tea & every requisite
Accomodation may be had in the Packet which sails daily betwixt
these Places, he has likewise fitted up the above Tavern with good
Beds, Wines, Spirituously malt Liquors for the entertainment of
Families, Travellers & the public in general whose Favors he humbly
solicits assuring them it will be his constant study to merit their
Approbation and support

Advertisement for the Canal Packet transcript

When Ackerley's lease was renewed in 1804, the Company laid down the following regulations under which the inn and packet boats were let:

The taverns are to be kept with regard to furniture, provisions and attendance, equal to the best inn in Chester.
Three stables are attached to the inn at Chester and one at Ellesmere Port.
Refreshments with Wine, Ale, Porter, Cyder or Perry are permitted but no liquors are to be kept, or any smoking suffered on board the boat.
Four sufficient horses and handsome harnessing are to be kept in good order, one pair

to stand at Tower Wharf and the other at Ellesmere Port.
The Captain and one assistant to be in the boat besides the woman who attends the kitchen, and a person to ride the horses and the horses are to travel at a rate so as to perform the journey in two hours.
In the Bathing Boat there is to be one person to steer, one assistant in the boat and a person to ride the horses...

These craft were given priority. They operated under the protection of company bye-laws which fined the captain of any boat that failed to drop its towing line or got in the way of the packet. There was occasionally trouble on the packet boat, as shown by this extract from the Ellesmere Canal Committee minutes of 1802, reminiscent of bus company regulations: *...that if any person shall use indecent language or in any respect behave offensively to the passengers... the captain of the packet has express orders... to turn any such person or persons so offending out of the said packet boat...*

The 'Courant' of 25th March 1828, gives a vivid account of one such incident: *Francis Merner, John Jackson, and Samuel Jones, all of Manchester, were brought before the Mayor on Wednesday, on a charge of attempting to pick pockets the preceding day on board the Liverpool Canal Packet Boat. It appeared that one of them was detected in the act of attempting to extract something from the pocket of a passenger on which the Captain ran the boat alongside the bank, in order to turn them out, which they stoutly resisted, and Merner drew a knife upon him. This caused the indignation of the passengers, some of whom proceeded to eject the fellows... while others called out to have them secured. They immediately took to their heels, and Jackson threw a jemmy (a small crowbar) into the canal. They were pursued and taken. They appear to be 'regular built' [typical] Manchester thieves, who came via Liverpool, on a marauding excursion, which they called 'a lark,' to our ancient city. The captain of the packet did not appear against them, and they were discharged on a promise that they would instantly leave Chester.*

Not all pick-pockets were apprehended of course. The 'Courant' of the 4th March 1834, informed its readers: *The city was visited by a greater number of light-fingered gentry on the fair day than for a considerable time past, and much money changed masters in consequence. They commenced operations on the day previous, and eased a person of about £35 as he was leaving the Liverpool packet.*

Occasionally, some of the canal-packet freight was stolen. The 'Chronicle' of 8th April 1825, for example, reported that a carter known as "Shifty" Edwards was gaoled for 18 months with hard labour, for stealing three casks belonging to Swainson & Co of Liverpool. He had "chucked" them into his cart at Tower Wharf, and sold them to a local small-scale brewer named Joseph Jones, "at a very inadequate price." After his arrest Edwards said, "it was a bad job, for if he had not been drunk, it would not have happened." In giving evidence at his trial, John Hickson, then the packet captain, said he had brought a consignment of eleven casks from Ellesmere Port to Chester. "I discharged them on Coffield & Co's Wharf. Next morning Roberts the carrier missed some... There were three missing, two half barrels and a quarter cask. The half barrels are worth half a guinea, and the quarter 6s or 7s." Hickson went to Jones's premises, and saw them there. Such consignments from Liverpool were regularly handled by the packet boat crew. He added, "We carry anything, man or cask, as we can get."

Returning to Samuel Ackerley's captaincy of the canal packet, we find that, in April 1807, he and his partner William Fairhurst, a Liverpool carrier, purchased Elizabeth Coffield's cross-river sailing packets. Just over twelve months later, one of them, called the 'Eliza', was put on sale, she being *well adapted for the fishing trade* according to the newspaper advertisement. Her replacement was the 48-ton register 'Telford', a smack-rigged packet with a sliding bowsprit, which measured 47.1 feet x 14.4 feet x 8.2 feet, and was launched from Cortney & Co's Roodee yard, at Chester in April 1808. The owners, Ackerley and Fairhurst, assured intending passengers that they had *selected sober and experienced Captains, and are determined that passengers shall meet with every civility.*

During Mrs Coffield's term the conditions on board these river vessels had left a great deal to be desired, as evidenced by the frequent complaints made about the generally unclean state of the packets. The Sub-Committee for the Wirral Line investigated the complaints and made the following report to the General Committee on 12 May, 1801: *Better end clean, but stuffy - no ventilation, also too small. Common hold, or worst end, filthy - not cleaned every trip. Small boat inferior to the other and as calves and other livestock are received in it and brought over the other boat, it delays the sailing of that boat and occasions dirt and inconvenience to passengers.*

It had been customary for the two river boats to be tied up abreast at Whitby Wharf, and the outer one to be loaded first with livestock, by driving the animals over a gang-plank across the inner boat and then, without cleaning the boats of filth, to take in the passengers. It was recommended that both vessels be berthed separately at the quays and cleaned out after each trip; also that cordage and sails be stowed out of the way of passengers.

Packet boat and sailing flats in the Chester canal basin of the Wirral Line
Grosvenor Museum, Henry Wyatt 1794-1840 pencil

Ferry across the Mersey

Nevertheless, the canal packet was frequented by many people in preference to the alternative route by the northern ferries and coach. Why? Because at Seacombe, Woodside, Rock Ferry, and New Ferry they were conveyed across the Mersey in boats of various sizes (some with and some without sails) which had *neither awning, cabin, or forecastle, sufficient to contain their complement of passengers; all of whom, are consequently exposed, in open boats, to be repeatedly wet thro', from head to foot, by the dashing of every wave, and the fall of every sudden shower: to faint with the heat of the noon-tide sun in the summer; to be pelted by hail, snow and sleet, in winter; to suffer without resistance the fury of the winds…*

Some of the ferry-boats were large enough to carry horses, carriages, cattle, etc. But all of them were of very unsafe construction with regard to the length of the passage, the frequency of strong gales of wind, and the strength of the current. Consequently, fatal accidents not infrequently occurred to the passengers. In June 1817, for example, it was reported: *On Wednesday morning last, a little after nine o'clock, the boat belonging to the Bang-up Coach, which meets the Coach to the Talbot, in Shrewsbury, left Liverpool on its way to the Rock-Ferry, (where the Coach to this city stops) having on board seven passengers, the coachman, and two boatmen. At the time, the wind blew a perfect hurricane, and the waves rolled with tremendous violence. The boat had scarcely reached the mid-way of its passage, about two miles, when it shipped an immense mass of water, filled and instantly sunk! The Coachman who was heavily clad in waistcoats, top-coats, and boots, instantly disappeared, and in a few seconds afterwards, Mr Jones, of Whitechapel, Liverpool, and a female, also found a watery grave!*

It is small wonder then, that observers had long called for the following improvements: *The vessels, at each of the four ferries, should be converted into covered boats… Their pilots should be mariners of experience. They should be sober, and strict regard should be had to the cleanliness of the boats, (a circumstance in which the Eastham-ferry can have nothing to boast, so long as man and beasts have one common apartment) as well as the good condition of the boat itself, its oars and tackling.*

True, the large Eastham boat, like the Ellesmere Port vessels, was decked over, with two separate cabins, which cost first class passengers only 1s; and second class 6d. Moreover, the Chester long-bodied or *double stage coach* it met at that ferry could carry 16 inside passengers, at 3/6d each, *without the abuse of outside passengers, whose situation was not only hazardous, but in bad weather extremely unpleasant.* But this was not the case at the other ferries.

Worse still, the road between Chester and the Liverpool ferries was very bad, even in summer time; and extremely dangerous for all travellers, particularly those who were obliged to travel in the dark, because the ferry-boats frequently and unavoidably left them on the Cheshire side of the water, in the dusk of the evening, owing to contrary winds and tides. To give just one example, the 'Courant' of 22nd January 1811 reports *One of the Liverpool coaches was overturned a few days since, from the falling of a wheel, we understand; when one outside passenger had her thigh broken, and was otherwise much injured; a second passenger had an arm fractured, a third outside had one of his legs severely bruised, and the coachman was very much hurt. - There certainly are no better horses, carriages, or drivers, than on the Liverpool road; but the excessive overloading of the coaches, and the violent speed at which they are so often driven, render accident frequent at this season of the year, when the roads are in general comparatively bad. - In these conveyances expedition should be combined with safety, and that road is naturally calculated for this important purpose.*

The newspaper was damning the coach drivers with faint praise, for they were generally regarded as *insolent, imposing, and drunken.* By contrast, a frequent traveller between Cumberland and the south of England, observed that the Ellesmere Canal packet boat combined comfort, safety, and cheapness in a very superior degree. In a letter to the Chronicle of 30th June 1815, this man said he had made the last two trips by way of Whitby, and the canal to Chester: *The boat is a moveable inn; you pursue your travelling, whilst you experience every accommodation aboard, as it may respect good eating and drinking, and unusual civility. I therefore beg leave to recommend this conveyance to my perambulating friends, on the same track of road, as the most desirable which they could adopt.*

That is when the canal-packet service was in its prime. Indeed, Captain Thomas Crimes, who had been the tenant of the Ellesmere Canal Tavern at Tower Wharf since 1810, had to take a second inn, the 'Coach and Horses,' in Northgate Street, for the accommodation of his customers. His bathing packet was doing well, too. The 'Chronicle' of 25th August 1815 informs us that, to celebrate Napoleon's exile to St Helena after his defeat at Waterloo, a party of Cestrians hired the Whitby bathing-packet for a pleasure trip to Beeston, up the old Chester Canal. About 3 pm. *an excellent dinner* was served up in the boat, after which, some of the group went into what had once been the Keep of the ruined Castle, where they drank loyal toasts and sang patriotic songs. About 8 pm. the boat *weighed anchor*, and a little before 11 pm. arrived back at Chester.

But the post-Napoleonic era saw increased competition from the northern ferries, as well as improved road transport. The road to those ferries, which had been among the very worst in this part of England, would soon be classed among the very best, thanks to the improvements made after 1815. According to the 'Courant' of 31st May 1824, there were few roads in the country on which there was more travelling than on that between this city and the Liverpool ferries, and there were few roads kept in such good order.

This trend both reflected and re-inforced the rapid introduction of steam packets at these rival ferries. It is true that the Ellesmere and Chester Canal Company (formed in 1813) were quick to invest in a river steamer of their own. In June 1815, the first steam packet ever seen on the Mersey arrived from the Clyde, to ply between Liverpool and Runcorn. Twelve months later, the Canal Company's 32-horse-power paddle steamer, which measured 90 feet long by 31 feet wide, performed the first experimental trip to Ellesmere Port, reported the 'Chronicle' of 31st May 1815, *in the presence of an immense number of spectators and passengers. About half past ten, she set out from Liverpool town side, in a direction opposite to her intended course, to prove her power against the run of a spring tide, and adverse wind. Under these very unfavourable circumstances she proceeded nearly a mile with astonishing steadiness and celerity, to the entire satisfaction of every person present: she then commenced her* voyage, and performed it, without the assistance of a sail, in one hour and five minutes; the Engine making only twenty-five strokes per minute, its general rate being thirty…its principal cabin is spacious, elegantly finished and furnished for a large private party; there is a handsome private apartment for ladies; in short accommodation superior to any thing we ever saw on the river.

The next week's issue of this newspaper, under the heading *Steam Packet*, stated: *It is now in daily use, and runs the distance between Whitby Port and Liverpool (eleven miles) in ONE HOUR, and frequently in less time, against wind and tide!* While Thomas Crimes the lessee advertised *a large Steam Packet late the Greenock to sail daily and reduce the time for the journey to Chester from Liverpool to under three hours… it is presumed the passage will be found the cheapest, safest, and most expeditious, as well as most comfortable, of any hitherto offered to the notice of the public. From Ellesmere Port every Sunday one hour before High Water, wait two hours and Return.*

Two weeks afterwards, the ceremony of renaming the steam packet the 'Countess of Bridgewater' was held at Liverpool. The 'Chronicle' of 26th June reported that members of the Canal Committee living in Chester travelled there in two open landaus, drawn by four horses each, and returned by the paddle steamer in the evening; leaving Liverpool at 3.45 pm, and arriving at Ellesmere Port, a distance of ten miles, *in an hour and ten minutes, without the use of a sail, and with a very low neap tide; landing her passengers, the Packet immediately returned majestically at a rate of 9 miles an hour, against wind and tide, making a progress highly satisfactory to the numerous spectators collected on the Pier Head. - At Ellesmere Port, one of the Canal Packets was in waiting for the Committee, in which they sat down to an elegant cold collation, provided by Mrs Crimes. The wines were excellent, and the evening was spent in the utmost conviviality; the party prolonging their stay upon the water until one o'clock.*

The newspaper went on to say: *The fare in the 1st compartment (for 20 miles) is only 2s 6d; in the 2nd compartment, 1s 6d and the passage is insured [sic] in three hours!: but to prevent disappointment, passengers must be punctual to the time fixed for starting. The Packet now being independent of the wind, starts precisely at the appointed hours, and many have already been in consequence left behind. It is shortly expected to sail twice every day, having performed two voyages this day (between Chester and Liverpool) with great ease; a more frequent conveyance than heretofore is in contemplation, which will be highly advantageous to the public.*

That said, steam packets were more expensive to buy, maintain and repair than sailing packets. As early as 4th October 1816, Thomas Crimes, the lessee, was obliged to inform *the public that he has engaged a new and elegant Steam Packet to sail between Ellesmere Port and Liverpool, during the refitting of the 'Countess of Bridgewater'*. Moreover, an entry in the Ellesmere & Chester minute book, dated 30th July 1817, states that owing to the *enormous expence of repairing & supporting the Steam & other passage Boats belonging to this company and as Mr Crimes term expires in October next; This Committee beg leave to recommend to the General Committee the propriety of letting by public Auction at Chester the Houses & Packet Boats in four lots*, viz: 1. Canal Tavern; 2. Passage Boats to Ellesmere Port; 3. Houses at Ellesmere Port; 4. Boats on Mersey. They agreed.

Two months later, in September 1817, the Canal Company accepted Messrs Whittle & Co's offer to pay £1000 per annum for three years and *keep the Steam Packet, the Telford & Luggage sailing Boats with the two Canal Packets in complete repair, at their own expence* - and even replace the boiler if it failed. But because of mounting competition from the steam packets at the Tranmere and Woodside ferries, they offered to pay only £600 pa. when their lease came up for renewal three years later. This was unacceptable to the Ellesmere & Chester Committee, and on 7th July 1820 the properties and boats were let to the highest bidder in two lots: Lot I - Two Canal Packets and Canal Taverns at Chester and Ellesmere Port; Lot II - Sailing Packets and 'Countess of Bridgewater' paddle steamer.

A couple of weeks afterwards, an offer of £960 from Charles Hickson was accepted. Then it was discovered that the boats from Whittle & Co had dry rot, so the latter were liable to replace them. But Hickson offered to take the craft and repair them for £160. He also received the Company's permission to lengthen the luggage boat for his livestock to avoid *the inconvenience, expense and delay of trans-shipping at Ellesmere Port*. Clearly, Hickson wanted to build up that side of the business. Three years earlier, the Company stipulated that no parcel over 112 lbs should be accepted by the lessees of the canal packets, but no such restriction applied to *any live or Dead stock, as Calves, Pigs, Sheep and Fish*, carried in the luggage boat provided by them. However, he did not lease the 'Countess of Bridgewater' steam packet, which was sold on. Instead, Hickson informed intending passengers on 20th September 1820 that he had *Contracted with the Runcorn Steam Boats Proprietors to ply between Ellesmere Port and Liverpool*.

By the 1820s Ellesmere Port was a little pleasure resort, with Charles Hickson advertising bath houses for ladies, warm and shower baths, and a newly fitted hotel for those who wished to lodge there during the bathing season. Many years later, his granddaughter recalled:

My father, eldest son of Charles Hickson, kept the Canal Inn and Packet House on the Chester canal wharf, from which the Packet sailed every day. The Packet boat was very long, with many windows on each side, and first and second cabins, with a refreshment bar in the centre. An old blind man, 'Dick the Fiddler', played the violin, and it was very common to get up dances during the voyage from Chester to Ellesmere Port. On arriving at the Port, the passengers walked to the steamer for Liverpool. My grandfather, Charles Hickson, kept the Canal Inn at Ellesmere Port, and also a large private house, quite close to the pier. There were baths attached to both houses, which stood as it were on an island, having the canal locks and basin on one side, and the river locks and basin on the other, and the Mersey in front. The docks later occupied the site of the hotel.

Unfortunately, Hickson suffered heavy losses in December 1822 when one of the Runcorn steamers chartered to him (the 'Prince Regent') sank in the Mersey during a terrible storm with the loss of eight lives. This tragedy had shaken public confidence in steam boat safety, as the 'Chester Chronicle' of 13th December noted: *In the mean time, we understand, that fine sailing Packet, the Telford, is preparing for service; and, upon the whole, during the winter season, we think it fully as desirable to employ such vessels, particularly at ferries so far distant from Liverpool.*

Hickson's lease expired in 1823 and he went bankrupt the following year, still in debt to the Canal Company.

Earl of Bridgewater

Hickson was followed by William Johnson of Runcorn, whose steam packet the 'Earl of Bridgewater' was already operating between Liverpool and Whitby Locks. Johnson rented the packet boats for 3 years at £750 per annum, and promised to build a new canal packet and repair the (smaller) bathing boat. The new canal packet cost £439, and was built by Joseph Evans of this city. In May 1824 it started running to Ellesmere Port, where it was advertised to meet the 'Earl of Bridgewater': *Her accommodations are of a superior class, having three Cabins elegantly fitted up, with every convenience suited to the taste and comfort of passengers; which, together with her superior power of Engine, and unequalled speed, it is hoped will merit the patronage of the public. The sailing of the Canal Packet and Luggage Boat, will be arranged to make the passage in as short a time as possible.*

However, the 'Earl of Bridgewater', with James Radley as master, failed to keep to that arrangement on the first day of the Chester Races. The steam packet was supposed to sail from Liverpool at 5 am.; but the captain, wanting to take in as many race-goers as possible, did not start until 5.45 am., when he had 200 of them on board. This delay meant that Captain Radley would be too late for the canal packet at Whitby Locks, so he made all his passengers disembark one and a half miles away at Pool Rocks, *in a small boat crowded with 15 or 16 people at a time*, and left them without any means of transport to Chester. One of the passengers, a Liverpool merchant named Gardiner, who walked the rest of the way, was subsequently awarded 1 shilling damages - the canal packet fare to this city - and costs at the Cheshire Assizes, in a case he brought against Captain Radley for breach of contract. The court heard that: *The passengers were highly indignant at this treatment; and the misconduct of the master was considerably aggravated by landing them in a most inconvenient place, where they had to wade through dirt and mud for a considerable distance...[in order] that he might be back in time in Liverpool to take a second cargo of passengers to Chester and put more money in his pocket.*

The 'Earl of Bridgewater' was in the news again after her boiler exploded from excessive pressure at the George's Pierhead, Liverpool in August 1824, killing the 12-year-old fireman, a woman passenger, and seriously injuring many more. An 'Eye-Witness' wrote to the 'Liverpool Mercury' a week later, complaining about two accounts of this *awful catastrophe* published in another newspaper, *which are evidently drawn up, in the first, as a most trifling accident; in the second, to take off all blame from the managers of the vessel. As it is stated that the persons 'leaped' overboard through fright, I should like to be informed, if the deck planking and one of the knees... 'leaped' overboard through fright and next, if the vessel had not been without an engineer for some days? It is a case, I conceive, that the public should have a strict investigation into, and that the sufferers should be recompensed, if gross blame attaches to the managers.*

At the inquest, it was fully proved that someone had tampered with the safety valve on the boiler. Moreover, the engineer had, some time previous to the accident, informed both the agent and the master of the vessel of the dangerous state of the boiler, and its unfitness for use. The 'Liverpool Mercury' declared that *the deceased fireboy was in the act of exhibiting some parts of the engine to strangers, when the catastrophe took place. He was, we learn, ignorant of the nature of the engine; and a boy (aged 17) who, it appears, was the only engineer of the ship, was, at the time, on shore. If such youths are to be trusted with engines, of which they can have but little experience, we know not how the proprietors can expect the encouragement or confidence of the public.*

The 'Mercury' might have had plenty to say about their canal packet to Chester, too, if this interesting (and amusing) letter from *A Timid Traveller* had been sent to it instead of the

'Chester Chronicle's' editor, in September 1824:

Sir… I took my passage in a canal packet, which was so badly moored, that in getting into the cabin, I had the misfortune to be plunged into the bason; but being an expert swimmer, I saved my life, but entirely spoiled some valuable jewellry. When arrived the day following at the other end of the passage, myself and other passengers of both sexes, were deserted by the crew, and had to leap three or four feet to reach the quay. It seems that stepping stones had very properly been placed to accelerate the entrance and exit; but the packet was moored without any reference to these conveniences. Upon these considerations, Sir, I do not mean to stir from home again, until either the balloon convenience becomes practicable, or the projected rail-roads are extended in the course of my peregrinations. If you can give me any information when either of these means of conveyance, especially the former, is likely to be established, I promise the projectors I will be one of the first to take a fare.

History does not say whether our *Timid Traveller* ever stirred from home again, but we can be sure he was not taken in by a newspaper advertisement assuring the public that the canal packet would meet the steam packets 'Duke and Earl of Bridgewater' for Liverpool during the Chester Race Week of 1825; and that *the Proprietors can with confidence recommend it as an extremely pleasant, cheap, and expeditious conveyance.*

Nor were such assurances enough to stop increasing numbers of passengers using road transport to and from this city, and the other Liverpool ferries instead. Johnson, who was £602. 10s. in arrears, lasted only two years before he pleaded to be released from his contract in 1825. His plea was granted on condition he paid £200 and continued to work his steam packet 'Earl of Bridgewater' without payment on the Ellesmere Port station, at least until a new tenant was found. Subsequently, a notice appeared in the 'Chester Chronicle' of 14th October 1825:

TO BE LET BY TENDER:
The Canal Packets, now navigating upon the Wirral line of the Ellesmere and Chester Canal, to and from the City of Chester, and Ellesmere Port.
Also, the privilege of Conveying the Passengers and Luggage carried by the said Boats, to sail from Ellesmere Port, and the Town of Liverpool, by means of a Steam Boat on the River Mersey.
Persons desirous of renting either or both of the above concerns, are requested to send in proposals, sealed up, and endorsed proposals for Renting the Canal Packets, the Mersey Packet, or both, as the case may be, and addressed to Mr Crimes, Tower Wharf, Chester, on or before Tuesday the 18th day of October next. Thomas Stanton, Agent to the said Canal Company.

The tenancy of the packet boats was then taken by Samuel Smith of the Eastham Ferry House. Following his death, aged 78, in 1827, the business was continued by his widow and it appears that, by this time, both the routes from Eastham and Whitby Locks to Chester were controlled by the Smiths as, in 1829, *Peggy Smith's Conveyance* was running four times a day between Eastham and Chester. She was succeeded in March 1834 by Messrs Whaley & Smith, whose initial offer of only £250 pa. for three years proved unacceptable to the Ellesmere & Chester; but they were allowed to rent them on a yearly basis for one year. On 13th December that year, however, a Company minute states *Whaley insolvent will pay £125 and give up Tavern & boats & house. Fairhurst, Tilston & Co to rent at £250 pa. for 5 yrs (unless either party give 6 months notice).*

By then the packet-boat service was on its last legs. Sir George Head, in his book 'A Home Tour in the Manufacturing Districts of England' in 1835, made one voyage along the Wirral Line, from Chester towards Liverpool, by the packet boat, and wrote that *the indications of business, both in the office and on board the packet-boat, were fewer than might be imagined;*

Ellesmere Port Docks, *early 20th century*

129

that is to say, there were not more than twenty or thirty passengers, and the inland produce chiefly consisted of live fowls. Indeed, Head went on to complain: *A chicken merchant on board, who had under his charge upwards of twenty baskets of live fowls, that while the annoyance of their cackling extended to every corner of the vessel, those who sat to leeward were covered with dust and feathers.*

The incidents of this short voyage were but commonplace, he continued, *though it behoved each passenger to exercise some degree of watchfulness to prevent his brains being beaten out by the arches of the numerous bridges across the canal. These are so low as not to allow a man to stand upright [on the small deck] when passing underneath, and they are encountered at the rate of five or six in a mile. The boat was towed by three horses, of which a boy rode the hindmost, driving the other two before him without reins. The animals thus free of control, were, nevertheless, like men in the same predicament, not quite so independent as might be imagined, the towing-path being straightened and narrow, that they were unable to turn round; and as the boy was what is called 'sharp', whenever the leaders were deaf to the crack of the whip, he jumped off and flogged them up to the mark.*

Head's fears regarding low bridges were not exaggerated; the Canal Company Report for 1821 calls for immediate repairs to Caughall Bridge and bears the following gruesome note - *Many accidents have happened and some lives have been lost by the Packet Boats passing under bridges.*

Stage coaches

As we know, the stage coaches connecting with the Liverpool ferries had been involved in many accidents, too. But a new safety coach, reported in the 'Courant' of 23rd April 1833, was destined to put an end to canal-packet traffic: *On Friday last a new Patent Safety Coach upon the most improved principles, constructed by Mr Sandland of this city, commenced running from the White Lion and Mrs Smith's, the Eastham Ferry. It is without exception the most splendid coach we have ever seen; and reflects great credit upon the skill and talents of the builder.*

Ironically, this four-horse safety coach was started by Thomas Whaley, of the White Lion Inn, in the Market Place, Chester (where the Town Hall now stands), who leased the packet boats in 1834. The 'Chronicle' of 2nd May that year advertised Whaley and Chalton's safety coaches leaving for Eastham, *with experienced and careful drivers, generally remarked for their attention and civility.* Although Whaley himself went bankrupt, his partner Samuel Chalton continued the service.

The historian Joseph Hemingway, in his 'Panorama of Chester' (1836), wrote that Eastham Ferry *is very much travelled, the coach conveying passengers to and from Chester five or six times in a day, usually well loaded.* In addition, *the vehicles running to the [other] Mersey ferries, and returning the same day, generally crowded with passengers, are not less than eighteen or twenty; while the passengers going and returning, do not amount to less in number than three hundred and fifty persons!*

The opening of the Chester-Birkenhead Railway soon put a stop to the coaches running to the northern ferries, if not to Eastham. According to the 'Courant' of 3rd November 1840, *Those who are not devotedly attached to the railway speed of the times in which we live, and who delight in viewing the various objects of nature and of art, which present themselves in such pleasing alternation, en route to Liverpool, from this city, will rejoice to find that it is intended to continue the customary coaches, by careful drivers, to Eastham Ferry, and thence to that great entrepot of commerce - Liverpool. Those who have been so long accustomed to the advantages and pleasure of travelling by these well-regulated coaches, will not fail to continue availing themselves of that safe, old-fashioned, and pleasant mode of travelling, so much in vogue in the time of our forefathers.*

However, there was to be no reprieve for the canal packet. It lay under a shed in the Chester dock basin for many years; the last occasion on which it was used being at the funeral of Charles Hickson, junr. in 1842, when it conveyed his body and a large number of mourners to Stoak Church. (There was no church at Ellesmere Port in those days, and the residents used to go to services at Stoak in a boat towed by donkeys.)

Yet passenger carrying had not become extinct on the Ellesmere & Chester Canal. The 'Chronicle' of 2nd August 1844, under the heading *Irish Reapers*, states: *Within the last fortnight large droves of these useful annual visitants have made this city, en route from the Mersey to the midland counties. The canal company are driving a large traffic, by conveying them from Chester to Wolverhampton, per canal-boat, the charge for the trip being eighteen-pence. The time occupied in the voyage is from eighteen to twenty hours.*

In Victorian times also, excursions and Sunday school trips were often made in a hired narrowboat. Even the children (up to 70 in number) attending the Sunday school of the Chester Boatman's Chapel, or "Bethel", enjoyed an annual treat by canal boat to Beeston Castle in the 1880s and 90s. Sadly, one such trip was marred by sectarian violence, when *a boat load of Sunday School children were stoned in [Boughton] Chester, because they happened to be singing a hymn adopted by 'The [Salvation] Army', and to which, in their religious fervour, the Irish element objected."*

The Chester Canal nowadays sees many types of pleasure craft: hotel boats and trip boats, as well as narrowboats hired or owned by individuals. The boats may change, but the life of 'the cut' goes on.

The former 'Lord Clive' paddle steamer c1950. *The iron-hulled 'Lord Clive' was built in 1875 at Seacombe, Wallasey by Bowdler & Chaffer. It carried passengers and towed barges between Liverpool and Ellesmere Port. Later it was itself converted, in 1889, to a dumb barge and continued to work on the Mersey. At 18 ft wide and 112 ft long the boat would not have been used on the canal. When the SU stopped carrying it was sold to Nicholsons of Liverpool and then, in 1947, to Harris Barges of Liverpool, before being broken up in Preston during 1967. In the rear is the famous Telford's Warehouse at Ellesmere Port built in the 1830s and destroyed by fire in the 1970s.*

Boat Museum Trust

CARGO-CARRYING FLATS AND BARGES Terry Kavanagh

A broad canal

The Chester Canal was built as a broad canal with locks 14 feet 9 inches wide, to accommodate the traditional coastal and river barges of the northwest, known as 'flats' or 'flatts'. But the Canal Company were obliged to build a few primitive narrow-beam boats to negotiate the river lock at Chester. This stood on land owned by the River Dee Company, who had insisted that the tide gate should only be 7 feet wide. Later, after a court case in 1776, they agreed to the erection of another floodgate, at the Canal Company's expense, which allowed sailing flats or barges in and out of the tidal basin at the foot of the Northgate Locks (see page 46).

By now the Chester Company were in financial difficulties, and many of the shareholders were unwilling to advance any more money towards completing the line to Nantwich and Middlewich. A correspondent in the 'Chronicle' of 10th January 1777 wrote:

Great complaint is made of the enlargement of the Canal and Locks; but I am persuaded that it will be found to be such an improvement, as will fully answer the extraordinary expences. - Indeed the narrowness of the first plan would have been such an obstacle in the way of trade, particularly in the articles of salt, cheese, and all kinds of merchandize, passing to and from the Port of Chester, as must have diverted it into another channel. In navigations that have an immediate connection with larger rivers, where the boats are to be navigated in the tide-way, they are required to be of a different construction from those that are navigated in Canals only.

The earlier type of square-sterned gaff-rigged sailing flat on the Mersey, c1908
Boat Museum Trust

133

'A Proprietor' sent this reply to the paper a week later:

I agree with the writer that the execution of the Canal, on the plan of making it navigable for barges of 14 feet wide, capable of carrying from 40 to 60 tons, was a most judicious measure, and must be approved of by all persons conversant in commercial affairs. Many more reasons may be given in favour of large barges than are there adduced, particularly the conveniencies of such boats being always decked over; having accommodations for the master and his family to lodge in; and all the goods kept dry under lock and key, free from pilferage; so that they may be as safe and free from damage as in any waggon. Seven feet boats have in general no decks; in such cases the goods are only covered with tarpaulins, and such great pilferages and damages have been experienced, that many goods still go by land-carriage. Some have been lately built with decks; but these are so incommodious, that few goods can be stowed under the decks, and of course the vessel cannot be properly loaded; they are, besides, apt to be strained, to break their backs, and to sink, with all the goods on board, even on Canals, and much more would they be liable in the Tide-ways, though the greatest care be taken in loading and conducting them.

This 'Proprietor' had a point about pilferage; it was well known that goods transported by water were less secure than those carried by land. He may have exaggerated the inadequacies of seven feet boats on inland waterways. However, some of the early narrow boats seem to have been of clinker construction – that is, with overlapping planks which were then clenched together - and it was soon found that carvel boats were easier and cheaper to build, as well as being more suitable for canal use.

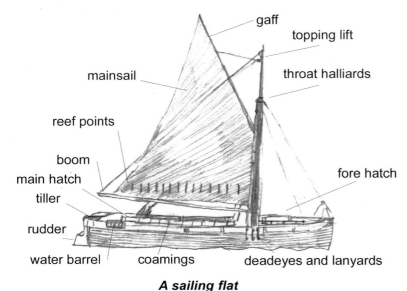

A sailing flat

The sailing flats, of course, were always carvel built; that is, the planks were laid edge to edge and the gap between filled with oakum. Moreover, these flat-bottomed and round-bilged barges were very strongly built with heavy oak timbers and planking to withstand the frequent groundings at low water in tidal regions - essential for loading and unloading where there was no wet dock. Little of the keel projected, although the massive internal keel, or 'keelson', gave the flats longitudinal strength. The early sailing flats were horse-hauled when working on the canals. They usually had a heavy square stern to make the most of the space in the lock-pits; and a mast that lowered was essential for passing under bridges. The rigged flats had two hatches, a small one forward of the mast and a long main hatch, which was always a point of weakness in heavy weather. But their efficient if simple high-peaked gaff rig, with heavy tanned canvas main and foresail, was easily handled by a small crew and stood up to hard usage. At the stern they had a stout post, bored out for a pump and fitted with a large cleat for the mainsheet.

The pioneering Duke of Bridgewater had built his canal between Runcorn and Manchester to provide access for his fleet of sailing flats, so that exports and imports could connect with (Chester's rival) Liverpool and the Mersey without further transhipment. Initially the Duke built his flats at Worsley; but from 1765-75 he set up a boatyard at Bangor-on-Dee in Flintshire, with the wood for the flats coming from his own estate at Ellesmere. The flats were delivered by being sailed down the River Dee and round the Wirral to the Mersey. One of the last flats built at Bangor, the 'Dantzick' of 1775, was later registered at Liverpool as a coaster, so we have her dimensions. She measured 65ft 10ins long x 13ft 10ins beam x 5ft depth of hold, and 50 tons burden.

The Duke's flat-building activities had not gone unnoticed. In July 1774, the Chester Canal Co's managing committee ordered: *Two Boats be immediately Contracted for such as are Generally built at Bangor for his Grace the Duke of Bridgewater.* One - probably the second - of these two 14ft flats or barges, called the 'Egerton', was launched into the canal near Cow Lane Bridge, in this city, on 27th December 1774. Five weeks later, on 3rd February 1775, the Chester Committee resolved that a third *Barge to be built same dimensions as the 'Egerton' on the lowest Terms, to be Carvel built.* This flat appears to have been completed by the beginning of September 1775 when *Inquiry [was to be made] of the Proper Person to go Master of a Barge on the Canal.* Eventually the Company built six flats of 40-60 tons burden - the 'Egerton', the 'Peploe', the 'Bootle', the 'Speed', the 'Powell', and the 'Bird'. The last reference to flat-building in the minutes dates from February 1779, and says: *That seven feet Boats be broke up* and replaced by *a Boat similar to the 'Powell' as soon as Edw'd Bird can.*

Now, one of the flats went up with coal as soon as the first section of canal, from this city to Beeston, opened for navigation on 16th January 1775 - a sharp drop taking place in the price of this commodity formerly carried by road waggons, the transport cost of low-cost, heavy, bulky commodities like coal being a large part of the price. But it would be almost two years before any of the Chester Co's flats could sail out of the tidal basin and down the Dee to the Flintshire collieries.

The 'Chronicle' of 13th December 1776 reported that, *for the first time one of the Canal barges, of the burden of about 60 tons, navigated out of the Canal, thro' the five-fold lock lately compleated at this city, into the river Dee, to proceed on her voyage to the colliery, to load coals for the use of the interior parts of the country.*

Not only coal came up from the river into the canal. The 'Chronicle' of 11th April 1777 reported that two vessels passed through the staircase lock at the Northgate with pig-iron for Doddington Forge, at Doddington near Nantwich. But the line of navigation to the latter place would not be completed for another 19 months or so. The 'Chronicle' of 8th August 1779 announced: *The canal is now opened between this city and Nantwich in this county and in consequence two boats loaded with timber, iron, and other goods were navigated last week through the whole length, being eighteen miles.*

In the meantime, at least two of Canal Company sailing flats were employed in the coasting trade. The 'Chronicle's' shipping reports in 1777, for example, show that the 'Egerton' and the 'Peploe' carried cargoes of lead and oats to Liverpool, and returned with sundries. Then, in October 1778, it was ordered that *the 'Egerton' and 'Bootle' Flats Bee in Proper Repair fit to be stationed on the Nantwich Line as soon as finished.* Thus, they became two of the Company's *regular Stage Boats of Sixty Tons Burthen, decked over, and perfectly dry, for the Conveyance of Goods and Merchandize…on this Navigation.* (See page 138.)

With the line to Middlewich not built, however, little traffic used the canal. Several schemes were implemented in order to attract traffic to the canal for Chester and even Liverpool. First, the Company started rock salt mining at Nantwich. Then they placed two of their boats on the Trent & Mersey, and tried to compete with Liverpool for the Potteries and Birmingham trade by carrying once weekly by boat to Wheelock, transferring the cargoes there to road waggon for Nantwich to be freighted in the 60-ton canal flats, or 'stage boats', to Chester, where they would be rigged, if necessary, for consignments to Liverpool.

It all ended in failure, however. In May 1780 salt mining operations were stopped, as no salt had been found; in August the Company decided to take off the boats plying on the Trent & Mersey, and in October to lay up the (unrigged) flats 'Bootle', 'Peploe', 'Speed' & 'Egerton' in the basin opposite King Charles' Tower at Chester.

The first-named flat was subsequently engaged in the coasting trade. A Company minute in June 1781 states: *The 'Egerton' and 'Peploe' Flatts to be rigged to go to Rhyddland to raise*

'The flats 'Bootle', 'Peploe', 'Speed' and 'Egerton' were laid up in the basin opposite King Charles' Tower' Old engraving

the Flatt 'Bootle'. The salvage operation at Rhuddlan was evidently successful, for, in May 1782, it was resolved that *the 'Peploe' and 'Bootle' with all Materials be advertised and sold at auction.* But for some reason the sale did not go through. In June 1783, however, it was ordered: *Flatt 'Peploe' and her Rigging, Sails, Cables, to be sold by Public Auction on Friday 27th inst.* It was hoped to raise £80 to pay for the repairs to Tilston lock, but a William Hughes later paid only £55 for the vessel. Then, in December it was reported: *Flatt 'Bootle' seized by Custom House Officers for bringing Kernel [grain] from Liverpool,* without declaring the cargo on arrival. The ultimate fate of this flat - and the 'Egerton' - is not known. As for the 'Speed', she was advertised for sale in the 'Courant' of 30th September 1783.

Chester Canal Navigation

The Company having fixed regular Stage Boats of Sixty Tons Burthen, decked over, and perfectly dry, for the Conveyance of all kinds of Goods and Merchandize: Likewise Passage Boats, with comfortable Accomodation for Passengers, and for the Carriage of small packages and parcels on this Navigation.

Goods and Merchandize will be conveyed between the undernamed places at the following prices: -

	per ton £. s. d.	Distance in Miles
Beeston Brook	0. 4. 0	1from Tarporley, 2 from Bunbury
Nantwich	0. 6. 0	
Audlem	0.10. 0	
Drayton	0.15. 0	
Newport	1. 3. 0	
Shrewsbury	1. 6. 6	
Whitchurch	0.13. 4	
Wheelock, on the Staffordshire Canal	0.10. 0	1 from Sandbach, 9 from Congleton
Lawton, Red Bull	0.11. 6	
Etruvia & Burslem, the Staffordshire} Potteries}	0.13. 4	2 from Newcastle
Skelton Wharf, junction with the Caldon Canal		Goods are here forwarded from & to Lock, Cheadle, Ashburn, & places adjacent.
Stoke Wharf		
Stone	0.15. 6	2 from Newcastle
Bromley Common Wharf	1. 1. 0	4 from Lichfield. Goods are here forwᵈ from & to Uttoxeter, Tamworth, Atherton, Coleshill, Coventry & places adjacent
Hornington Wharf	1. 5. 0	Near Burton-on-Trent
Shardlow, the junction with the } River Trent }	1.10. 0	Goods are here forwᵈ from & to Derby, Kegworth, Loughborough, Leicester, & placers adjacent; likewise on the River Trent to Nottingham, Newark, Gainsborough, to Hessle & places adjacent.
Radford Bridge	0.19. 0	2 from Stafford
Wolverhampton	1. 5. 0	
Birmingham	1.10. 0	

Between Chester and

138

| | per Ton |
| | £. S. D. |

Between Chester &

Stourport, the junction with the
River Severn 1.10. 0

Gainsborough & Bristol 2. 0. 0
Hull 2. 5. 0

Goods are here forwarded from & to
Bawdleys, Bridgenorth, Worcester, Gloucester & places adjacent
upon the River Severn

Between Liverpool by way of Chester and

*The Land Carriage from }
 Birmingham to London }   4.10.0
And from London to Birmingh 3. 0. 0
At other places detached from }
 the Canal .... } 0. 1. 0 per Mile
 Beeston Brook 0.8. 0
 Nantwich 0.10.0
 Audlem 0.14.0
 Drayton 0.19.0
 Newport 1. 7. 0
 Shrewsbury 1.11. 6
 Whitchurch 0.17.4

N. B. Packs of Wool, Bark, and such very Bulky Articles, must be
charged one fourth per Ton more than the above Rates.
Iron in Barrs or Pigs, Lime & Free Stone, & other Goods not perishable
will be carried at a lower price.

Corn will likewise be conveyed between the undermentioned
places at the following rates: £. s. d.

Between Nantwich and Chester

Barley 0. 0. 2
Wheat 0. 0. 2 1/2
Oats 0. 0. 1 1/2
Malt 0. 0. 2

Between Nantwich & Liverpool by way of Chester

Barley 0. 0. 3 1/2
Wheat 0. 0. 4
Oats 0. 0. 3
Malt 0. 0. 3 1/2

The Passenger Boat between Chester & Nantwich sets out every Tuesday Morning
exactly at Eight O'Clock: and from Nantwich every Friday Morning at the same Hour.
 A Market Boat sets out every Saturday Morning from Beeston Brook for Chester,
exactly at Six O'Clock, & returns to Beeston Brook the same Evening at Three O'Clock.
Canal Office Chester, January 3, 1780.

Chester Canal Company Minute Book   Pages 42 & 43
The National Archives RAIL 816/6 transcript

There were still a few flats or barges trading on the Chester Canal, as evidenced by this advertisement in the 'Courant' of 22nd April 1783: *To be sold by Auction, in the Canal Yard, near Cow Lane Bridge, Four Tenths of three large Boats, now in constant Work on the Canal, with their Anchors and Cables, and other Materials. Particulars of which will be given at the Place and Time of Sale. The 'Jackson', 'Sutton', and 'John', burthen 50 Tons or upwards.*

But there was to be no reprieve for the two remaining Canal Company flats. The following advertisement appeared in the 'Courant' of 16th March 1784:

> *To be Sold by Auction, by Mr T. Powell, Two Good FLATS, called the POWELL, and BIRD. Now lying in the Canal at Cow Lane Bridge, where they may be viewed by applying to Thomas Clayton, Exchange Coffee House, Chester.*

By selling at least four of their flats (and the odd piece of land) the Company just managed to keep the canal open. But in November 1787, Beeston Lock collapsed, and all traffic above it stopped for a time, because there was no money for repairs. Only the junction with the eight-mile-long Wirral Line of the Ellesmere Canal at Chester rescued anything from this abortive project. Thus 'Projector's' plan in the 'Chronicle' of 28th May 1779, of a new communication by water from Chester to Liverpool, *not subject to the present necessity of a tedious, expensive, and dangerous passage round the West Point of Wirral or the expense attending a land carriage of seven miles between Ince Boat-house and Chester*, became a reality.

The Wirral Line

The Ellesmere Canal Company wasted no time in establishing goods and passenger craft on this new inland waterway. An entry of October 1794 in the minute book states: *two Passage Boats & two Barges for the carriage of Goods to be provided for the Wirrall Line of the Canal so as to be ready for use as soon as that part of the Canal is completed*. The Ellesmere Canal packet-boat service began on 1st July 1795, but the three locks into the Mersey were not finished until early the following year. This has led canal historians to suggest that the initiation of goods traffic was made by four flats laden with Lancashire coal, which reached Chester from the Mersey in February 1796.

However, the Ellesmere Company inserted a notice (opposite) in the 'Chronicle' of 2nd October 1795, informing the public, amongst other things:

That Boats are now established on the Canal, for the conveyance of heavy goods and articles of merchandise, and that regulations are made with the His Grace the Duke of Bridgewater, and on the Mersey, for forwarding goods between the towns of Manchester, Liverpool and Chester.

All goods delivered at his Grace's quays, at Manchester or Preston Brook; at Pat. Coffield & Co. Dry Dock, Liverpool; or the Canal Office, Chester; will be forwarded according to directions, with the greatest care, and regularity.

But the Ellesmere Canal Company, who are at present the sole carriers on the canal from the City of Chester to the river Mersey, will not be answerable for the safety or delivery of any goods, until the same shall have been received into their boats on the canal, or after the same shall have been delivered out of their boats into any other boats or vessels for the purpose of conveying the same upon the river Mersey to the places of their destination.

The passage between Liverpool, by this conveyance is perfectly safe, and goods will be delivered the same day they are received.

The two Ellesmere Company barges then, were the only commercial traders on the Wirral Line itself, goods being transferred to and from river flats at the Whitby end. But Coffield & Co's vessels entered the canal soon after the tidal entrance into the Mersey was finished. The first of these, the 53-ton flat 'Ann', with Joseph Hayes as master, was registered at Chester in 1796 under the name of Thomas Whittle, a partner in the firm. Others followed in her wake.

A notice in the 'Chronicle' of 31st March 1797 reads:

> *P. Coffield & Co return their sincere Thanks to the Merchants, Dealers, and others, for the Encouragement they have met with since they commenced Business as carriers by the Ellesmere canal to and from Liverpool and Chester, and beg to inform them, that they continue carrying Goods as usual.*

The 16th May issue of the newspaper tells its readers that Manley & Co, of Runcorn, had *provided a set of good vessels to navigate weekly, along the Ellesmere Canal and river Mersey, from Chester to Runcorn, and from thence to Manchester, and to carry goods, merchandise, etc...* According to a report by Telford dated 27th 1799: *Eleven flats were working to Liverpool and Manchester with four more on the stocks.*

By then both carrying concerns were trading between Chester and the two Lancashire towns. Successive toll reductions almost from the opening of the Wirral line had encouraged such trade, and the regular carriers had established installations at Chester, where a new basin was constructed next to Manley's in 1809. In this period, cargoes of timber, lead, iron, bricks, coal and general goods passed along the canal, mainly towards Liverpool.

By 1805 the Ellesmere and Chester Canals were connected near Nantwich, and narrow boats at Chester began to receive and deliver goods to and from the river flats, trading between this city, Liverpool, Manchester, and Preston Brook. The 'Courant' of 4th February 1806 advertised that Manley, Hiles & Co of Tower Wharf had established a *new and Substantial set of [7ft] covered boats*, for all merchandise between Chester, Nantwich, Whitchurch and Ellesmere. Coffield & Co's flats were also loaded and unloaded in this city, *substantial covered boats having been built for the purpose* of forwarding goods between those places, by Whittle, Trevor, Lewis & Co.

Pilfering

The flat traffic to and from Chester provided ample opportunity for pilfering over the years. For instance, William Jones, a flatman, was arrested by a police constable, who saw him in the streets one night, at twelve o'clock, with a sack upon his back, in which was found a small bag containing 45lbs flour. Jones, aged 33, was captain of the 'Perseverance', which had left Chester a few days before with best quality flour from Messrs Frost; although he denied stealing it from them. Later, Thomas Fleet, aged 18, a hand on the flat was taken into custody, and he admitted that Jones stole the flour from Messrs Frost's sacks, as suspected, taking a little from each, the young flatman holding the bag to receive it. But Fleet retracted his statement in court, and Jones was acquitted. But Fleet himself was found guilty of the robbery on the evidence of his written confession, and was sentenced to seven years transportation. Frost's had suffered considerably by thefts from flats, and on one occasion, it was found that 242lbs of flour had been taken from 16 sacks.

On another occasion, about two o'clock in the morning, John Jones, master of the flat 'Moses', was seen at Tower Wharf by a watchman, who, observing his pockets were bulging, stopped and searched him. The watchman found some sugar wrapped in a handkerchief, which he returned to Jones and let him go. About twenty minutes after, the watchman came back to the same place, in the course of his round, and within a few yards of where he had searched the flatman, found some soap which had come out of the flat's cargo. Immediately afterwards, the watchman saw Jones approaching, apparently looking for something, and the latter said "he had lost a good knife." The watchman showed him the soap and said, "There's the soap you are looking after." Jones then tried, but failed, to get away, and offered the watchman sixpence to let him go.

Others, it seems, were prepared to offer violence to the watchmen in order to get away. The 'Chronicle' of 9th January 1807 reported: *On Wednesday morning one of the watchmen of this city, named Boulton, was found drowned in one of the Ellesmere Canal locks, at Tower Wharf.- It appears that his lanthorn [lantern] was found in the cabin of a flat, his hat and stick in the graving-dock [dry dock] adjoining, and his rattle swimming right over the spot where the body was found; from these circumstances two flatmen (now in custody) are suspected of throwing him into the lock. The coroner brought in a verdict of 'wilful murder'.*

Pilferage remained a serious problem for carriers and the owners of goods, throughout the era of canal carrying. Carriers provided some flats with no means of access to the hold except by a hatchway, which was padlocked with a key kept by the captain. The lock itself could be sewn up in a canvas bag to make it less accessible. In the 'Chronicle' of 15th May 1812, for example, we find Coffield & Co informing local merchants, *that for the more expeditious conveyance of Goods, they have appointed a regular Market Flat, to Lock Up – to load every Saturday and*

Tuesday, in Liverpool, and deliver at Chester, every Monday and Thursday. – All Spirits, Tobacco, etc. are particularly requested to be ordered by this vessel, as this will be only one Day upon the Road. The following week Ralph Manley countered by saying that he too had *established a regular MARKET FLAT, to <u>Lock up</u> and <u>Seal up</u>… she will only be <u>One Day</u>* on her passage.

There was a similar flat trading from Liverpool through to Nantwich around that time. This advertisement appeared in the 'Liverpool Mercury' of 10th January 1817:

> *The NANTWICH, of Liverpool is a new vessel, intended as a constant trader between the above places, and to sail from hence once or twice every week, as goods may offer.*
>
> *She will be a lock-up vessel, and is the only one by which goods can be conveyed from hence to Nantwich without being transhipped at Chester. The owners therefore presume that this circumstance may entitle them to a preference, on the ground of its being in the shippers' interest. The same charge of freight and tonnage as made by Messrs Coffield and Co. and Messrs Manley and Co. will be required.*
>
> *Applications to ship goods made to James Brooke, brewer, or to the Master (Thomas Ashworth, publican), on the New Quay near the bottom of Chapel Street, will be duly attended to, and gratefully received. 10 Jan. 1817.*

Later that year another firm, Shanklin & Co, commenced business as carriers, on the Ellesmere Canal, to and from Liverpool, Chester, and the different towns on the line of the Ellesmere and Montgomery Canals; *and having provided good new Lock-up Flats and covered Boats, they shall be able to forward all Goods trusted to their care with the greatest punctuality, safety, and dispatch,* according to the 'Chronicle' of 27th June 1817.

Four years later, one of their competitors, Manley & Co inserted the following advertisement in the 'Courant' of 23rd January 1821:

> **CANAL FLATS, BOATS, etc. TO BE SOLD BY AUCTION** At the Canal Tavern, Tower Wharf, Chester.
> **Nine excellent Flats, in the Most Perfect State of Repair, completely rigged, and well found in cables, anchors, etc. fit for immediate Navigation.**
> **Also, Eight capital canal Boats, five of which are fitted with tarpaulin coverings, and double bottoms, for the carriage of Commercial Goods.**
> **The whole of the above vessels have been regularly navigated upon the River Mersey and upon the Duke of Bridgewater's, and the Ellesmere and Chester Canals, and are now lying in the bason of the latter Canal, at the Tower Wharf, Chester.**

In the event, however, they joined forces with Shanklin & Co, who then moved from Cow Lane Wharf to Manley's premises at Tower Wharf. In the 'Courant' of 27th February, M Manley, widow of Ralph Manley, who died in 1815, informed the public that *she has entered into a Partnership with some respectable Persons, with the view of continuing the Carrying Concern for the benefit of her Grand-children; and that it will be carried on under the firm of SHANKLIN, MANLEY & Co.*

Goods traffic

By then the goods traffic had become relatively more important than passenger carrying on the Wirral line. Indeed it had increased so much by 1823 that flats carrying commercial goods and grain were allowed to travel by night for the first time. But the Ellesmere & Chester Canal Company (formed in 1813) had pursued a policy of maintaining their revenue by adjusting tonnage rates to fluctuations in traffic and, in 1827, they decided to encourage long-distance traffics at the expense of short-distance ones. However, this caused considerable outcry among the Chester merchants and traders who removed their Liverpool traffic to the Dee estuary for a time with considerable loss of revenue to the Canal Company.

Sailing flat sunk in the lower basin
Photographed in the 1880s
Grosvenor Museum

In 1830 the Ellesmere & Chester obtained parliamentary powers to carry goods across the Mersey, though they gave the contract to two firms, Fairhurst, Tilston (formerly Coffield & Co) and Shanklin & Co, which later became one concern. After the opening of the Birmingham & Liverpool Junction Canal in 1835, the Canal Company decided to investigate complaints about favouritism and inefficiency on the part of the carriers and it was agreed that the Canal Company should take over responsibility for carrying. Finally, in 1836, they took over the trade along with Fairhurst, Tilston's wharves, warehouses and equipment - which included 26 flats @ £500 each - at Ellesmere Port and Liverpool for the sum of £25,000.

From 1836 the Ellesmere & Chester began to cheapen its Mersey barging operations by hiring the Liverpool Steam Tug Co's tugs to tow unrigged, and therefore fully loaded, flats and floats (barges decked for their full length to carry deck cargoes only, in this case timber). The doubling of revenue between 1832 and 1839 enabled the Canal Company to purchase new vessels, and by 1840 they possessed thirty flats and timber floats, as well as two steam tugs of their own. The Company intended to dispense with all the fleet's sails, masts and rigging. But a few flats still worked under sail; indeed, two of their sailing flats, the 'Earl' and the 'Eliza', were among the first vessels to enter the new dock at Ellesmere Port when it opened in 1843.

Flats under tow on the Mersey in the 1930s
Boat Museum Trust

In the same year much of the transhipping between river and canal craft was transferred from Chester to Ellesmere Port, which had specialised wharves for particular commodities like iron or pottery clay, and warehouses for grain. ('Fly' or express boats were still unloaded at Chester and the goods there transhipped to Mersey flats.) Tariff cutting wars with the Bridgewater Trustees enabled the latter to lease the Ellesmere & Chester Co's carrying trade in flats and floats for five years in 1844; the Chester trade excepted. This arrangement was terminated in 1852.

Shropshire Union

It was terminated by the Shropshire Union Company (formed in 1846) who then began to build up an impressive carrying business. During the 1860s and 1870s their fleet of river flats and floats was greatly enlarged. In June 1871 there were 81 Mersey flats and 12 floats; by 1889 these numbers had risen to 101 and 15 respectively. The company was engaged in cross-river barging not only from Liverpool to Ellesmere Port but also to Birkenhead. In 1869 they suggested that the L&NWR should transfer to them the railway's cross-river trade with private carriers. This was agreed, and the SU thereupon, in 1870, bought William Oulton's lighterage business, which included 13 barges varying in size from 80 to 130 tons. In 1883 the business of the Mersey Carrying Company was also taken over. Apart from flats being purchased elsewhere, more were being built on the Company's own stocks at Chester. The 'Chronicle' of 27th November 1875, for example, reported: *On Saturday last a new flat built by the SUCo,*

under the superintendence of their boat inspector, Mr Hulse, was launched from the Chester yard. The ceremony of christening was performed by Miss Jones, daughter of the company's general traffic manager. The vessel was named the 'Harriet,' after its fair sponsor, and is destined for trade between Liverpool and Chester.

The 'Ellesmanor' float
c1930 at Taylor's Yard
Geoff Taylor Collection

At that time the Shropshire Union's Cow Lane Bridge office was considered the premier goods' agency of Chester. The grain trade with the Chester millers and dealers, F A Frost & Sons, John Wiseman, William Johnson (Dee Mills), and William Gamon was exceptionally heavy. Moreover, practically the whole of the grocery traffic, averaging 40 tons a day, came from Liverpool to Chester by canal. In addition there was the traffic for wine merchants.

The importance of the grain trade to the Shropshire Union is clear from this long report in the 'Chronicle' of 14th July 1894:

If the shipbuilding trade of Chester has left the river Dee the canal company apparently has no intention that it shall leave the canal, as on Wednesday another new river flat, which has been completed by the company, was launched into their canal. The new boat has been three months in building, and has been specially designed upon the newest principles for the growing requirements of the company's trade in the canal and river Mersey, by Mr Beard, the company's boatyard superintendent, and Mr Hulse, foreman. It is 71 feet in length, and has a beam of 14 feet 7 inches. It is capable of holding 110 tons, and will be a valuable addition to the company's large fleet of vessels. She will be under the charge of Captain John Thomas, one of the Company's oldest servants. Out of compliment to the firm of Messrs F. A. Frost and Sons, who have for so many years done a large business with the company, the vessel is named the 'Sir Thomas Frost'. The ceremony of 'christening' was performed by Miss Hales, daughter of the manager of the company, who as the vessel gracefully glided down the ways into the water, gave her her name with the time honoured custom.

Like other more modern flats designed for canal work, and those working under sail, the 'Sir Thomas Frost' was round sterned. These canal or 'cut' flats all had a single long hatch spanned by a middle beam and forward of this the main beam. They were also fitted with hatch coamings (raised sides), hatch boards and cloths because they worked on to the tidal Mersey. They were equipped with anchors and windlasses for the same reason. The 'Sir Thomas Frost' was a great success. In August 1894 the Shropshire Union minute book states: "*Reported that she had brought up to Chester 60 tons [of grain] compared with 44 tons carried by old type of Boat and that the cost per ton in working was proportionately reduced.*"

The late Pat O'Brien, in his book 'Looking Back at Ellesmere Port' (1986), had this to say about the flats carrying grain in bulk from Liverpool to Frost & Sons Steam Flour Mill at Chester: *In those days before grain elevators, all the grain had to be bushelled by two men and it was the duty of the flatmen to hold the sacks into which the grain was emptied. The bags were then tied, two at a time, by nippers and hoisted into the mill. The foreman at the mill was a man named John Smith, who resided at Steam Mill Street, Chester. When the flats were drawing up to the mill wharf, he would be waiting with a bread tin for the flatmen to get him a sample of the grain. John Smith was a kind old fellow, but very asthmatical which he thought a drop of gin would cure, and the young flatmen who desired to remain in Chester for the weekend, and whose flat was likely to finish discharging before Saturday evening, found that by interviewing John and taking him to the 'Cross Foxes' [in Boughton] for a drop of gin, the matter was satisfactorily arranged.*

A Mr J Williamson, of Ellesmere Port, on the other hand, recalled how a Shropshire Union foreman used to give him a drop of gin when he was a young flatman trading in goods between Liverpool and Chester in the early 1860s.

The Tower Wharf was the depot for discharging goods in Chester. The Wharf was a very primitive affair in those days and consisted of a landing stage built and covered so that the flats could get under to unload their goods without damaging the cargo if it rained, wrote Mr Williamson in 1930.

The flat 'Catherine' lying derelict in the Lower Basin in the 1880s Geoff Taylor Collection
The 'Catherine' was broken up in the 1890s.

Four special flats were picked out from amongst the fleet of flats owned by the Shropshire Union Company for this work, named 'The Joseph', 'Swallow', 'Emma', and 'Catherine', the cargoes that these flats carried consisted of wines and spirits that went straight to the bonded stores. They also carried goods that went to the shops in the town. It was all hustle and hurry, as much of the goods were perishable, or were badly wanted in the shops. The flats which were towed from Ellesmere Port by a pair of horses would arrive at one o'clock in the morning. The flat would be berthed at the stage and all got ready for six in the morning when the men would arrive and immediately commence work.

I must not forget to mention that amongst the goods in the cargo was a large consignment of fish and boxes of eggs. The fish was carried in barrels and boxes, and for convenience and quick handling these were placed on the top of the hatches ready for the merchants to get them ashore. The merchants who were mostly Irishmen came from Boughton, and would arrive at the depot at 4 a.m., and after getting permission to take their stuff they would ask the flatmen for a hammer and a bucket, and of course, we knew from previous experience what this meant. It would not be very long before he would be lowering the bucket down again when the bucket would contain a couple of dozen fine herrings or some other kind of fish, and a basin full of eggs. One does not meet with that class of men very often nowadays.

The men who were engaged to work at the depot would be mustered up at six o'clock prompt by the stage hands, four elderly men named Thomas Charmley, Thomas Davies, John Williams and John Jones, the foreman named Henry Forester was a very kindly man, and

149

The flat 'Chester' in the Mill Arm at Ellesmere Port in the early 1900s
Boat Museum Trust

highly respected by all who knew him or worked for him. Orders would be given for Gin and Tobacco up first; it was one of the duties of the foreman to take samples of all excisable goods. When he had tapped the casks he would hand the men a good stiff glass of spirits, and I can assure my readers that we found it very beneficial especially on cold and frosty mornings.

However, some of the merchants shipping goods at the busy Tower Wharf were experiencing long delays. So the Shropshire Union built a new dock at Frodsham Street Bridge (known later as the Cheshire Farmers' Arm), to accommodate flats and narrow boats loading and discharging in the city. Sheds were erected over the docks to prevent damage to goods, and covered accommodation provided for carts and drays employed in their conveyance. The Company also bought two iron steam tugs, called 'Dagmar' and 'Dreadnought', to replace the slow-moving flat-horses on the Wirral Line.

These powerful craft made a lasting impression on one late-Victorian schoolboy. Many years later this old Cestrian asked: *Do you remember the vast amount of traffic handled by the Shropshire Union Canal 60 years ago? How each evening a convoy of flats and barges assembled at Tower Wharf to be towed to Ellesmere Port by the steam tug 'Dagmar' or 'Dreadnought'? What a delight to us boys to be invited on one of the flats by a kind-hearted skipper for a voyage as far as Eleven Arches or Backford Bridge, and then walk home.*

Unfortunately, the Shropshire Union had to sell the canal tugs 'Dagmar' and 'Dreadnought' in October 1917, because the flat traffic on the Wirral line to Chester had greatly declined. To some extent this was accounted for by the development of road transport - motor transport having taken away a certain proportion of the canal business. But a major factor here had been Messrs Frost's decision to transfer their milling operations to Ellesmere Port in 1910.

In 1921 the financially-troubled Shropshire Union Company stopped carrying on their own account. The main reasons given were the extension of the eight-hour day to boat and river men, increased wages,

Above:'**Richard Abel' in the Mill Arm at Ellesmere Port in the 1930s**
Boat Museum Trust

Below: **'Betal'** *(Harris Barges)* **c1920 in the Dry Dock, Chester**
Geoff Taylor Collection

and the higher cost of materials. The Chester & Liverpool Lighterage Company stepped in and began a general carrying business between Liverpool and Chester; their cross-Mersey services were handled by an associate company, named Harris Barges, whose flats included the 'Betal', seen overleaf under repair in the dry dock at Chester.

Meanwhile, the Shropshire Union river barges had been tied up at Chester awaiting disposal. The Company sold many of their newer flats straight away, the 'Lord Stalbridge' of 1908, for example, going to the Bishop's Wharf Carrying Company of Liverpool in November 1921. But it proved more difficult to dispose of the older barges. In May 1932 the Canal Company obtained £45 for the flat 'George', aged 67 years, which was only £5 below the valuation placed upon her by their former boatbuilder in 1927. A month later, an official reported that he had *succeeded in getting an offer of £50, which I have accepted, for the barges 'Grosvenor', 'Swan', and 'Ann'. The first named barges are of an antiquated type, and the last is in bad condition, and we have experienced considerable difficulty in keeping her afloat.* In January

The flat 'Lord Stalbridge' *c1920s*   Geoff Taylor Collection

Surplus craft laid up in the Lower Basin 1935   West Yorkshire ArchiveService, Wakefield. ref. C299

1936, however, the Company's flats 'Hector' and 'Batavia' were sold at Barrow-in-Furness for only £2! The purchaser was shown photographs of the surplus fleet at Chester, but the vessels were too far away for him to consider.

In the years leading up to the Second World War, no one else would consider buying the flats, either. But the exigencies of wartime Britain led one Cestrian to complain in the 'Chronicle' of 12th June 1943: *The papers are telling us to save iron for weapons. Why aren't the railings in front of Chester Castle on the offside of the river pulled up? Also why aren't about two dozen barges lying in the Canal Wharf broken up and the timber used instead of rotting in the water?*

Stung by this letter one Company official suggested that a reply be sent intimating to the correspondent that they would be willing to hand over to him or anyone else who would break up or remove the craft free of charge to the Company. But his boss felt it was not worth worrying about.

In 1946, however, Messrs Boden & Nelson of Paradise Row, Chester, were prepared to undertake the cutting and removal of those old craft from the Dee Basin. The portion of the craft then above water level would be cut off, and when the remainder of the hulls, all of which were lying on the mud, were to be removed, the water in the basin would be temporarily lowered to facilitate the operation. They were given the go-ahead, although several previous similar attempts by contractors had resulted in failure financially. For that reason, a Canal Company official had earlier proposed *laying it down that one flat must be dealt with completely before another is commenced, otherwise we may be in the position of having a number of the bottom sections of the hull left on our hands.*

This is exactly what happened. The work was not completed, and the remaining hulls were simply buried under the rubble when the Dee Basin was filled in about 1952. The basin was later earmarked for housing development, and in 1996 Chester Archaeology recovered the bottom section of the 'Earl', which was the oldest ex-Shropshire Union flat on the site. She was built for Coffield & Co by George Edwards, at Frodsham Bridge in 1802. The square-sterned 'Earl' of Chester registered 64ft 2ins x 14ft 2ins x 5ft 3ins, and 56 tons burthen.

So much for the Dee Basin, now for the other well-known flats' graveyard in the North Basin at Tower Wharf. In the late 1990s there was talk of preserving three of the ex-Shropshire Union flats abandoned there. Archaeologists from British Waterways uncovered these vessels and consulted experts from York's Archaeological Trust to see whether there was any way to preserve them. It was hoped that eventually they would be put on permanent display employing similar techniques to those used on Henry VIII's flagship, the 'Mary Rose', after she was brought up from the sea bed in Portsmouth harbour in the early 1980s. In December 1999, however, the skeletal timbers of the flats 'Herbert', 'John' and 'Onward' were removed to the Ellesmere Port Boat Museum instead.

At least one of these vessels, namely the 'Onward', began her career under sail. On the 1881 Census she is down as a 70-ton sailing flat employed in the Mersey river trade between Manchester Basin, Liverpool and Ellesmere Port. The Shropshire Union bought the 'Onward' from John Smith, a Liverpool flatowner, in 1869. He also supplied the flat 'Mossdale' (then called the 'Ruby') which is preserved at the Ellesmere Port Boat Museum. She is well worth a visit.

'Mossdale' formerly *'Ruby'* at the Boat Museum
Boat Museum Trust

SALLY BOATS AND FLY BOATS Terry Kavanagh

To sally or fly

In 1921 the Shropshire Union Canal Company of Tower Wharf, Chester abandoned its carrying activities, and tied up its large fleet of canal and river craft. The stoppage of canal traffic proved to be only temporary, as most of its horse-drawn narrowboats were acquired by other carriers. But many contemporaries had been concerned about the possible demise of the family-crewed 'Sally boat', and with it the boat people's way of life. On 4th June that year a 'Cheshire Observer' correspondent wrote: *The canal bargees present a picturesque phase of the life in Cheshire. Who has not been interested in the barge community, the family crews and the hard-working, though somewhat thin, horses? It would perhaps be difficult to find the derivation of the name 'Sally boat', but, to hazard a guess, a solution might be found in the fact that in most cases it is associated with the stalwart lady who usually is found at the tiller.*

Originally, the name was used to distinguish the slow-moving horse boats from the express boats running 'fly' or non-stop with relays of horses. (J Wright's 'English Dialect Dictionary' of 1904, states that *Sally out* means *to walk with an idle, trailing gait*.) There are, for example, five 'Sally' boats - which carried the heavy cargoes - and three 'Fly' boats shown on the 1871 Census Returns for Tower Wharf.

The Shropshire Union Co was noted for its fly-boat services which handled perishable and high value goods. The main service, between Ellesmere Port and Birmingham ran twice a week in each direction, took about thirty hours and lasted until after the First World War. Horses were changed en-route at Tyrley, Norbury and Autherley. There were also fly services to the Potteries, which took 24 hours, and to Shrewsbury, Trench, Llangollen, Welshpool and Newtown.

Family life was inevitably very difficult. Invariably the three- or four-man crews of the latter-day Shroppie fly boats were young or unmarried or both, although the skippers were often older and married – veterans like Captain John (Jack) Woolley, whose life and times I wrote in 'Waterways Journal' (vol. 5), and which forms part of this chapter. T W Cubbon, in his famous book 'Only a Little Cockboat', published in 1928, observed: *These barges (sic) are run by men only, three forming the crew; one to steer, another to drive the horse and open the locks while the third turns in to sleep. Speed is the feature of these express boats, and young rollicking fellows usually take on the job, leaving the older fraternity, and married folks, to manage the daylight service. Where the canal is specially wide, mooring posts are ranged along the bank for the daylight barges (sic), which start off in the morning at the first sign of daybreak, doing as much as thirty miles by night-fall, if the huge staircase of the Audlem locks is not included. The fly-boats cover as much as fifty miles or more in twenty-four hours, making their best time at night, when there is not much traffic; and sometimes the crew are well primed with 'courage' before leaving Chester.*

The earliest narrow-beam boats built by the old Chester Canal Company had no cabins as such. In a letter to the 'Chronicle' of 17th January 1777, one of the proprietors referred to the large 14 feet river barges as having *accommodations for the master and his family to lodge in*, whereas the *seven feet Boats* did not. Many trips were short so the crews would get home, but family boating was a means of economising. When freight rates fell, owing to the trade depression after 1815 and later railway competition, the captain's wages fell. He could not pay his mate so took his wife aboard as unpaid assistant with the children as useful helpers, particularly with the horse. The 'Chronicle' of 12th December 1817, for example, describes a boatman's wife named Furber, as *a middle aged woman… belonging to a small boat which trades on the Ellesmere and Chester Canal.* And a report in the 'Courant' of 21st August 1838, states that John Price, aged 8, son of Robert Price, captain of a Staffordshire boat, was *driving the horse* attached to it, whilst on the way to Ellesmere Port; also, that William Thomas, aged nine years, was *steering a boat* at Hurleston Locks.

Captain John (Jack) Woolley

The centre of family boating lay in the Midlands, in the long distance narrowboats. Their cabins were not ideal for families, being about six feet by eight feet long, but they survived to breed a race of specialist boatmen. Narrowboat people became a close-knit community. They intermarried and sons succeeded fathers as captains after unofficial apprenticeships. On the Shroppie it became the norm for a boy of 14-15 to leave the family boat and go as mate or boat-lad to another captain, who would feed and clothe him. After a few years the boy would have a boat of his own with a mate or a wife. Boating skills were taught from a very early age, three-year-old boys would learn how to steer a narrowboat standing on a stool.

Construction

Historically, narrowboats seem to have evolved from the little mine boats at Worsley, measuring 48 feet long and 4 feet 6 inches wide, nicknamed 'starvationers', whose boxed coal cargoes were transferred at Worsley basin to craft of similar shape but larger dimensions for the journey to Manchester.(See page 91.) Some of these 'box' boats were in use until recent times, unchanged in hull form for two hundred years. The huge fleet of Birmingham and Black Country 'day boats' followed a similar design with few refinements, but later long distance 'cabin' boats were given more shape, particularly if they were fly boats. This is borne out by the following sale by auction at the Crown Inn, Nantwich, advertised in the 'Chronicle' of 1st June 1830: *Four new barrel sided, and Three new upright sided 7 feet Canal Boats, with cabins and forecastles complete; built of the best seasoned English oak timber and plank.*

Some thinner timbers were used on fly boats, which could carry up to 18 tons, as a means of saving weight and thereby increasing speed. Later Shropshire Union fly boats had thicker bottoms for the first 16 feet, the remainder being of reduced thickness. The thicker timbers were the ones that took most of the wear because narrowboats were always loaded a little by the head; the pull of the horse bringing them almost level.

Narrowboats were built to fit the 74 feet by 7 feet locks James Brindley had chosen for the central section of the Trent & Mersey Canal as being cheap to build and economical of water in relation to their carrying capacity of 20-30 tons depending on depth. Such boats were usually about 72 feet long and 6 feet 10 inches broad, though dimensions varied slightly in order to fit local locks. Like most canal craft, they were generally built with ordinary open holds, fitted with side and deck cloths for wet weather. Decked boats were provided for valuable cargoes, and the later oil boats; but the first narrow boats coming onto the broad-gauge Nantwich Canal off the Ellesmere were open holded.

The 'Courant' of 31st December 1805, reported *the arrival of six vessels, heavily laden with oak timber, from the Ellesmere Canal, along the old Chester Canal, at the Tower Wharf, in this city yesterday, being the first that have gone by this conveyance since the communication between these canals. Five of those vessels were from Shade [Shady] Oak, about two miles distant from the extremity of the Ellesmere Canal, at Weston, and 50 miles from this city, and belong to the firm of Manleys, Hiles & Co; the other was from Montgomeryshire.*

They were the first of many. The 'Chronicle' of 27th June 1806 declared:
The junction of the Ellesmere Canal with the Chester Canal at Nantwich, has already introduced a very considerable trade on the latter canal, and opened a direct communication from the remote parts of Montgomeryshire to Liverpool, and been the means of bringing by water carriage, immense quantities of timber, bark, corn, and other produce of the rich and fertile counties of Salop, Denbigh, and Montgomery to Chester, Liverpool, and the adjacent country, and supplying those counties, with all kinds of West Indian produce and other articles from Liverpool, at a moderate expense, compared to the uncertain and expensive navigation of the Severn from Bristol.

Birmingham & Liverpool Junction

The opening of the Middlewich branch at Barbridge in 1833, followed by the Birmingham & Liverpool Junction Canal two years later, brought yet more narrowboats onto the Ellesmere & Chester Canal system. One of the main traffics was manufactured iron products from the Midlands to Liverpool, via Ellesmere Port. A return traffic would be iron ore and pig iron imported through the latter port. But the local press devoted more space to the arrival of fly boats freighted with premium goods. The 'Chronicle' of 6th March 1835, for example, reported that eight or ten deeply laden express boats had arrived at Chester, from London and elsewhere, along the newly-opened B&LJ Canal. Six of these fly boats were owned by the well known Midlands carriers Shipton & Co., who had wharves at Wolverhampton and in the City Road Basin on the Regent's Canal. The 'Chronicle' of 10th and 24th April, carried advertisements from rival carrying companies. Robin, Mills & Co, for example, reminded the public that their fly boats continued to leave London and Manchester every night, *by which means goods are delivered in Chester from London in five days, and from Manchester in one.* Crowley, Hicklin, Batty & Co also sent fly boats along the new main line of canal to and from Chester, Nantwich, Audlem and Market Drayton; some carried Cheshire cheese to the Midlands and London, others were *Lock-up Boats for safe conveyance of Wines and Spirits.*

The first fly boat to reach the new canal basin at Shrewsbury belonged to this last concern, and brought a cargo of goods direct from London through the new B&L Junction Canal. Whilst

Hugh Henshall & Co., sent the first fly boat throughout the new line of Canal from Shrewsbury to Manchester; *the boat had a full cargo of cheese and butter from Shrewsbury Fair, and left that town late on Wednesday night week arriving in Manchester on the Friday following,* according to the 'Courant' of 24th March 1835.

As stated in an earlier chapter, ten years later, in 1845, the Birmingham & Liverpool Junction Canal Company was absorbed by the Ellesmere & Chester, which became excited about the prospect of railway conversion. So much so that it changed its name in 1846 to 'The Shropshire Union Railways & Canal Company' (SUR&CCo) and promoted several railways of its own. But the London & North Western Railway had also been formed that year and regarded the SU's expansionist activities as a serious threat. Accordingly it leased the SU in 1847, but it continued to develop canal carrying as parts of the 200-mile system penetrated into rival railway territory. The SU's canal offices, which had been installed in newly-acquired premises in Wolverhampton upon the expectation that it would be the hub of its railway and canal system, were now transferred to Tower Wharf, Chester.

Chester was still a thriving inland, though not a sea, port. Fly boats were unloaded here and the goods transhipped to Mersey flats. Indeed in 1864, the SUCo was building new docks at Frodsham Street (Cow Lane) Bridge, to take flats and canal boats loading and discharging in

Shropshire Union fly boat 'Mail' in Northgate cutting. *This photo taken c1907; the boat was cut up in 1925.*
Boat Museum Trust

Northgate (Water Tower) Locks c1910
Note the narrowboat under cargo in the lock and the wider flat in the background.
Grosvenor Museum

this city. Sheds were erected over the docks to prevent damage to goods, and covered accommodation provided for carts and drays employed in their conveyance. *By this plan the annoyance experienced by parties shipping goods at the Tower Wharf will be avoided, and no delay will be caused to boats passing by the bridge as heretofore*, reported the 'Chester Record' of 9th July that year.

Assault

It did nothing, of course, to stop the annoyance experienced by the boatmen at the hands of the mischievous street urchins, who were continually untying and larking about the boats. William Carter, captain of the Griffiths Bros narrowboat 'Crane' was so annoyed by this that he grabbed one of them by the scruff of the neck and ducked him in 'the cut'. Carter was summoned to appear before the local magistrates, who then acquitted him because he had evidently received great provocation. There was laughter in court when the Chairman said they advised him not to take the law into his own hands again by *re-christening people* in the way he had in this case.

On another occasion, even more drastic action was taken to deal with the problem. A 14-year-old boat-lad, named Ephraim Williams, had been left in charge of the boat 'Alfred', which was tied up for the night under City Road Bridge, when a number of boys on the towpath began to taunt him, and some stones were thrown at him. So he went into the cabin and brought out a fowling piece loaded with powder and shot, and fired it at them, slightly wounding a ten-year-old boy who refused to get off the boat. Ephraim was arrested; but the charges against him were later dropped, as he had acted in self defence. William Williams, his half brother, and master of the 'Alfred', intimated afterwards, that he kept the gun on board as a means of protection when travelling by night with his boat. But there is little doubt he used it for poaching, about which more will be said below.

Most of the boat-lads like Ephraim, were well-treated by their captains. There were exceptions, however, as evidenced by a report in the 'Courant' 9th October 1867. Henry Parry, master of the Shropshire Union canal boat 'Kestrel', plying between Ellesmere Port and Shrewsbury, was summoned, and fined for assaulting his boat-lad, Billy Gallant, aged 14. This boy had been on Parry's boat for six months, when he left and joined the boat 'Salisbury', at Whitby Locks. He left because Parry had *ill-used him and given him no pay*. (Strictly speaking, the Canal Company employed only the captains or steerers of horse boats, who had to get what help they needed.) Billy was on the 'Salisbury' when Parry went over to him and kicked him and tore the clothes off his back, leaving him *all tattered and torn*. The 'Chronicle' of 16th March 1872, reported that George Wale, a boatman, was fined 5s and costs, 13s 6d. for assaulting a boy in his employ, named Joseph Poole, aged 13. The assault took place at Backford when the lad failed to throw the towing line just at the right time when a boat was passing.

Time was money to boatmen: stoppages of any kind, or delays at locks, wharfs, and elsewhere, cost them money because they were paid by the trip. That is one reason - it was also an ego thing - why they disliked being overtaken by other boats, especially when approaching locks. Such incidents, as rival craft racing to get through the lock first, often resulted in a fight, or *skirmage* (skirmish). One boatman would accuse another of *trying to bounce him out of his turn; You will have to fight for it,* came the reply; and they would settle the dispute with their fists and boots.

Assaults on lockkeepers by boatpeople, who resented their intervention, were commonplace. For instance, Isaac Hammond's wife Emma, of the SU boat 'Bosworth', used a horse whip on the locktender at the Audlem flight when he tackled them - yet again - about wasting water at the locks. A boatman named Latham threatened to shoot the lockkeeper with a revolver when he said he should report him for damaging Wharton's Lock at Tiverton, by running his boat into it before it was ready. Another lockkeeper there gave preference to a Bridgewater Trustees' fly boat, and Tom Hodgkiss, a SU slow-boatman, quickly grabbed him by the head and *munged* (punched) him very severely about the face, and kicked him repeatedly.

Cruelty

Fly boats had absolute priority over other craft at the locks. Even that was not enough for some fly-boatmen, particularly if they were trying to make up for lost time. On one occasion Frank Meredith, of Acton, had his boat in the locks at Audlem, and the lockkeeper was opening the gates for him, when he made his horse attempt to draw the boat out of the lock before the gates were fully open. He thrashed the animal so unmercifully with his whip that it fell, and after it got up he continued to beat it. The lockkeeper reported him to the Canal Constable, so he was prosecuted and sentenced to two months' hard labour.

Another callous boatman, Henry Hodson, former captain of the SU narrow boat 'Tench', plying between Ellesmere Port and Wolverhampton, was sacked for kicking a Shropshire Union Company horse into the canal. The horse afterwards swam to the other side of the water, when Hodson tied a rope round its neck and pulled it across the canal. He then drove it to Bunbury Locks, where the horse was taken from him and he was supplied with a fresh one before a SU boat inspector could stop him.

Boat people were kicked by their horses sometimes, of course, but that does not excuse the following act of wanton cruelty, as reported in the 'Chronicle' of 13th June 1891. It appears that a Shropshire Union horse keeper went into the Company stables by the Northgate, Chester and saw Henry Rowlands, a hand on the *Brummagem* (Birmingham) fly boat 'Crescent', striking a horse which had been in his charge a few days before with a stout stave in the ribs, causing it much pain. The horse keeper told him to stop, but he would not. When summoned Rowlands admitted having beaten the animal, but said it had kicked a fellow boat-hand and put him in hospital, and he was now having his revenge.

Generally speaking, the Company's horses were in better condition than those belonging to the steerers. The latter were sometimes called *thirty shilling horses*, because only the boatmen and the knacker would put in a bid for them. Indeed, Thomas Wagstaff, captain of the SU boat 'Gowy', had only paid twenty five shillings for his, as he had given an old one in part exchange. The replacement horse was *a very small animal, was lame, suffered very much from sore shoulders, and was in a wretched condition.* But there were a great many worse horses worked on the canal in the 1870s.

One such animal belonged to John Pritchard, captain of the SU boat 'Hind', who was charged with working the horse with sore shoulders, at Church Lawton. When an RSPCA Inspector stopped Pritchard and asked him his reason for working the horse in such a state, he replied that the wounds were caused the day before by the wet, and he was obliged to work the horse that morning as the 20 tons of grain he had on board was wanted very badly at Leek, on the Caldon Canal.

The bad condition of these animals was often the result of poor feeding. But when an old SU employee, John Wood, captain of the boat 'Rover', was charged with working a sore-shouldered horse at Bunbury Locks in May 1879, he claimed that the animal had been *over-corned*, which had caused it to have *heat-lumps*! This was an unconvincing reference to a practice of keeping boat horses moving by feeding them well. Because his horse had not been very well kept; it was, in fact, very emaciated.

Being constantly on the go, even the better-kept Canal Company horses suffered from sore shoulders at times and had to be rested. But the SU horse keepers were under pressure to send them out before they were fit for work. One day in May 1877, an RSPCA inspector examined two such animals on the aqueduct at Nantwich. He had been watching Mary Ann Cooksey flogging one of the horses, which was attached to a light (empty) boat, captained by her father, Bill Cooksey. After the RSPCA man stopped the animal, he found two old wounds, one on each shoulder, which had not healed properly. Bill Cooksey told him that Mr Young, the SU horse keeper at Hack Green, had 'geared' (harnessed) the animal, and ordered him to take it out. But Young denied this at first, claiming that the boatman had geared the animal himself, *although the bridle was reversed, which showed the horse wasn't fit to go out*. In court, however, Young changed his story, and stated that the horse having been in the stable some time, he allowed it out for exercise. At that point Bill Cooksey's wife Martha, stated that her daughter Mary Ann had not flogged the animal; she was only striking the ground with the whip. In the end the magistrates dismissed the case, as they considered Young was to blame for allowing the horse to go out.

The other unfit horse examined that day by the RSPCA inspector, was drawing the SU boat 'Hawk', with John Bates as master. Bates said it had been sent out by Peter Johnson, the horse keeper at Audlem. The inspector afterwards saw Johnson, who told him that he was short of horses, and had to send it out. The RSPCA man went into the stable where the canal horses were kept, and *a worse lot of sore-shouldered animals he never saw in his life*. A bottle of stuff called *red bottle*, was used to dry up the wounds and produce a false skin, which broke open again when the collar pressed on the sores. The magistrates fined Bates 10s and costs; and Johnson £1 and costs - though that did not stop him sending the same animal out in an unfit state a couple of weeks later.

Posed for the camera *Twenty years ago, the author met Mrs Dolson (nee Littler - the girl in the photo).*
*She remembers her father had told her to, "Take that b****y 'orse over there"*
Boat Museum Trust

Solving the problem of horses with sore shoulders was proving extremely difficult during a period when the SU's fleet of narrowboats nearly doubled in size, from 213 in 1870 to 395 in 1889. In 1882, Thomas Hales, the SU Manager, reported *that everything possible is being done to prevent them from being so injured*. Then, to make matters worse, two steerers were each fined 5/- and costs at Wolverhampton, for working sore-shouldered horses. Although their fines (and others) were re-imbursed by the Company, Hales issued a notice *ordering the steerers under no circumstances to work a horse in an unfit condition*. This measure did reduce the problem for a time, but it was never solved. In 1893, for example, so many horses had sore shoulders that two of the Company's steam tugs were operating a shuttle service between Autherley Junction and Tyrley.

Although this measure helped, a number of boatmen were summoned for working horses in an unfit state into the early 1900s. Two of them were brought to court in one day by an RSPCA inspector at Tarporley. One was Frederick Price, master of the boat 'Peak', whose horse was found to be incurably lame in the near hind leg from a diseased hock, which was very much swollen. Price had bought the horse two months before and it was lame when he first had it. The other was Evan Powell, captain of the boat 'Dot', and his horse was painfully crippled on the near foreleg. The knee, which was bandaged with sacking, was highly inflamed and double its normal size. When Henry Green, SU boatman of Audlem was charged with a similar offence in July 1904, he apologised and pleaded ignorance, adding: *He had had a great deal of trouble with his horses lately, and had lost five*! In another case, an RSPCA inspector described the horse belonging to Bill Trow, of the boat 'Countess', as *a physical wreck*.

That description also fitted an old grey mule a police officer spotted at Ellesmere Port attached to a canal boat, captained by John Evans. The mule, although it was a warm day, had a sack on its back, and was staggering along as if it was in an exhausted condition. The policeman on seeing this, examined the animal, *and in loosing the rope, the mule fell to the ground exhausted. It was with great difficulty that it could be made to stand on its feet.* The mule had sore shoulders, and was very lame in both hind legs, caused by injury. It was also in a poor condition, and was nearly a skeleton. The driver William Johnson said that the mule belonged to Evans, and although he had told Evans the mule was unfit for work, Evans had told him to use it. Johnson added that to stop the RSPCA inspector from seeing him work the mule, he and his wife had bow-hauled the boat through Chester, and sent the mule on in front. Johnson had bought the animal two months before from the SU for £2, and had sold it to Evans for 14s. Johnson was ordered to pay 3s 6d and costs, while Evans was fined 40s and costs, or in default one calendar month's imprisonment.

The magistrates in these cases were astonished that the SUR&CCo did not exercise some sort of supervision, so that such animals could not be worked. That was easier said than done, of course. But one way of exercising more control was to use Company horses instead. It was also cheaper, apparently. In May 1898 it was reported that the cost of working slow boats between Ellesmere Port and the Potteries, for which the steerers provided horses, could be reduced if the Company's horses were used. So the horsing of 3 additional boats was approved. Three months later, Thomas Hales stated that the trial had been satisfactory, and it was expected there would be a saving of £200 per annum to the Company. Three years on, he submitted a statement of the comparative cost of working the boats to Shropshire and North Wales by Company horses as compared with steerers horses during September 1901, showing an increase in the weight moved of 1239 tons, and a reduction in the average cost per ton of 12.5d. There were then 147 boats worked by Company horses against 108 the previous year. In 1905 the SU owned 328 horses and the steerers 94; and it became the Company's practice to provide more steerers with horses rather than give them loans to buy their own.

Moreover, the SU knew that most boatmen looked after their regular horses, but were less particular about temporary ones. In 1902 Hales reported with reference to *the new arrangement for working the boats to and from South Staffs, by which the boatmen had continual charge of their horses, that it had worked well, and that the veterinary surgeon stated that the horses were now in better condition than formerly.*

Unfortunately, the SU could do little about the condition of those horses which belonged to independent carriers on the canal. Take, for example, the horse attached to a Foster's of Wolverhampton boat. The animal was in a wretched state. It had a new collar on, which pressed on the sores. The fetlock was also very inflamed, and the animal was covered from head to foot with mange. The boatman said that he had come from Tipton, stayed the night at Barbridge, on to Chester, and was going to Ellesmere Port with 25 tons of corrugated iron. When he started out they gave him a new collar, and some oil to rub on the sores so that they would not hurt. After the boatman was summoned at Chester, and fined for working the horse in an unfit state, the court heard that he had lost his job as a result of the charge. After imposing the mandatory fine, the magistrates stated that Fosters had shifted the responsibility from themselves on to the steerer in this case.

Things were very different, however, in the cases involving two callous Shropshire Union boatmen. One was Tom Boswell, an ill-tempered fly-boatman, who had flogged his horse from Seller Street Bridge to Hoole Lane Bridge, while trying to pass two other boats and get into the lock first. The horse fell on its knees exhausted in consequence of this cruel treatment. The other boatman, William Copeling of Ellesmere Port, was summoned for throwing heavy stones at his horse, which was drawing a narrowboat at Waverton. As the result of one blow the animal dropped into the hedge, and it was shivering with fright. When Copeling was charged he admitted the offence, but said that he had lost his temper because the horse broke the tow line by snatching.

The Canal Company condemned this practice, which had serious consequences for the horses. Sometimes the animals got into the canal, and they received only the explanation of the men themselves as to how it had happened. Occasionally the horses fell in when they got tangled in the lines of boats passing in the opposite direction. In 1901 the steerer of the Salt Union Co's canal boat 'Gothland' sought to recover £5 for loss of his horse, pulled into canal through the alleged misconduct of John Woods, captain of the Shropshire Union's fly boat 'Minnie'. Judgment in this court case was given for the Canal Company, however. Three years later, Harris Bros of Brierley Hill claimed £19 10s to replace one of their boat horses drowned in the Canal at Tattenhall Road, through being met by one of the Company's horses at the entrance to a bridge. The claim was settled for £10, one half of which would be recovered from the steerer.

Very occasionally boatpeople were seriously injured through getting entangled in their own lines when a boat passed in the opposite direction. This happened to William Williams, a 54-year-old hand on the boat 'Madge', with Henry Lyth as master, which carried iron ore from Ellesmere Port to the Shropshire Iron Works. They were passing another boat near Beeston at the time, and Williams lifted the line so that his boat should pass the other. Instead, the rope came off the towing mast and wrapped round him, the horse dragging him along the towpath for about 300 yards. George Talbot, the Shropshire Union boat superintendent, commented that clearing the line over the other boat was a quicker way than allowing the line to sink and letting the other float over it, but it was a breach of the Company's rules.

Welfare & Worship

While all this was happening, the SU had become increasingly concerned about the material and spiritual welfare of its boatpeople. From the 1870s onwards they loaned money to steerers to tide them over difficult times - stoppages, sickness, injury, the death of a horse, and so on. Under special circumstances, these loans were even written off. In addition, the Canal Company began granting pensions to long-serving boatmen who were incapable of working their boats through age and injury. This, at a time when such boatpeople often ended up in the Workhouse. Witness John Atkins, a 74-year-old boatman, of Queen Street, Chester, who was sent into that dreaded Institution after being arrested for begging at several houses in Boughton, in late 1881.

That would have been the fate of a middle-aged boatman named Henry Wilday without the support of his wife Frances, who lived with him on the SU narrow boat 'Crane'. Her husband was disabled through injury, and *she had been practically looking after the boat for 30 years and of earning whatever had been earned*. But she may well have ended up in the workhouse herself, for it would be many years before boatwomen like her received an old-age pension.

Another boatwoman, a 60-year-old widow named Elizabeth Swift, formerly captain of the SU narrowboat 'Ranger', was determined to avoid such a fate. Being unable to work her boat any longer, she went to live with her daughter Elizabeth Oakley and son-in-law Thomas Oakley on board the SU canal boat 'Mastiff'. She had been ill off and on since she had been with them, and would not let her daughter fetch a doctor or take any *doctor's stuff*. Instead, she took some gin and treacle for her breathing problems. She ate very little, and what she did eat consisted mainly of bread and lard. Elizabeth Swift had been asked on several occasions to go into the

Workhouse, but she said *she would beg from door to door rather than do so,* according to the 'Courant' of 28th March 1877.

1877 was the year when the first Canal Boats Act reached the statute books, thanks to the vigorous campaign led by the reformer George Smith, of Coalville, Leicestershire. The three main objects of the Act were: 1) The separation of the sexes over twelve; 2) To bring the cabins under the sanitary laws of the country, so as to prevent the terrible overcrowding in the cabins and the spread of infectious disease; 3) The education of boat children.

In 1878 the SU Manager reported that the regulation which mainly affected the Company was that of providing more air space in the cabins, the interior of which, if used as dwellings were required to contain not less than 80 cubic feet, or 180 cubic feet if a rear cabin, and explaining that this would not materially affect the Company's Boats. Then the Town Clerk of Chester, where most of its canal craft were registered, wrote to them in November 1879, drawing the Manager's attention to the Pritchard family living on the boat 'Hind' consisting of 7 persons whereas the boat was only allowed to contain 4 persons, and stating that, this being the third breach of the Canal Boats Act, the Corporation would be forced to take proceedings if a similar breach of the act occurred again.

Not an easy task for Thomas Hales, judging by this return of the Company's registered boats and the condition of the boatpeople, compiled in 1882:

Boats registered (as dwellings)		269
Men in charge of boats		321
Men, Women & Children, dependent for support upon employment furnished by the Canals		1,441
Men, Women & Children living on board boats		862*
Men, Women & Children habitually resident on shore		579
*Men & Boys, 13 years of age and upwards		466
Women & Girls		186
Children, up to 13 Females	92	
Males	118	210
		862

Canal people were virtually a race apart. *They could scarcely be recruited from other occupations and it seemed as if they were necessarily, so to speak, bred to the work*, said one SU official. That is why the Company co-operated with the religious agencies at work among their boaters. They shared the optimistic Victorian belief *that anything which tended to elevate the [boat] people through the knowledge of the Bible and education tended also to provide them with more trustworthy and better servants [employees].*

As early as 1874, in order to prevent Sunday Trading and to give the boatpeople an opportunity of attending places of worship, the SU Company issued instructions prohibiting their boats from working on Sundays, except those specially required to work 'fly' with urgent stuff on board. These regulations were strictly enforced. Indeed, they were supplemented, five years later, by having the locks at Chester closed entirely from 9am to 7pm, thus preventing any boats passing on Sunday between those hours.

In 1877 the SU handed over an old timber float, called the 'Oak', to the Minister of the Queen Street Independent Chapel, Chester to be used as a Boatmen's Floating Mission House or Bethel, *the religious body undertaking the expense of fitting up, & also the carrying on of suitable services for both adults and children.* The building subsequently erected on the converted barge was divided into two portions - a small room for a school for the children, and a larger one for the adults. The latter could seat, when filled with chairs and forms, about eighty to one hundred persons. When the Bethel opened on the first Sunday in May 1878, a free tea was given to all the boatpeople who might be in Chester. They were *shy at first*, but a *goodly number came*, and *sat at the long tables and enjoyed what to most of them were luxuries in the shape of sandwiches and currant bread.* The organizers were not sure whether the numbers at the Sunday and other services could be maintained without such an attraction; but they found that those numbers were considerably increased.

It is worth mentioning that this was the only Floating Bethel for canal boatmen in Britain, with the exception of the Bishop of Lichfield's Missionary Barge, which actually went up and down the canal. But the Chester Bethel could not leave its usual moorings at the end of Queen Street during the severe winter of 1878-9. It was among the 50 or 60 canal boats frozen up in the neighbourhood of Chester. Fortunately, the benevolent friends of the Bethel distributed soup, bread, coal and groceries week by week among the boatpeople in distress. Moreover, on the first Sunday in January 1879, another free tea was provided, and 70 boatmen and women sat down at two long tables, running the entire length of the Bethel. *Their great favourite appeared to be ham sandwiches which they called 'bacon and bread,' and the number of these which they succeeded in stowing away was truly astonishing.*

At the same time, about 60 of the boatchildren were treated to a good tea, in the Queen Street Independent Chapel schoolroom near to the canal. When the frost broke early in February,

270 boatpeople, a considerable proportion being children, were given another free tea in the Queen Street schoolroom.

Meanwhile, at the Nantwich Mission in a small canalside warehouse, a tea had been given to the boatmen and their families who were frozen up in the Basin End, Acton over the Christmas period. *About sixty men, women, and children sat down to the good fare with which the tables were supplied, consisting of cake and currant loaf, and plain bread and butter.*

The Nantwich Mission opened in August 1877, and the first Sunday afternoon service was attended by some 15 to 20 persons out of the boats. Average attendance was 20; sometimes as many as 30 attended. A Sunday school was also established *for scholars young and old*. According to the Mission workers, the early results had been very encouraging. Four or five couples from the boats, who previously lived together, although unmarried, had been married. Another four couples, in similar circumstances, were being persuaded to tie the knot at Acton Church. Temperance meetings were also held at Nantwich and six of the boatpeople signed the 'pledge'.

Siphoning off the profits

Whether one is religious or not, it is undeniable that boatpeople could do with improvement, especially in the matter of theft. In January 1877, local newspapers reported that Joseph Maddocks, captain of the SU boat 'Cygnet', and Edwin Owen, of the 'Gull', had been ordered to convey pig iron from Barbridge to Wolverhampton. After loading the boats, Maddocks, Owen and another boatman, were seen busily engaged filling two carts, the property of three Nantwich marine-store dealers, with about 3 tons of pig iron from the boat 'Gull'. The police at Nantwich were informed, and they were on their way to Barbridge, when they met the two carts broken down on the road within a short distance of each other in consequence of being overloaded. The three marine-store dealers (who had paid 30s for the stolen pig iron, whereas its market value was about £15) were arrested without a struggle. But the three boatmen involved were only apprehended after a free fight with about 25 boatpeople, both men and women, in the King's Arms, Barbridge.

Boatmen had few qualms about sampling the boat's cargo. It was an invariable practice to draw wine, spirits, and beer from the casks, by means of siphon pumps, which were in common use in the boats. The boatmen would knock one of the hoops off, get a brace and bit, drill a hole, plug it, and then bore another one. The drink would be siphoned off, and the requisite quantity of canal water substituted to make up the weight.

One evening in July 1880, the fly boat 'Eyton' came up to the wharf at Nantwich with a cargo of porter. John Evans was driving the horse, and William Roscoe, the captain, was steering. The two men were *in drink*, but were capable of working the boat. Richard Colley, the second mate, popped his head out of the cabin and invited two boatmen, Edward Dean and Moses Hamer, on board for a drink. In about half an hour the boat left the wharf and went on towards Wardle. An hour or so later, as he was leaving his office, Benjamin Clay, the SU agent at Nantwich, spoke to Dean, who was *staggering drunk*, and got an evasive reply. Clay's suspicions were aroused, so he decided to follow the boat. He overtook it at the Tile Works at Wardle, and ordered the boat to be stopped. After examining the cargo, Clay allowed the boat to go on to Calveley, where he had the 10 porter barrels taken out, and found that a couple of them had been tampered with. Roscoe was sacked afterwards. Moses Hamer, though, always protested his innocence, saying that *he went into the cabin to dry his time bill!* But everyone knew he went aboard to wet his whistle.

Others got away with it, too. Take, for example, Thomas James, master of the fly boat 'Snipe', who took casks of sherry to Newtown (Montgomery) in April 1877. On the return trip to Chester, James ran part of the way with the fly boat 'Usk', worked by John Probert, his wife Jane, and a boathand, or *chap*. Probert it appears had agreed to *butty him [James] down the locks*. (These fly boats shared the locks but they worked as single craft travelling in close company rather than two boats behind one horse as was the normal practice with, say, slow boats in the fluxing stone trade from Trevor to Nantwich.) Before they got to Bates's Mill Lock, according to Jane Probert, James called her husband on to his boat for a drink of sherry: *When we came to the lock, there was a pair of boats in the lock. While waiting for these two boats to come out, the wind blowed our boat and the 'Snipe' to the outside of the canal. I got off and went on Thomas James's boat to look at what they was doing. They had got a brown can full of what I thought was ale, and there was a tea basin full on the table. Tom catched hold of the basin and asked me to drink. I said 'No thank you, I don't drink ale.' He said 'It's not ale. Do you drink? This will do you no harm'. and I did drink.*

When the matter came to light, however, James claimed that Probert and his wife only had a drop of the *swillings* of water shaken in some empty casks. It might have been sherry *swillings*, he conceded. The empty casks were brought from Newtown (Montgomery), and he had taken casks there, but he had no idea what they contained. These *swillings* were not the produce of what boatpeople called *sucking the monkey* (-boat), or tapping the casks, he said. Nor could the SU prove otherwise.

Woman and child on Thomas Clayton horseboat 'Pearl', *c1940.*
The boat was No 81 in the fleet registered at Daventry on 4th February 1935.
Thomas Pickthall - Chester History and Heritage

Lasses

It was not unusual to find women like Jane Probert on express boats in those days. Mary Jane Hodson, for instance, assisted her husband William Hodson, captain of the SU fly boat 'Raven', plying between Ellesmere Port and Wolverhampton. Hodson also employed a 17-year-old boat-girl, named Isabella Roper, who had been with him for a considerable time. He paid her 3s. per trip, and all found; she steered the boat and drove the horses by turns. Hodson, his wife and the girl used to sleep in one cabin, without any division -- which arrangement contravened the Canal Boats Act of 1877. As it was, the boatwomen regarded Isabella as something of *a loose character*, though Hodson had not been aware of it. He was quite a character himself; he enjoyed *a good sup of ale* in the 'Dock Hotel', whenever he was at Ellesmere Port. He had fallen in the Dock many a time afterwards, *and the water was deep enough to cover him overhead.* But his wife Mary Jane boasted that she had *kept him straight since* she married him, adding: *Her husband would not go into a public-house without she went with him!*

Even after the introduction of the Canal Boats Act all-female fly-boat crews were not unknown. Mary Evans, with the assistance of two other women, worked the SU fly boat 'Merlin', between Barbridge and Manchester, for a number of years after her husband's death in 1878.

The Act applied to slow boats, too. One of these had been crewed by Samuel Walker and Johanna Banks, aged 24, who originally came from Kidderminster, where she worked as a carpet weaver. She had been *messing about* the country on boats for three and a half years, according to the 'Chronicle' of 27th October 1877, and came to Nantwich on Walker's boat to fetch a load of fluxing stone and bring it back to the 'Hat holes' near Bilston. But she had left his boat, and joined Hannah Clarke on the SU boat 'Tern', before the Act came into force.

Thereafter, Walker would have to pay a mate or take a wife on board. Perhaps that is why he decided to get married at Acton, near Nantwich in August 1885. He certainly made a remarkable choice of a second wife, as shown by this report in the 'Cheshire Observer' of 10th June 1895: *The extraordinary negotiations for a wife, in which the*

Mother and children on Shropshire Union horseboat 'Irene'. *Northgate Lock c1910*
Waterways Trust

captain of a canal boat, plying between Nantwich and Ellesmere Port, engaged with the authorities at the Nantwich workhouse about three weeks ago, had a gratifying sequel on Monday. The man, whose name is Samuel Walker, a native of Wolverhampton, had called at the workhouse and asked the authorities to recommend one of the female inmates for a wife, explaining that he had been six months a widower, and was desirous of remarrying. His

application was conceded, and the banns having been published on three Sundays, the couple were married at Acton Church on Monday morning. The bridegroom attended in his boatman's attire, but the bride, who is 45, fifteen years younger than the bridegroom, was rather smartly dressed in a print dress and a bonnet in which there were arranged a number of roses of rather brilliant hue. The bride was given away by the Clerk of the church (Mr Provost), while the relieving officer (Mr Pooley) officiated as best man. Several other workhouse officials also graced the ceremony with their presence. The vicar at the close of the ceremony delivered a long address on the subject of the marriage vows. As the captain and his wife left the church they were the recipients of a number of gifts, and they left the village amid a shower of rice and old slippers.

Patience

Horse boats like Walker's - the 'Berlin' - were often towed by steam tug on the broad-gauge Wirral Line. One day in April 1894, John Woods, the steerer of the Pottery fly 'Minnie', got tired of waiting for the steam tug 'Dreadnought' to tow his boat from Ellesmere Port to Chester, so he went for a drink in the 'Canal Tavern' instead. The tug started before he had finished, and in revenge he cut the towrope, worth eight shillings. If there had been any other boat passing there might have been a bad accident. Accordingly, the magistrates fined him 20s and costs, plus the value of the rope, with the option of a month's imprisonment.

A couple working a Fellows, Morton & Clayton boat
c1950
Waterways Trust - M Ware

John Woods would have had a much longer wait in February 1895, when a number of canal boats were frost-bound at Ellesmere Port. With the greatest difficulty the SU Canal had been kept open down to Chester. Beyond this city no goods were sent from the Port by canal as the waterways were blocked. No less than 47 boats were frozen up at Bunbury Locks and Calveley Station. Keeping the Wirral Line open to Chester, was costing £6 or £7 a day. The icebreaker was drawn between Whitby Locks and Chester daily, and on one particular day fifteen horses were required for the work. The iron canal tugs 'Dagmar' and 'Dreadnought' followed, with the flats. The intense frosts continued, and the large blocks of ice which had been accumulating for a fortnight became impregnable, and traffic by this canal route had to be suspended.

Once the thaw came though, life on 'the cut' returned to normal. At Calveley, for example, William Lloyd and Henry Howard, SU boatmen, were bound over to keep the peace, after an affray that had seen them *stripped and abusing each other shamefully*. Lloyd was frequently mentioned in police annals. In January 1896, he and John Owen, were charged with being drunk and riotous, and also with assaulting the police on the canalside near the end of Queen Street, Chester.

All three men were tough customers. However, they were no match for John Sadler, the captain of the SU fly boat 'Wren'. He was a powerfully built man, and known as the 'King of canal boatmen'. Sadler was the boaters' champion - a bare-knuckle fighter, who took on all-comers. He was an army reserve man, having left the army twelve months previously, and was in receipt of 6d a day. But he came from a boating family; and had been brought up on the boats.

One evening in August 1896, Sadler was in a group of boatpeople who got very drunk in the 'Jolly Tar', Wardle. Then they visited the 'King's Arms', Barbridge, and asked for beer. But the landlord refused to serve them, and asked them to leave the premises. Sadler refused to quit, and a police sergeant was called to take him back to his boat. On the way there Sadler suddenly launched a savage attack on the officer. Meanwhile, a crowd of about 40 boatpeople watched the struggle; no one but the landlord and his brother apparently thinking of helping the sergeant by pulling his assailant off. Sadler again attacked the police officer *like a madman*, but with their assistance he managed to handcuff him.

When Sadler appeared in court a number of boatpeople were there to give him support. Not that it did him much good. For being drunk and disorderly Sadler was fined; and for the assault he was gaoled for a month. Bill Thomas, a boatman on the 'Wren', was also fined for

obstructing the police sergeant, whilst he was apprehending Sadler. "Give it the --, Sadler," Thomas shouted, . "I'll see he doesn't take thee." In sentencing the two men, the magistrates said Barbridge had been a law abiding place before the boatpeople settled there, and that they were determined to put an end to their *rowdy and lawless conduct*.

Education

Not everyone in authority shared their views. John Davenport, the Canal Boat Inspector at Nantwich, welcomed the fact that since the introduction of the 1877 and 1884 Canal Boats Acts, there was a greater tendency among the boatmen to take houses on shore. Barbridge, which was one of the most important canal stations in his district, had become quite *a little boatmen's village*. At the same time, he had *found a considerable improvement going on amongst the canal boat population.* Generally speaking, he had *met with every facility* for his work, and *every courtesy* from the boaters, who were *a*

Thomas Clayton boat
Northgate cutting c1930
Waterways Trust

176

hardworking and interesting body of people. His one regret was that he continually saw a large number of children on the canal who were receiving little or no education.

The SU, however, believed that some progress had been made in the education of its boat children. On board 409 boats there were 753 men and women and 249 children, in 1897. *Nearly three-fifths of the children between five and thirteen years of age were able to read and write, which was a great advance, and it was one that would be assuredly carried further.* In 1902, a report on the subject was read, showing that in 1884 there were 151 children of school age on 363 boats, there were now only 97 on 433 boats, and of this number 32 could read and write. (There had been 763 adults, male and female, on 363 boats, while now there were only 802 on 433 boats.) True, some of the steerers had been summoned to appear before the magistrates at Chester for not sending their children to school, but in 1903 the SU Company engaged *a Lady Inspector who would be able to visit the Cabins and exert a beneficent influence, especially in seeing that the children attend school.*

The boat children were not welcomed with open arms in this city; a number of them had been refused admittance to local schools. This came as no surprise to the Mayor of Chester: *These children were exceedingly unpleasant he might say, to the masters and mistresses of the schools to have anything to do with. They were absolutely untaught, wild and uncared for, and when they were driven to the schools they were a perfect nuisance to masters and mistresses - so much so that in their experience as magistrates these poor children when they did present themselves at the schools had been driven away from the doors, and told by the masters and mistresses that the school was no place for them.*

A local school teacher said that in some cases this was true; *but generally the children were not in a fit state of cleanliness to be admitted.*

Now the majority of boatpeople had clean habits; most of the women took great pride in keeping their cabins and children clean. But unfortunately some boaters were summoned for neglecting their children, notably William Slater the steerer of the SU boat 'Norah' and his wife Mary. They had three children - two boys aged four and three, and a 15-month-old girl. In July 1900 an NSPCC officer inspected the boat at Ellesmere Port, in company with two police officers.

They examined the three children, and found that they were badly vermin bitten. Their heads were caked with dirt, their scalps being so black that they had obviously not been washed for a very long period. Each child was wearing an old black frock, stiff with dirt, and there was no

177

other clothing on them at all. The man, wife, and three children occupied the cabin. It was horribly foul and offensive, the bed clothing was filthy, and simply alive with bugs.

In court Slater said: *You cannot keep childre' (sic) clean in a canal boat.* But the NSPCC Inspector, in giving his evidence, stated: *Some of the other boats I visited were palaces compared with this; they were perfectly clean.*

Another case of family neglect a week later, involved Edward Moore and Annie Moore, husband and wife, of the SU boat 'Eleanor': *Although the boat contained two cabins (fore and aft) only the one aft was used for habitation and sleeping. A number of dirty sacks, which formed part of the boat's cargo, did duty as beds, and on these the children were lying at the time, their bodies being in a state of filth that almost baffled description. They were poorly nourished, and their clothing was ragged and infected with vermin.*

The magistrates in both cases were quite surprised that the SU Company, which had a virtual carrying monopoly on its canal system, did not look after the cleanliness of its boats. But the cabins of the boats were, of course, treated as the homes of the boatmen, and while the Company's officers had instructions to see that the boats were kept decently clean, every care was taken not to intrude on the privacy of the boat families.

Poaching

The police, on the other hand, did have powers to search boat cabins if they had reason to believe a crime had been committed. In January 1898, the police found the skin and head of a sheep in the canal at Middlewich. So all the narrow boats were searched afterwards, and James Minshull, captain of the SU boat 'Starling', and James Turner, boat-hand, were arrested at Chester for stealing the sheep out of a field at Minshull Vernon. On being charged with the offence, Minshull replied, "Well, we can't get out of it; we did it", while Turner rejoined "We did it, and both are as bad as one another". Both men had been seen in the 'Horse and Jockey' at Ellesmere Port, where Turner had given Minshull's mother-in-law 3 or 4lbs of mutton, saying, "it would make a bit of stew". The men also pleaded guilty to stealing a number of fowls, and were sentenced to six months' imprisonment.

If they were not poaching themselves, the boatpeople were aiding and abetting others in unlawfully taking game. Canal boats assisted gangs of poachers from Chester morning after morning, and the police had the greatest difficulty in apprehending the offenders. But one day in September 1905, plain clothes police officers saw a notorious poacher get off the SU boat 'Fyfe' at the Northgate. He recognized the officers and ran away when approached. The master of the boat 'Fyfe', William Goode, and his wife Ann, denied any knowledge of poaching. But on making a search of the boat, the police found 63 dead rabbits, along with driving lines and nets, which had been put on by poachers between Ellesmere Port and Backford. In court later, on a charge of assisting poachers, Goode said *rough looking men put the rabbits and nets on his boat, and he was frightened to say anything to them*. Not surprisingly, this plea was rejected, and the magistrates fined him and his wife 20s. and costs each, or in default one month's imprisonment.

Strike

Six years later, in September 1911, all the SU boatmen refused to work their boats and went on strike, demanding increases in the rates of pay, and improved conditions of working. The men wanted the company to equip the boats, pay full money for full tonnage conveyed, and in addition were asking for an increase of one penny per ton on all cargo.

The other SU employees - warehousemen, truck porters, flatmen, and general dock workers - had decided to stand by the boatmen by refusing to handle any cargo which was intended for the Midlands or North Wales, per the narrow boat canal route. The general stoppage of all traffic on the SU Canal was a serious thing, and a threat to the distribution of food stuffs, as the congested railways could not handle it. The men were

Boats moored at Barbridge during the SU strike, 1911
Boat Museum Trust

allowing narrow boats to transmit galvanised iron from the ironworks to the flats in the Ship Canal, but nothing beyond that was permitted. About 60 boats were lying idle at Ellesmere Port, and 70 were held up at Barbridge.

It was not a bitter dispute, even though the SU management refused to 'recognise' the men's union. The boatmen's conduct during the strike was exemplary. When they resumed work two weeks later, the police at Ellesmere Port sent a message warmly thanking the men for the quiet and respectable way in which they had transacted their negotiations. And a correspondent there wrote that *Instead of men idly lolling about or playing football, horses could be seen being brought from the stables, and attached to the boats, many of which had resumed their journey before 4 am.*

The General Manager, Thomas Hales, had had several interviews with deputations of the boatmen, and promised that, if the men returned to work, he would carefully consider their claims for increased wages. True to his word, he agreed to the following alterations:

Staffordshire & Humber Arm Trade. Steerers to be paid on 2240lbs to the ton, instead of 2400lbs.
Pottery Trade. To be allowed 2/6 each voyage for legging through Harecastle Tunnel North to South
Trench Trade. To be allowed 2/6 per week in addition to present pay.
North Trade for Shropshire and North Wales. To be allowed 2/6 per week in addition to present pay.
Llangollen & Welshpool Flys. To be allowed 3/6 per week extra.
Provision of nose tins, water cans, and boat hooks to all boats.

Narrowboat art by Harry Taylor, 1920s *'Sir John Jellicoe' was bought from the SUR&CCo, and retained the carved name from the company, in its new, but similar, livery.*
Tony Lewery

The steerers still had to find their own towing lines, which cost 5s 6d each and lasted for about three round trips from Ellesmere Port to the Midlands. A fly boat captain got 3.1/2d per mile, and was paid on 83 miles for the SU's main service between Birmingham and Ellesmere Port, fresh horses being provided in relays along the route. The timetable for fly boats between these two places ran to 48 hours actual working time, and the steerers had to do the trip in three days. In one particular stage 22 1/2 hours were worked at a stretch, and if the boats failed to keep to the timetable they were paid on the slow rate of 2 1/2d instead of 3 1/2d per mile. What a splendid sight the fly boats must have been coming down the canal with their bows all awash!

Decoration

On the Shroppie fly boats the bows were painted white and a black disc was added in the middle on both sides, producing an effect like a pair of eyes. All their narrowboats had black cabin sides with red beading, a white border and white lettering giving the company's name, usually abbreviated to Shropshire Union R & C Co', the fleet number in a panel at the after end, and the registration details on a white strip at the top of the cabin. In the First World War it seems some of the boats were painted in a drab khaki.

__More artwork from Taylor's Yard,1920s__
This signwriting and artwork is also by Harry Taylor. When he died, his son, Wilf Taylor took over and he used to copy a picture of the King Charles' Tower instead of the traditional castle.
Geoff Taylor Collection

181

Carrying

The Canal Company received a government subsidy during the 1914-18 War, but that payment came to an end on 31st August 1921. This, together with higher wage claims from the boatmen's union and demands for an eight-hour day, meant that the Shropshire Union's financial position was hopeless; so it stopped carrying on its own account in 1921. At that time there were still over 200 narrowboats in the long-distance fleet, although the numbers had fallen substantially since the beginning of the twentieth century. The Company had boat families on 202 boats: the total boat population was 592, 415 of them having no home except the boat and 177 with a home on shore. There was a great deal of uncertainty about the future of traffic on the Canal, but many of the boats were purchased by other firms.

Fellows, Morton & Clayton Ltd of Birmingham, for example, bought no less than twenty-five boats and later introduced a service from Ellesmere Port to Wolverhampton, flour being an important traffic. The Chester & Liverpool Lighterage & Warehousing Co Ltd, of Cow Lane Wharf was established to purchase forty boats, renaming many of them after local meres. These boats plied regularly to the Midlands and also on the Montgomery branch. The Midlands & Coast Canal Carriers Ltd of Wolverhampton was formed in 1922, and bought around 30 boats which worked mainly to Ellesmere Port. A & A Peate Ltd purchased eleven boats to import grain from Ellesmere Port for their Maesbury Hall Mills near Oswestry. (One of these was 'Cressy', which later achieved fame in Tom Rolt's book 'Narrow Boat'.) Arthur Sumner of Wrenbury Mill took at least one of the boats, and several of the Shropshire Union boatmen purchased single boats to stay in carrying.

One ex-Shroppie boatman, Henry Wood, of 15 Bishop Street, Hoole, Chester bought the narrowboat 'Sedan', and carried for Fellows, Morton & Clayton. Early one morning in February 1924, Wood and his mate were involved in an alarming accident on the canal near to the Water Tower by Canal Street, according to the 'Observer' of 1st March: *The horse-drawn boat 'Sedan', which was carrying a load of 20 tons of aluminium from Ellesmere Port to Birmingham, suddenly capsized. The two men in the cabin were awakened and luckily escaped. There was practically no damage to the boat, but the cargo will suffer through the immersion. The clothes and personal belongings of the men also will be lost... The Chester and Liverpool Lighterage and Warehousing Co were asked to salve the vessel, which is by no means an easy task. We are informed that the cause of the accident was that the boxes of aluminium all slipped to one side of the boat during the night, and thus disturbed its equilibrium.*

Older boatmen retired of course when the Shropshire Union sold off its fleet. The 'Observer' of 6th January 1934 reported that the second oldest man at a party held in the Town Hall for 1,000 'Old Folks' was the 86-year-old retired boater, William Williams, of Charlotte Street, *who still wears the earrings which used to be the boatman's trade mark.*

And the 'Chronicle' of 23rd December 1933, interviewed the seventy-five-year old, Mr Thomas Owen Nicholls, in his home at 7, Alms Houses, Pepper Street, Chester, and he looked back on a lifetime of hard, but never dull, work on the Shropshire Union Canal. Born near Bilston, Staffordshire, he left home early and had found his way to Chester 57 years before. He began work on the Shropshire Union, and for forty years journeyed on the horse boats from Ellesmere Port to Victoria Dock (London), the Midlands, Montgomeryshire, the Potteries, and Manchester.

His most vivid memories hinged upon an old windlass, which he kept above the fireplace. Over forty years earlier, while he was working his boat through Nantwich, he became involved in a dispute which ended in his receiving a heavy blow from someone wielding a windlass. He fell with the windlass into the water and the windlass remained at the bottom of the canal for ten years before it came into his possession. On another occasion he captured a fox cub at Gnosall, took it with him to Ellesmere Port, and when he next touched Gnosall there was the vixen peering from the bank, apparently sensing the fact that the cub was on the boat, although it was hidden below. He did the decent thing and released her cub. *A grand life*, he reflected, while he recalled how in winter he frequently had to harness the 17 horses to an ice-boat and afterwards help to rock the craft in order to break the ice.

Coincidentally, the 'Chronicle' of 9th December, had reported that a boatwoman had to smash the ice on the frozen canal with a pole only the week before. She was the wife of John Bannister, captain of the motor narrowboat 'Norway'. While he was tying up the boat at Market Drayton on the Thursday, his feet were badly crushed. His wife called a doctor, who advised her to take him to the Chester Infirmary as soon as she arrived in the city. Mrs Bannister took charge of the boat, and although at times she had to cut the ice in the canal with a pole, she arrived in Chester safely the next day. She immediately took her husband to the Infirmary and he was detained. She continued her journey to Ellesmere Port alone. She stated that after loading up she would return on her own to Birmingham. *We have to do these things,* she remarked*, although I must say I have been a bit fed up at cutting a way through the ice since Thursday.*

This severe weather must also have delayed the boats belonging to the last regular carriers on the Shroppie: Thomas Clayton of Oldbury. They carried petroleum products, especially fuel oil, from the Shell refinery at Stanlow usually to Shell's depot at Langley Green, Birmingham, but with a few trips to Walsall, Saltley and Leamington Spa. This traffic started in 1924 and at first it was handled entirely by horse boats working together in pairs. The horse boats used to work very long hours on the run, sometimes travelling from 4 am to midnight. They did the 160 mile round trip in a week. The boatmen arranged their journeys so as to be moored at one of the canalside pubs each night. Often at closing time the towpath near what is now the Mill Hotel witnessed fights between Griffiths Bros, the millers' bargemen and the Clayton oil boat men who tied up there looking for trouble.

In 1938 Claytons had 26 horses on the route, but thereafter motor boats started to appear. By 1952 there were only two horse-drawn boats left on the run – 'Oka' and 'Kama' – which worked as single craft travelling in close company rather than as two boats behind one horse. Both were under the command of Steve Dulson, a horse-boating die hard, who, after much persuasion, eventually took charge of the motor 'Severn' with 'Oka' as his butty. By the end of April 1953 Claytons had eight pairs on the run, including 'Towy' and 'Kubina' crewed by 37-year-old Skipper Leslie Berridge, his wife and children.

The 'Birmingham Weekly Post' of 11th September 1953, contains an article entitled 'By Canal from Birmingham to the Mersey', written by Vivian Bird, a journalist who accompanied the last named motor and butty on a six-day round trip to Stanlow on the Manchester Ship Canal, whence the Berridge family returned with 45 tons of fuel oil, earning £11 for the trip. The Berridges travelled without pause for 15 hours, covering 45 miles through three counties, and tied up behind the Royal Oak at Beeston. They had encountered the many deep tree-shaded cuttings and high embankments of the 'Shroppie' main line, *yet had not entered a sizeable town, merely glimpsing Market Drayton and Nantwich from outside,* wrote Bird. *This remoteness is the charm of the canal - a veritable world apart.*

However, Bird conceded that *the idyllic turned to the gruelling* as he had bow-hauled 'Kubina' down fifteen locks at Audlem in heavy rain, while Gertie (12) and Anne (13) Berridge *plied their windlasses to draw the paddles, and strained to open and shut the lock gates.* But at Hack Green they negotiated the last narrow locks, and for the remainder of their journey their boats could enter the double locks 'breasted-up', and navigate the intervening pounds under 'Towy's' power. At Christleton Lock, Annie bought a bowl of apples from a woman in a canalside cottage who always saved her illustrated magazines for the Berridges - none of whom could read, apart from Skipper Leslie, he not having been born to the 'cut'.

Thomas Clayton, laden pair (motor and butty 'Peel' no. 83) in Northgate cutting c1950.
Edward Chambré-Hardman 770 ECH/1/1/0443

Soon they reached Chester: *through the heart of the city we chugged, a street on our left open to the canal like a Dutch quay, without even a railing betwixt roadway and water. A deep trench carried us spectacularly beneath the red city walls and under Northgate Bridge, to emerge at Nor'gate Locks with a superb view across miles of Cheshire lowland [actually Wales] into Flintshire with its gracefully rolling Clwydian Hills. Then down the treble locks, four gates to three chambers which droppped us 60 feet in three falls.*

They were now on their last lap of eight miles, and Bird celebrated with a huge breakfast of egg and bacon on the cabin roof in bright sunshine. *Annie at 'Towy's' tiller was threatened with the loss of her breakfast if she did not steer straight, as 'Kubina' was being thrown about and things upset in the cabin.* As they drew closer to Ellesmere Port the Berridges passed Clayton's motor 'Spey' homeward bound, towing its butty 'Ohio'.

With a 45-ton cargo of fuel oil shipped at Stanlow, the Berridges began their own return journey with barely a foot free board instead three feet when light (empty). Vivian Bird tells us nothing else about 'Towy's' home run, although he did mention that the Berridges' record round trip, some months earlier, was from 3am Tuesday leaving Oldbury, to 4pm Friday unloading at Langley Green.

In the 'Cheshire Life' of September 1954, however, Norman Ellison wrote an interesting piece, entitled 'Canal Craft', about a trip he had made on one of the Birmingham-bound oil boats travelling at 3mph from Ellesmere Port to Chester: *We were sitting on the cabin-roof of the 'butty' – a long-boat 72 feet wide, with 25 tons of crude oil in bulk beneath us, being towed by another long-boat powered with a 15 hp diesel engine. On our craft the skipper, his wife and two bonny children lived in a cabin 12 feet by 7 feet - their only home. It was scrupulously clean, every brass rail and knob shining in the reflected light from the iron galley-stove in the corner by the door. With one hand on the tiller, the wife could stir the pot on the stove or tend the fire. Not an inch of space was wasted; drawers and cupboards under side-bunks; a hinged table that lets down when needed and an oil lamp safely tucked away in one corner. Brightly patterned curtains could be drawn across the small window and door so that even in the depth of winter, I could imagine this a snug retreat when they tied up for the night. The swing-doors that led down to the cabin, were painted on both sides: outside, with castles of many red-roofed turrets against purple mountains rising from the bluest of seas: inside, with elaborate posies of gay roses. Even the water-cans on the cabin-roof were ornamented; the chimneys were banded with brass; the rudder-post, the sides of the cabin and the stern of the boat had coloured lozenges and squares, scroll-work and more flowers wherever they could be painted.*

Unfortunately the Stanlow oil traffic - amounting to 2,000 tons per month - was lost to the canal in the autumn of 1955 with Shell making other arrangements. The last motor boat on the run was 'Towy', which is now leased by the Chester Canal Heritage Trust and used for educational purposes (see page 4). 'Towy' was built by Fellows, Morton & Clayton at Uxbridge in 1938. It was one of a batch of eight wooden motor boats built to replace earlier horseboats.

Fortunately one of Thomas Clayton's wooden horseboats, 'Gifford', has been preserved by the Boat Museum Society at Ellesmere Port. Built in 1926 by Nursers at Braunston, it has a carrying capacity of 25 tons. By the late 1930s 'Gifford' was towed by a motor boat. Records show it often worked between Stanlow and Oldbury. It has a forecabin to provide extra living accommodation. The hold is covered to form a tank to carry the liquid. Access is by trap-doors which were covered by slides to keep the water out as the decks were often awash. But today 'Gifford' is high in the water, just as all the Stanlow-bound Clayton boats were half a century ago.

STEAM AND MOTOR POWER Terry Kavanagh

Steam Trains

The story of steam on the old Chester Canal begins in 1842, when the Birmingham & Liverpool Junction Company obtained powers to carry passengers and goods, and to provide haulage facilities for independent carriers. They did so on the strength of experiments carried out by an engineer named Henry Davies, from Stoke Prior in Worcester. These, along with an iron-hulled steam tug designed by him to tow narrow boats, seemed early in 1843 to indicate that *the expense of moving Trains of Boats by Steam Power is... likely to be less than Horse power.* Later that year the Canal Company - in collaboration with the Ellesmere & Chester - began working boats in trains through from Autherley to Ellesmere Port, each train hauled by one of eight tugs. But as we shall see, this very bold and novel experiment with canal trains ended in failure.

Seven of the steam tugs were constructed by Tayleur & Co., Vulcan Foundry, Bank Quay, near Warrington, in the summer of 1843, and *finished in a style much to the credit of that Company.* They were built after the prototype had undergone a series of trials, drawing water through the bow and expelling it through the stern to obtain motion, *by which it is clearly proved that steam-power can be safely and economically applied to boats of ordinary form upon narrow canals, without the much-dreaded wear and tear of the banks.* Each tug was fitted with eight screw propellers attached at intervals to two lines of shafting, both lines consisting of four screws on two shafts connected by a universal joint: one pair of screws near the bow, one pair immediately before and one pair abaft midships, and one pair near the stern. The shafts were placed in a false bottom built on to the tug so as to form a channel through which water was drawn in at the bow by the first two pairs of screws and forced out at the stern without a destructive wash, thanks to the 'contra-acting' effects of the last two pairs of screws running loose under the after deck. Because the mid-hull length of the false bottom was fixed below the water line in order to give the vessel buoyancy, each of the four screws amidships had a smaller diameter (2 feet 8 inches) and a higher pitch (6 feet 6 inches) than the four screws near the extremities of the tug (each 3 feet 6 inches in diameter by 5 feet pitch) so that they could deal with the increased velocity of water in the constricted part of the channel.

They were common or helical screw propellers, each consisting of two half turns of a double-threaded screw, which had wide tipped blades and a small cylindrical boss. The common screw, which was in general use until 1860, had two main disadvantages. First, the portions of the blades nearest the boss served no useful purpose and were in fact a source of weakness, for the boss was made as small as possible. Secondly, the wide, fan-shaped tips

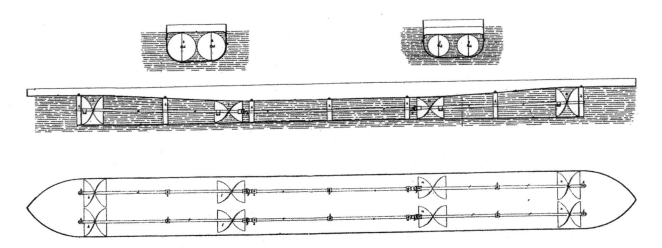

Arrangement of screw propellers

of the blades absorbed a large amount of power without adding to the thrust of the screw, and they also contributed to vibration.

In 1849 an engineer named Robert Griffiths began a series of investigations on the action of marine propellers, and this work was carried on until 1855. The outcome was the patenting of a propeller that overcame the disadvantages of the common screw and incorporated a number of other improvements. The central portion of Griffiths' propeller was filled up for about one-third of the diameter by a spherical or ellipsoidal boss. From this boss the blades widened to a maximum width about two-fifths along the radius from the centre and then tapered off again to a flattened end.

This leaf-shaped propeller blade came too late for Henry Davies to use it. But he was fully aware of the vibration problem and its causes. After the practicability of screw propulsion had been demonstrated, it was the convenience and efficiency of the screw in comparison with the paddle wheel that led Davies to adopt it. But the screw required a higher speed of rotation than the slow-running (and bulky) paddle-engines which were then available; hence the earliest screw steamers were fitted with geared engines to obtain the required multiplication of speed, and the toothed gearing wheels used inevitably created noise as well as vibration. That is why Davies' tugs were fitted with an engine for driving the two screw shafts directly - in this case a 16hp high-pressure disc engine (with direct rotary action), which he and another engineer, William Taylor, of Smethwick, patented in 1836.

This type of rotary engine, according to John Bourne in his book 'A Treatise on the Steam-Engine', published in 1868, *consists substantially of a disc capable of moving in a globular vessel in the way it would move if every part of its edge were sucessively pressed down, and an arm extending from this disc therefore moves in a circle, and will turn round a crank when the disc is thus moved by the steam.* The first disc engines were *both leaky and noisy*, but Henry Davies, and an inventor named Bishopp (1850) did overcome these defects. Even so, *a nicety of workmanship is required in the construction of disc engines*, which proved very difficult to obtain in the context of the technology of the day.

The disc engines for the B&LJ Co's tugs were constructed by the Patent Disc Engine Company of Birmingham, and Henry Davies installed them at Norbury Junction where a workshop had been erected for the purpose.

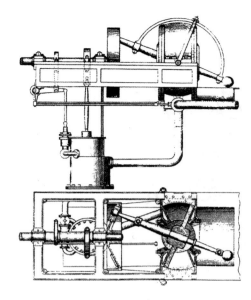

Disc engine as improved by Bishopp

Three of the steam tugs took part in the opening ceremony of the Ellesmere & Chester Canal Co's new dock at Ellesmere Port in September 1843. One of these towed *an elegant barge*, in which the Canal Committee and others had embarked at Chester's Tower Wharf, at a speed of 6 mph for most of the way; *but very little material displacement of water took place, and there certainly was no visible tidal action on the banks.* Another tug towed a narrow boat, specially fitted up for the occasion, along the length of the Wirral Line. And a third towed nine boats, containing 104 tons of goods, joined together at their extremities by Davies' patent 'H'-shaped troughs, so as to form an 'articulated' train of boats which was steered by just one man, upwards of one hundred miles, at an average speed of 3 mph.

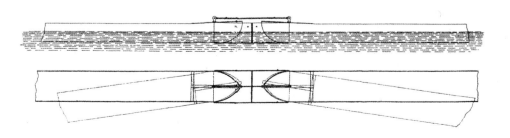

Davies' patent 'H'-shaped troughs could form an articulated train of boats.

The B&LJCCo's superintendent, Robert Skey, who directed the whole operation, said *plans were already underway to send luggage trains along the line of canal both day and night, with the same regularity as post office and railway conveyance*. There was even talk of *establishing an equally regular system of passenger traffic; and as it is now ascertained that a speed of eight or ten miles can be attained, and the cost of transit so economised as to be perhaps the lowest yet devised, falling very short of locomotive power on railways, or horse power either on roads or canals, there can be no doubt that the public will soon have the advantage of a cheaper medium of transit than any heretofore enjoyed, and which will again revive the passenger traffic on canals, and to an extent hitherto unknown.*

This was a mere pipe-dream – even though Slater's 1844 Shropshire Directory, under Market Drayton, states: *To Chester, Ellesmere Port, Birmingham etc. the B & LJC Co's Steam Boats three times a day for the conveyance of passengers from the old Wharf.* Few then knew that the speed of the steam tugs was governed, not by the engine, but by the width and the depth, that is, the cross-section, of the waterway itself. Any attempt to increase the speed beyond what the section of the waterway permits merely causes a waste of power, heaps up the water in front of the vessel, creates a breaking wave which damages the canal banks, and renders the vessel too difficult to steer.

In November 1843, one of the steam tugs, called 'Powis', was tried on the Duke's Canal. Although the Bridgewater Trustees did not order a similar craft, they were particularly impressed by the apparent simplicity, durability, cheapness, and fuel economy of its disc engine: *there are few complex movements and the few which are required are of small dimensions.* They found that 'Powis' could haul a train of five boats at a speed of just under 4mph *without any observable washings against the banks of the Canal.* Why? *The formation of the Boats, the position and mode of working the propellers, rendering it impossible for the water to run otherwise than immediately in the wake of the Train. Beyond the rate of 4 miles an hour, a wave makes its appearance on the Banks, and increases in size in proportion to the increased speed of the Steamer... at one time... we went rather more than 6 miles per hour when the waves along the banks were not less than 3 feet high.*

A few days after these trials, the steamer 'Powis' set off from Autherley Junction with a train of 16 boats containing 320 tons of goods destined for Ellesmere Port, at the rate of 2mph, and was relieved by other tugs or 'engines', as they were called, stationed at various places on the voyage, which was *performed in good style throughout.*

By the end of 1843, the B&LJCCo's engineer, Alex Easton, could report that for the previous two months the steam tugs had been *hauling trains of boats from 8 to 12 in number, containing 160 to 240 tons of goods, daily between Autherley and Ellesmere Port and back the same route; and all with perfect safety to the Boats in the Train and to other Boats hauled by horses and using the navigation.* He went on to say that, *Under all the disadvantages which naturally attend the commencement of a perfectly novel system of Trade the Steam Engines and Tug Boats whether as regards speed or load or consumption of fuel answer fully as well as they were intended or expected to perform. In conclusion I have to add that from the experience we have already had in the working of the Tug Boats and Trains of boats with Goods have perfect confidence in the correctness of the plans that have been adopted.*

Indeed three months later, Easton reported that the 80 boats employed in the goods trade were inadequate to meet the demand, adding: *The Tug Boats and Trains have hitherto been worked successfully and from the short experience we have had of the system my opinion of its merits is confirmed.* And, in August 1844, another report stated that *the Steam tugs of the Company have been actively at work throughout the main line of Canal and the System of hauling Boats in trains has been carried out to a considerable extent.*

Under that system, *Two trains, usually consisting of six or eight loaded boats, are started from each terminus of the above line every day, and, by this means, a quantity of merchandise, averaging between 2,000 and 3,000 tons per week is conveyed by the use of steam-power on canals. The average weight conveyed in each train exceeds 100 tons, and the haulage of this for one mile is effected by the consumption of less than 1/2 cwt [56 lbs] of coal; consequently, the power of hauling one ton of goods one mile is yielded by the consumption of less than half a pound of coal. The engine is managed by one man; the train of boats is steered by one man; and the sole additional attendance is that of a conductor (whose chief duty is to prevent pilferage), except in passing locks, when extra assistance becomes necessary. An equal quantity of goods could not be moved by horse-power, without the continued employment of six horses, with the requisite relays for changing these, and at least twenty-four men on board the boats.*

However, such glowing reports cannot disguise the fact that the experiment was a failure. Although the B&LJ Canal (later the Shropshire Union main line) had long straight pounds of water and regularly spaced locks in each flight, the steam tugs only achieved an average speed of 2mph, owing in part to *the difficulties encountered in passing the locks, and getting through the shoal-water sections of the canal.* Some years ago Dr E A Shearing, a canal historian, wrote: *Having watched working boats slowing down and virtually drifting through the many narrow bridge holes on the B&LJ section, to avoid bottoming, I find it difficult to believe that Davies' boat trains could have worked satisfactorily under routine conditions. Just think of the administrative problems in assembling trains and attaching boats at intermediate points on the way. Horses had to be made available, too, to hal [an old-fashioned term for haul] the individual boats through the lock flights.*

Back in June 1845 the Ellesmere & Chester conceded that *the system of working boats in Trains though used with great advantage... is not cheaper than locomotive power now is upon Railways with a good gradient*. As a result, the Canal Company and its successor, the SUR&CCo, became more interested in railway conversion than canal trains. Early in 1846 Skey was directed to arrange a gradual withdrawal from the carrying trade and by 1848 haulage by horses was let out to a single contractor, William Bishton. It seems that at least one of the tugs continued to tow lighters on the lock-free, broad-gauge Wirral Line for a few more years, albeit at rather less than half the anticipated speed of 8mph. But this almost certainly came to an end in 1854 when one of the *Old Steam Canal Tugs* was sold to a Mr. Williams of Chester for £80, the sale value of the remainder being estimated at £53 each as scrap metal.

Even so, the Shropshire Union minutes show that the Company continued to toy with the idea of replacing horse with steam haulage over many years. In 1861, for example, the Manager considered it desirable to extend the haulage contract with William Bishton *in consequence of the probability of substituting steam for horse power on this canal*; and the former was authorized to spend up to £300 in purchasing *an Engine* (or tug) for steam traction. The following year the Manager was directed *to have plans and estimates prepared of a suitable Steam Tug for the Liverpool and Chester trade*. By 1863 Bishton was operating two wooden steam tugs, 'Test' and 'Magnet'; later that year the Company purchased them. In 1864/6 they were joined by the iron tugs 'Dagmar' and 'Dreadnought', which came from the Lancaster Canal Co. They were built in 1858 for work on the Leeds and Liverpool Canal, and sold on two years later. Both tugs were sixty feet long by eight feet beam and five feet deep. Their horizontal geared 12 hp high-pressure engine, with steam supplied by a cylindrical tubular boiler, drove Joseph Burch's patent screw propeller *the blades of which can be removed if broken in a few minutes.*

The wooden tugs were of narrow beam and could operate south of Nantwich, for in February 1868 it was minuted that the steam tug at Autherley was tied up through badness of traffic. In September 1871, so many horses were suffering from sore shoulders that assistance was being given by the tug 'Test' working between Tyrley and Autherley. Then, just over two years later, in 1873, *the Company Secretary reported on the condition of the canal tugs which on account of the state of the boilers were consuming more coal than was considered necessary.*

It was recommended that new Boilers be obtained [from the LNWR Co's Crewe Works] for the Iron Boats 'Dagmar' and 'Dreadnought', they being most suitable for the Company's Trade and the Wooden Boats 'Magnet' and 'Test' be only repaired to make them available as Change Boats.

In December 1875, however, it was decided that the Canal Tug 'Magnet' which had been in use by the Company for a number of years, having become quite unfit for work, the Boiler requiring renewal, and the Hull in need of repair, had sold the Boiler and transferred the Boat to the Stone Trade, for which trade it could be made suitable for a time. Moreover, As the Tug ['Test' ?] which was now employed would not be fit for the service much longer it was Resolved That Tenders be obtained for a New Canal Tug to be specially adapted for service in place of the one reported by the Secretary broken up.

'Rocket' *Also see page 197*
Boat Museum Trust

This last tug was replaced by the powerful canal steamer 'Rocket', which the Shropshire Union built, most probably at Crewe Locomotive Works, in 1877. It was constructed of quarter-inch iron plate, was 65 feet long and 6ft 11in beam. Draught 3ft 3in forward, 3ft 8in aft. High pressure engine 12in bore x 16in stroke, horizontal with mitre gear drive to the propeller shaft. The boiler was 4ft 9in diameter and 12ft long with one furnace.

Narrowboat steamers

During October of the previous year the SU experimented with the Grand Junction Canal Company's steam cargo tug boat 'Wolf' between Ellesmere Port and Wolverhampton and found it had reduced the cost of haulage by 3d per ton, besides performing the trip in four hours less time. So this narrowboat steamer was purchased for £150 two months later.

In September 1877, *it was reported with reference to the working of the Tug Boat 'Wolf' plying between Wolverhampton and Ellesmere Port, that the saving in Haulage during the last month had been 2 1/2 d per ton, and recommending the derisability of having 1 or 2 Boats of a similar class with a view to a further reduction in the cost of Haulage.* The SU Manager was directed to enquire about the cost of a new cargo tug boat.

'Vulcan' Although the 'Vulcan' ran primarily on the Grand Union Canal it was similar to a handful of narrowboat steamers operated by the Shropshire Union Railways & Canal Co. Registered in Birmingham no. 1243, Vulcan was built in July 1911 and converted to diesel in September 1927.
Scraper board by Gordon Emery

Then in August 1878, he reported the London & Staffordshire Carrying Co's offer to sell their cargo steam boats (which also originated with the GJC Co) and was instructed to have them examined and if they were in good condition to negotiate for their purchase. Subsequently a Company official reported that *the Engines of those examined were fair second class ones with some good points that they appeared to be in Good Condition and likely to go for some time without large repairs.* It was also stated that the use of these boats would reduce haulage costs and assist in meeting the difficulty of working under the Canal Boats Act, and it was resolved that the two best steam tug boats, namely 'Nettle' and 'Pioneer' be purchased for the sum of £255 each. The latter had iron knees, oak planking, cross-bottom built, and was fitted with a 12-horse power inverted 10in diameter cylinder direct action engine, and vertical flue boiler, 7ft by 4ft 6in diameter, copper water heater, double action force and lift donkey pump; driving a Griffith's 2-bladed wrought iron propeller with cast iron and gun metal boss.

In November 1878, the Manager reported that *in consequence of the employment of additional tug boats between Wolverhampton and Ellesmere Port he was looking out the Old Horses and expected to dispense with 16 or 18 at an early date.* He had also been authorised to purchase an additional cargo tug boat similar to 'Pioneer', and called 'Havoc' for £160. It was intended that with this and the other three steam narrow boats *a daily service to and from Wolverhampton would be arranged, and that the Birmingham fly boats and about 24 horses could be dispensed with.* Two months later, it was found that *the employment of Cargo carrying Tug Boats will permit of 12 additional Horses being disposed of* and the Manager *was authorized to arrange for the sale of that number of the oldest Horses.*

However, those early successes could not be sustained - and the reason is simple. With their powerful yet bulky steam plants, these cargo-carrying narrowboat steamers could tow one or two 'butties' (towed boats), but they could only carry 12 or 13 tons themselves. Hence the need to keep them continually on the move day and night to earn their living. In other words, the successful results were obtained by working these steamers really hard. Inevitably, as time passed the amount spent on repairs and maintenance grew dramatically. True, 'Havoc' had been used only as a change boat, the hull having been in a bad state from the start - the new SU-built cargo steam tug 'Avoca' took its place in 1881. But 'Pioneer' was also rebuilt or replaced three years later; and 'Nettle' and 'Wolf' were cut up in 1887.

Two years earlier, in February 1885, it was reported that *with a view of reducing expenses, three of the Coys Cargo Tug Boats working between South Staffordshire & Ellesmere Port had been put out of Commission.* (It was also stated, that *Mr Chubb, the tenant of one of the Co's coal wharves at Shrewsbury, had been making trials of the haulage of his Tub Boats on the*

195

Shrewsbury Canal with one of the Company's Cargo Tug Boats, and the results being found satisfactory, he was arranging for a small steamer to haul his traffic between the points named.) In September 1886, Thomas Hales submitted a statement on the comparative cost of horse and steam haulage, from which *it appeared that the advantage was in favour of Horse power.* Meanwhile, G. R. Jebb, the Engineer, had warned that the wash from the screw propellers was damaging the canal banks - a problem that neither the trial of Taylor's patent screw propeller nor the raising of existing ones could solve. Accordingly, in November 1888, the SU Management discussed *the desirability of continuing the use of the Cargo Tug Boats on the Canals and in view of the effects on the Banks they ordered that they should be discontinued as soon as possible for general use. Mr Hales & Mr Jebb to consider whether they can be employed on the Wirral length as Tug Boats or if the engines should be taken out and the Boats converted into carrying Boats.* A month later it was reported that the steam cargo boats had been put out of commission.

Their days on the southern section of the SU Canal were not over, however, for the year 1893 saw the canal tugs 'Avoca' and 'Nettle' shuttling back and forth between Autherley Junction and Tyrley, so that the large number of horses suffering from sore shoulders could be rested. Two years later it was reported that the cargo steamer 'Avoca' was worn-out; but the shuttle service continued for a number of years. In 1899, for example, the owner of Tyrley Wharf was pressing the Company to rent it as he claimed their steamers were using it for coaling, ash heaving and turning round, seven days a week.

Locomotive haulage
Eleven years earlier, an interesting series of steam haulage experiments were carried out over about a mile of the Middlewich branch near Worleston, according to the 'Cheshire Observer' of 26th May 1888: *A number of canal boats had been drawn up near where the length of [18-in gauge] rails had been laid, and upon which stood an eight-horse power locomotive ['Dickie'] from the railway works. One canal boat was attached to the engine by a stout rope about thirty yards long. Other canal boats were placed behind, at a distance from each other of several yards. Eight canal boats were thus attached to the engine, their aggregate weight being upwards of 140 tons, most of them being laden. A man was placed in each of the boats to steer it. The engine started with the eight boats, but it did not get along very satisfactorily, oscillating somewhat on account of the irregular motion. It, however, drew them along at about four miles an hour, which is about the speed at which the horses on the towing-path travel. Having traversed the section of rails, a return was made with four boats, and the speed and motion were altogether satisfactory, the boats going through the water steadily, and the engine working smoothly. Another experiment was then made with six boats, and this also appeared*

'The engine and the six boats were then photographed'
Locomotive trials on the Middlewich Branch.

to be satisfactory. The engine and the six boats were then photographed. The length of canal upon which the experiment was tried was the best that could be selected for the purpose. However, the 'Observer' of 6th October reported that the Company had *abandoned the idea of locomotive haulage for canal traffic because the carrying out of the proposal along the whole length of the canal would be a very costly undertaking, for not only would two sets of rails have to be laid, but the canal would require to be deepened, its banks made secure to withstand the wash, and considerable alterations would be necessary to existing bridges.*

Nevertheless, some Shropshire Union officals still harboured hopes of utilising steamboats for canal traffic, and a number of steel-plated boats under construction at Crewe Works were intended to have engines and boilers fitted. These small steamers could tow several boats, and although the state of the canal in many places in Cheshire and Shropshire then was such that only a small speed could be maintained, yet there would be a considerable saving of horse power and horse attendants. In the event, however, only one of the steel boats was fitted up with a compound engine. In January 1890 it was reported that this boat, *the Tug 'Luna' had commenced working between Ellesmere Port and Wolverhampton, but that it was not yet known with what results. Mr Jebb… to watch the effects of the [new] Screw on the Canal.*

'Rocket'
Eighteen months later, one of the SU's canal steamers stole the show after steam dredgers began removing the earth dam which separated the two completed portions of the Eastham section of the Manchester Ship Canal. A pleasure steamer that had been chartered to convey

dignitaries and officials was supposed to steam through the gap in the dam first. *Then it was,* reported the 'Cheshire Observer' of 18 July 1891, *that the small but powerful tug called the 'Rocket' steamed through the opening which the dredgers had made and, with its tail of seven barges, made its way to Eastham... It was not, however, a thing which was premeditated, and indeed there was just a suggestion of sharp practice on the part of the skipper...the 'Rocket' was seen to bend round the dredger 'Barry', and to dart towards the gap. Having such a formidable tail, it was impossible to check the progress of the little craft.*

'Rocket' was reputedly the best of the canal steamers. The SU's Superintendent Engineer, L. W. Lindop, supervised a normal towing trip on it, using a drawback gauge obtained from Crewe Works. Starting from Powels Bridge, Ellesmere Port towing 11 loaded boats. Total tonnage 208 tons 18 cwt. Average speed 2.85 mph. Coal consumed 9/16 cwt per mile. Arrived in Chester after three hours (8.5 miles).

Mr Lindop's note books also mention the elegant wood-built tug 'Leader', which replaced the narrowboat steamer 'Avoca' in 1896. 'Leader' cost £160 to build, plus £398 for the compound engine and boiler supplied by Messrs Wilkinson [probably George Wilkinson & Co of Wigan]. It was 64ft 10in. long, its draught being 3ft frd, 3ft aft. The test run took place on 22nd July 1896, and Mr Lindop wrote, *This boat no use whatever at 3ft draught.* The draught was then altered with pig iron ballast to 2ft frd, 3ft 8in aft.

Several trips were recorded in his notes, towing narrowboats loaded with grain between Powels Bridge and Chester, namely 'Cestria', 'Bateson' and 'Nelly'. The entry for 27th August 1896 reads: *Draught 2ft 4.5in frd, 3ft 8in aft. Left Ellesmere Port 10.45am, arrived Chester 1pm, towing 'Herald' 21 tons, also 'Phoebe' 16 tons 15 cwt and 'Dorothy' 16 tons 15 cwt. Burning coke fuel used 2 cwt 9lb. Steam 122 PSI 180 rpm.*

The tugs on the Wirral Line usually towed one flat or barge and perhaps two or three narrowboats. If they did not have a flat then they would take extra narrowboats. There was always one tug going each way at the same time. One of the canal tugs worked as a special 'flat engine', according to Bert Jones, a former SU employee at Ellesmere Port. *Well, that used to be a special barge, loaded at Liverpool and that would go straight through all the way up to Chester, and there would always be a tug standing by to take that barge up to Chester. What was in it I don't know, but it must have been a special cargo.*

The steam tugs had regular crews: Joseph Challinor was engineer on 'Rocket'; George Bishop and Richard Morris were the drivers on 'Dreadnought' and 'Dagmar' respectively. In December 1902 the SU Committee discussed the case of a 65-year-old tug driver, named T. Jackson, who received a weekly wage of 27/-: *As it was desirable that he should give up working the Tug, a pension of 5/- [per week] was ordered to be paid to him*. And in December 1910 they authorised the *£1 advanced to Steerer Mitchell while off duty through a sprained leg when starting the Tug on 10th October last*.

Motor power

That same year the steam cargo tug 'Pioneer' was cut up. The Company did not replace it, but experimented with motor power instead. *We hear on good authority that the SURCCo recently have been experimenting in the working of the traffic on their canal*, wrote the 'Observer's' Ellesmere Port correspondent on 26th November 1910. *A narrow boat, carrying about 25 tons, has been fitted for propelling power with the Gardner No.2 cylinder engine, the fuel being ordinary petroleum, the consumption of which is small for the power developed. The boat is intended for the Ellesmere Port and Birmingham service. The preliminary trials have been successful, under the superintendence of Mr L. Lindop, a speed of about five miles per hour being attained on certain portions of the canal. It is intended to build another boat on similar lines immediately. If the company go in, on a large scale, for the improvement, the canal carriage will be practically revolutionised.*

A month earlier, Mr Hales reported that *Messrs Gardner & Sons Ltd., Patricroft, had agreed to lend the Company a 10hp petroleum oil engine for six months, for trials as to its suitability for the Company's carrying Boats, if the Motor does not suit the Company's requirements, they will take it back, if purchased, the cost will be £114-10-0*. The offer was accepted, and it was put in the new fly-boat 'Water Lily' to work between Ellesmere Port and Birmingham.

In common with other fly-boats, 'Water Lily' was designed with fine lines and a rounded cross section for speed and stability. But there was an obvious difference between a horse boat and a motor boat like 'Water Lily': the latter had a counter stern overhanging the propeller and a balanced rudder, whereas the horse boat or butty had a sharp stern and heavy rudder. The motor's counter kept the screw immersed, which ensured the propeller worked efficiently.

In April 1911 Thomas Hales stated that now the crew of the fly boat 'Water Lily' *had got acquainted to the Gardner oil engine, it was working quite satisfactorily, being capable of taking the place of the Express Boat working between Ellesmere Port and Birmingham, and a comparative statement of the cost of working by Horses, 3s 2 1/2d, and by Motor Engine, 2s 8d, was submitted*. It was then decided that the engine should be purchased.

In October 1911, however, a Company minute refers to the 10hp oil engine supplied ten months earlier by the Day Motor Company to work experimentally in the fly boat 'Adonis', *but which, after trial was found to be unsuitable. It was recommended that it be purchased, and fixed in the Salvage Barge 'Lancaster' at Ellesmere Port, for the purpose of driving the Centrifugal pump, which will enable the pump to be operated in a much shorter time than can be done by steam, after consideration the Committee approved the purchase at the makers price £85-12-6, plus experimental charges for services rendered by the Motor Company.*

There was more bad news in April 1912, when it was reported that the Gardner motor engine fitted in the Birmingham fly-boat 'Water Lily' *was not proving a success, and owing to the frequent breakdowns, and increased cost of Oil, the anticipated saving of working is not being realised.* So the engine was taken out of the boat and put into stock until some other use could be found for it, *and horse power reverted to.*

One wonders what would have happened had the Shropshire Union Company followed Fellows, Morton & Clayton's example and tried the extremely simple and highly reliable Bolinder two-stroke oil engine instead. Adoption of this semi-diesel engine spelt the end of steam and horse traction as far as FMC were concerned. Not only was it cheaper to run but it occupied only half the space of the steam plant, thus increasing the carrying capacity of the motor boat by 5 tons, and as it did not require a full-time engineer it enabled boat crews to be reduced.

As it was, the Shropshire Union was becoming increasingly dependent on horse traction. In June 1912 *The hull of the Tug 'Leader' having been condemned, it was reported that her Boiler, No. 34, had been taken out and put into stock.* Again, in October 1917, it was decided to sell the canal tugs 'Dagmar', 'Dreadnought' and 'Luna', as they were no longer required in connection with the working of the traffic between Chester and Ellesmere Port. The two iron tugs were sold to Richard Abel & Sons, of Runcorn for £85 each in February 1918. But since the best offer received for the steel tug 'Luna' was only £75, it was decided to put the compound expansion engine and boiler in stock, and to cut up the hull. Then in December 1920, it was reported that *Tug 'Leader' on condemned list had been dismantled, and the Hull sold to B. D. Bate, Chester for £25.* Finally, the canal tug 'Rocket' was sold to the Chester & Liverpool Lighterage Company for £110 after the Canal Company abandoned carrying on its own account in 1921.

As we have seen, the narrow beam steam tug had a longer history than the cargo-carrying type on the old Chester Canal. But there was a 'hi-tech' narrowboat steamer built using the engine and boiler of the famous Sentinel steam wagon. This was the aptly-named 'Sentinel' of 1927, launched from J H Taylor & Sons in the old SU boatyard, Chester. The Super Sentinel engine used was a single-cylinder unit, half of a standard lorry engine in fact, but it still occupied far too much space. Although the 'Sentinel' also towed the butty 'Ever Watchful', it made no impression on the growing number of diesel-engined boats (some of which were converted FMC narrowboat

'Sentinel'
Geoff Taylor Collection

steamers) because it could not overcome the dual handicap of a larger engine-room and the need for an extra crew member. The experiment seems to have lasted only six months.

It is also worth noting that the Midlands and Coast Carrying Company, which took over some of the former SU Co services and boats, used the motor tug 'Energy' to haul boats in trains for a while. This tug was equipped with a windlass so that it could bow-haul boats through the locks. It was also fitted with a special shrouded propeller designed to prevent fouling and concentrate the flow of water past the rudder, thereby giving increased manoeuvrability.

Shrouded propeller on 'Energy'
in Taylor's Yard
Geoff Taylor Collection

The miller's tale

The Shropshire Union Company never operated steam or motor driven wide boats on its canal system. But a handful of independent carriers in the Chester area owned powered flats or barges. The best known by-traders were Griffiths Bros, corn merchants, whose mill at Queens Wharf, Canalside, Chester had a bucket elevator. They owned several steam barges, all but one of which continued to carry grain in bulk over from Liverpool until well into the 1930s. The exception was the wood screw-auxiliary sailing flat 'Bessie', of Liverpool. She had a registered gross tonnage of 36.66 tons, or 23.53 tons net, and measured 69ft x 14.2ft x 4.7ft. Her 8hp simple expansion engine of 6 1/2in

Steam flat 'Bessie', *built on the banks of the Leeds and Liverpool Canal at Lathom, Lancashire, by Richard Tyrer in 1877.*
Boat Museum Trust

diameter x 7in stroke was made by Lowry & Co of Salford in 1878. The steam flat 'Bessie' began carrying grain to Chester in the summer of 1883, her owners paying the maximum Shropshire Union Canal toll of 1/6 per ton until they got it reduced to 1/- by complaining to the Board of Trade.

Five and a half years later, Charles Price, the 'Bessie's' skipper, had cause for complaint as well. On 5th January 1889 the 'Cheshire Observer' reported that Captain Price, had summoned one Edward Davies for assault: *He now occupied a position previously filled by the defendant, who was discharged on account of drunkenness, and who in consequence seemed to entertain malice against his successor. On Monday the 24th December, he went in a state of intoxication to the mill where Price was engaged, took off his coat and challenged him out to fight. After using very threatening language he put his fist in the complaint's face, said he would rip him up, and if Price had retaliated a serious assault might have been committed. Subsequent to the issue of the summons, when the parties met Price offered to forgive defendant for the sake of his wife and family; but he again visited the mill while in drink, and repeated his abuse as much as ever. - Defendant was ordered to be bound over in his own recognisance of £10 and two sureties of £5 to keep the peace for six months, or in default one month's imprisonment; and he now had also to pay the costs, or suffer an additional seven days.*

Iron dumb barge at Griffith's Mill (now the Mill Hotel) c1900
Geoff Taylor Collection

Charles Price was in the news again when the 'Observer' of 18th July 1891 declared: _The steamer 'Bessie' of Liverpool, which was the first vessel carrying cargo to use the Manchester Ship Canal, and entered the locks of Eastham on Tuesday afternoon, was en route for Chester with a cargo of maize for Messrs. Griffiths Brothers, of Canal-side, Chester and Liverpool._ The 'Chronicle' of the same date added: _The captain also boasts that she was the last vessel to use the old exit, passing from Ellesmere Port into the Mersey on the way to Liverpool on Monday last._

In 1894 Charles Price took charge of Griffiths Bros' new iron steam barge 'Cestria', which did not originate with the Rochdale Canal Co, as some canal historians have suggested. However, Walkers, Parker of the Leadworks, Chester did purchase the iron steam barge 'Pioneer' from that Company in 1896, for the purpose of carrying lead to Liverpool via Whitby Locks. This vessel was built by John Woodcock, Castle Dockyard, Northwich in 1889; and it is possible that he constructed the 'Cestria', too. Certainly his successor, W. J. Yarwood & Sons Ltd, built three more iron steam barges for Griffiths the corn millers, namely the 'Cambria' (1900), the 'Scotia' (1903) and the 'Anglia' (1905). This last steam barge was driven by the high pressure engine and 5ft diameter x 5ft 8in boiler, of the builders' own make, taken out of the previous vessel. Thus, Yarwood's converted the 'Scotia' into a dumb barge, shortly after completing two other purpose-built towing barges, the iron composite 'Victoria' and the 'Alexandra', to work with the three steam craft.

203

The aforementioned steam barge 'Bessie' was sold to Stephen Walley, Steam Flour Mills, Egg Bridge, Waverton in 1896. A Shropshire Union minute dated 15th January that year states:

A Communication was submitted from the Board of Trade enclosing complaint from Mr Walley of Egg Bridge as to working his Steam Flat on the Canal, and a reply ordered to be made to the allegation.

Waverton Mill with a steam flat,
possibly the 'Petrel' when she was converted to Motor Power.
Ed Walley

We do not know why he complained, but it is significant that a SU minute of August 1883 states: *The proceedings of the Select Committee on Canals were reported. Mr Hales to get up the information as to the allegation against the Company of placing difficulties in the way of private Tenders on the Canal.* Then again, it may be connected with the shallowness of the Shropshire Union Canal. A company minute dated 14th October 1896 says: *Claim of Mr Walley, Egg Bridge, for Damage to Grain by leakage of his flat caused by striking a Stone at the Cow Lane Level, viz. £4-18-9 to be paid.* But we do know that his steam flat 'Bessie' when inward bound in ballast from Chester to the Langton Dock, Liverpool stranded on the beach at Seaforth on the 5th August 1898, and became a total wreck.

Stephen Walley replaced her with the steel steam barge 'Ceres' built at Northwich that year by Yarwood's, Castle Dock. She was registered at the Port of Liverpool on 14th July 1899, and was 71.4ft x 14.4ft x 4.83ft, giving a gross tonnage of 47.22 tons and 32.11 tons net. The 'Ceres' was powered by one pair of high pressure engines 6" dia. x 8" stroke of 8hp each, steam coming at 100psi from a steel boiler, of the builders' own design.

Her crew received the following rate of wages paid by owners of steam barges on the Chester Canal to Captain, Engineer & Youth in the early 1900s:

	Wages	plus	Trip
Captain	£1- 0-0		12-6
Mate	15-0		7-6
Youth	5-0		5-0

Rate of wages paid to crews of craft by Messrs. Griffiths Bros., Chester:

Steam Barges.	Captain	£1 per week. + 12/- per trip.	
		Towage 1/3 per barge light, 2/6 loaded.	
Barge.	Captain	£1 per week. + 10/- per trip.	
	Mate	15/- per week. + 7/6 per trip.	

These bargemen were paid in part by the trip, and so delays at locks cost them money. The 'Chronicle' of 20th July 1901, under the heading 'County Police Court', reported that:

Henry Rowlands, canal boatman, was charged with assaulting Walter Philip Lowe, lockkeeper of the Tarvin Locks, on the Shropshire Union Canal, while in the discharge of his duty ...the defendant came to the lock in charge of the steam flat 'Ceres', belonging to Mr. Walley, of Egg Bridge, and complainant, whose duty it was to regulate the water, came up for that purpose, as there had been many complaints of people wasting the canal water. Rowlands did not appear to like this, and began to use bad

A horsedrawn iron flat
(probably 'Jeanie')
at Christleton Lock.
c1920s

language, and threatened to smash his face. He attempted to seize hold of him, and ultimately assaulted him. - Complainant bore out this statement, saying that defendant tried to wrench his hand away from the paddle, and when he found he could not do that he got him by the leg and nearly threw him into the lock. Had witness not stuck firm with his hands he must have fallen into the water. There was plenty of water in the lock for the defendant to have got his boat in. The bench looked upon it as a serious offence, and fined the defendant 20s. and costs, or 14 days' hard labour. - Defendant: Oh, I'll pay.

'Stanley' beached up for repairs at Tarvin Mill *c1920s*
Geoff Taylor Collection

Henry Rowland's steam barge 'Ceres' was sold in March 1903 to Liverpool owners for lighterage work on the Mersey. Stephen Walley ordered a replacement from Yarwood's in the shape of the iron composite steam barge 'Stanley' of 1904. But after he moved to Imperial Mills, Ellesmere Port, this steamer was taken over (along with his Waverton premises) by Dutton Bros, of Calveley Mill, near Nantwich, owners of the sister vessel 'Petrel' built the year before. Both steam barges were powered by a two cylinder compound non-condensing engine (6in/12in bore x 8in stroke), steam coming at 100 psi from a 5'0"dia x 5'8" boiler. They were *fitted with the latest transhipping gear to enable the cargoes to be dealt with expeditiously and satisfactorily*. Moreover, *the whole of the machinery, including engines, boilers and winches were designed and built in the Castle Dockyard*, according to the 'Chronicle' of 10th April 1904. These two steam barges were similar in size to the iron composite but dumb Yarwood-built barge 'Jeanie' of 1913, which measured 70ft 7in x 13ft 11in x 5ft 3in and 45.66 tons register.

'Jeanie' was built to the order of the Cheshire Farmers Assocation, of Calveley after they had absorbed the Dutton Bros' premises. The steam barges 'Petrel' and 'Stanley' were also taken over, and sold in 1926 to a sub-contractor named Joseph Davies, who lived in a wooden caravan he had constructed in Brown Heath, near Egg Bridge, Waverton. They were subsequently converted from steam to motor power.

Gordon Davies' memories

In 1991, his son Gordon Davies, who had emigrated to Australia, recorded his fascinating recollections of the early 1930s when he shared the hardships and adversity of canal life:

At the time I was only a boy of 7 or 8, and I can recall he [Joseph Davies] would make a trip via two barges from Waverton via Chester, to Crane [Tower] Wharf, on to Ellesmere Port. He would then proceed to cross the river Mersey to Huskisson Dock in Liverpool, and take on a cargo of corn, UVECO, bran or thirds, and sometimes coal, and return to Chester.

Regarding the canal trip beyond Waverton, I can recall my father saying he had been on a couple of trips to Calveley, but with what cargo I cannot say. He did remark that the conditions of the canal were not good, and could do with dredging. This was done occasionally with a long craft from Waverton to Ellesmere Port, mostly during winter months.

I might add that it is only now that I realise what a hard, lonely life my father had, with long hours of labour, via the trip, the appalling weather conditions at the time, the severe winters. My only involvement amounted to what help or assistance I could do, at the age of 9 to 11, which I had to do on the instructions of my dear mother; sometimes working through the night, not knowing next day what time I would get home, and of course I missed school on occasions.

I was, of course, delighted at the time to partake in doing what jobs were necessary, such as lighting the fire in the two berth cabin, which was small and damp, making tea, frying bacon and eggs, and going to the shop for whatever was necessary, taking off the hatches, which had to be done by two persons before the sacks of corn, bran, UVECO or thirds were slung via a chain hauled up into the mill. Offloading 40 tons would be almost a day's work. It would be necessary to sleep aboard sometimes for an early start, 6 a.m., in view of the fact that at least one hour's preparation was necessary to start up the engine, which was a Bolinder engine, which had to be heated up by 6 blow-torches and started with compressed air and paraffin. After about 15 minutes the change-over to diesel…

I was only privileged, in my school holidays, to make these trips on about 2 occasions. I say this because it was an exhausting trip from start to finish, and I found that the hours on one's legs were very tiring. I look back now and really admire my father for his efforts, in all weather conditions, leaving our country residence, doing this to support us. At Waverton he would leave at 6 a.m. on Monday, with luck, to see him return around 8 o'clock the following Friday evening… My father lived for his boats, [they were] his life, and, of course, he drank a lot; and I recall the barges carried 40 tons capacity approximately.

Gordon Davies also remembered the three iron steam barges operated by Griffiths Bros, but not all their names. *If you stood on the Cow Lane Bridge, in Frodsham Street, Chester, you could see the corn mill on the right hand side. The two men that operated the 'Cambria' I have forgotten. They were quite senior, but the barge was steam operated and carried its cargo loose; you would see operating from the mill a conveyer belt with small cup type bins taking the cargo out via the conveyer belt.*

SUR&CCo narrowboats 'Brocklebank' and 'Cheops' in front of steam barge 'Dale', *early 1900s.*
Waterways Trust

It was my duty to assist my father on occasions, when the labour he employed let him down. Sometimes he would send me to get help, and I would go to various addresses in Chester in the hope of procuring someone. One man who lived in Lower Bridge Street, by the name of Josiah Thomas, he had a large family and lived in a house that had to be permanently lit by electric light.

We would proceed to Cow Lane Bridge; the 'Petrel' would be at its moorings near the Gaumont Cinema; it was then necessary to start the pump and pump up to get the air bottle up to at least 500 pounds per sq. in.; and ignite the 6 paraffin burners on top of the cylinders. This would take about one hour's preparation, during which time the engine would start - and the engine-room, I might add, was extremely hot.

208

The engine was a Bolinder engine from, I believe, The Wash... Being installed in the barge at Egg Bridge, this was quite an event, and I did see a number of people taking photographs, with a great roar and cheer when the engine started, after being fitted in the particular barge, which took, I believe, about 3 or 4 days. And the look of satisfaction on my father's face. This was the first step from the days of horse drawn barges, during which time my father did a number of trips. I can recall at the time my father saying his price for the conveyance of corn was round about 13s 6d per ton.

Returning to Cow Lane Bridge, Josiah Thomas and myself would proceed to Waverton, via the locks - one at Hoole Lane, and Tarvin Road and then on via Christleton. Sometimes we would have a clear run, and it took us from about 5 a.m. on Saturday to 3 p.m. to reach Egg Bridge, turn the barge around and set it in position ready to be off-loaded. If the water level was low, it was impossible to proceed, only at a drag. Owing to lack of water, it would be necessary to get to the next lock and open the by-pass gate to let water from the higher level into the lower level to proceed on - which, incidentally, would be extremely low, with the flat bottom of the barge just gliding along the base clay mud of the Canal. As I was not too strong at the time, the tiller, which was long and horizontal, with a round end, which to me was large and made of cold steel. It was necessary to stand and brace one's legs against the tiller, to achieve the leverage to control the steering of the barge. At the approach of the bridges, it was necessary to lower the funnel. The journey from Chester to Waverton was possibly the best part of my early experience, and providing the weather was reasonable, it was not too bad. I have reason to believe my father, having got the barge from Liverpool to Cow Lane Bridge, Chester, had by that time had enough, and was glad to retire to his draught Bass beer.

Gordon Davies' father only carried for the Cheshire Farmers Association, so *his life was somewhat governed by the supply and demand. Some weeks he would not get a trip, owing to the fact that the mill at Waverton had enough stock. In fact, I can recall, whilst living at Brown Heath, Waverton, my father bringing in a cargo of coal. A small Ford wagon with solid wheels which was used to convey bags of coal to the local community. He did this himself with the help of another man, especially in the winter periods. The canals were busy with narrow boats at the time, with families aboard. These were horse drawn in most cases. Others had motors towards 1934, with the name '[Fellows] Morton & Clayton', Birmingham, written on. My father did in fact tow the narrow boats on a number of occasions through ice conditions, which they were thankful for, and I might add were certainly glad to get to Waverton. After this, sometimes they would be tied up just beyond the mill at Waverton for quite some weeks before they could proceed on.*

'Ellesport' c1930
Built by Yarwoods and registered 17/2/1925 no.146401, powered by a 72hp Gardner diesel, the barge was sunk at Liverpool by enemy action in 1941.
Geoff Taylor Collection

Also, on a number of occasions my father's barge, 'Petrel' would be brought to a standstill owing to the bed mattresses that were thrown into the Canal. Sometimes, it would be a human being, sometimes it was a beast [animal] that had fallen into the Canal, and we had to go and help on many occasions, prop up with oil drums and fenders, the section of the Canal being drained out between locks. We would have to get into the Canal to get the mattress from around the propeller. The spring steel from the mattresses presented problems, as you may realise being wrapped around the propeller. The steel was hard and tough, taking around 2 to 3 hours. Sometimes it was a dead person or a beast which would have got tangled up with the propeller.

To change over from steam to paraffin… the diesel did present problems, and I do recall breakdowns which resulted in a complete engine overhaul, which would take a week, especially over big ends and white metal fatigue. Owing to long periods of running the engine, these big ends did present some problems… and quite obviously it caused my father a number of headaches, and did actually get him to such an extent that he was very upset - costing money which he could ill afford, trying my father's patience plus the cost involved.

This is almost certainly the reason why Joe Davies took out 'Stanley's' semi-diesel Bolinder engine, according to a Ken Macgregor, who worked on his motor barges for a time. She was horse drawn for the rest of her working life, which ended abruptly when she sank in the Dee while being used by the contractors laying the two syphons across the river in connection with the Bumpers Lane Sewage Disposal Works Scheme. The sunken barge 'Stanley' was raised, and disposed of for £6 in March 1934. The motor barge 'Petrel' was probably broken up some time after 1937.

Eleven years earlier, in October 1926 the dumb barge 'Jeanie' was sold to the Wolverhampton Corrugated Iron Co Ltd, owners of a large fleet of steam, diesel and towing barges. But their works was only half a mile up the Canal at Ellesmere Port, so they will not be considered in detail here. It is worth mentioning, however, that a Gardner 6L2 Engine purchased by this company is exhibited in the Power Hall at the Ellesmere Port Boat Museum. The engine was used in either the 'Ellesburn' or 'Ellespool', which were steam barges converted to diesel propulsion in 1935. Description:- 6 cylinder compression ignition (diesel) engine. 57hp. RPM:- 1000. Bore:- 4in (110mm) . Stroke:- 5in (146mm)

The museum also has a Bolinder engine on display in the Island Warehouse. And the former Fellows Morton & Clayton iron composite motor 'Shad' in the boat collection there, was originally driven by one of those legendary engines. The ex-FMC narrowboat steamer 'President' - the only remaining working narrowboat steamer of its kind - is preserved at the Black Country Museum in Birmingham. Some years ago this unique craft steamed into our 'ancient city', taking us back to the days when steam-driven boats and barges plied the old Chester Canal.

'President' in Chester, 1990s. Built and registered in 1909 but converted to diesel in 1925, the narrowboat was reconverted to steam in the 1970s by Nicholas Bostock and Malcolm Braine, and is now run from the Black Country Museum, Dudley. Photo: Gordon Emery

Rowing on the Whitchurch Branch
c1914

LEISURE Gordon Emery

Pleasure boats

The attraction and use of inland waterways for leisure slowly increased. Trip boats on the Llangollen Canal have run since at least 1884.

One intrepid sailor, Preston Witter, after having made a pile on cotton options, arranged, in 1903, to buy a 17 foot open-top river launch on the Thames and cruise it to the River Dee. He set off in 'The 'Option' at Twickenham and arrived, with the single cylinder petrol engined launch, in Chester 11 days later, having navigated the working waterways, carrying cigars for the boatmen and chocolate for their children to help him get through the locks. He, his wife, his sister and brother-in-law stayed at pubs and hotels on the journey but these were often hard to come by. The log records a night at Wightwick, near Birmingham: *Preston and Henry slept four in bed with a soldier and a flea.*

'The Option' 1903   Nigel Witter

75 years later the journey was repeated by his son who had the log and a brass lamp from the original voyage. He traced the boat to a junk yard in Wrexham and refitted her with a temperamental steam engine. A century after the first voyage, the journey was made again, this time by his great-grandson Nigel, who tried, wherever possible, to stay in the same hotels, now flealess.

Canals were often used for boat trips. A local resident, Florence Pickthall went to the Chester, Garden Lane Methodist Church Sunday School. In the First World War the annual seaside outing was impossible. Instead, the children went on a canal boat to Stanney where they were each given milk fresh from the cow and a bun. She remembers that two of the boys who 'scrumpied' some apples had to walk home, this was ironic because they lived in Orchard Street.

Cadburys' chocolate factories were situated on canals as they had to bring cocoa beans and sugar from the docks, milk from the countryside, coal from the coalfields to burn in their boilers, and engineering products from the Black Country. In 1917, this Quaker firm started to take the children of employees on boating trips for educational holidays, making trips to towns and cities, studying natural history and experiencing life on a working boat. Each year one of their narrowboats was used as a *camp school on a barge* and travelled a different route letting over 200 boys explore the waterways every summer. Leonard Ball, an employee at Bournville all his life, remembers that in 1947 he travelled to Nantwich and Chester.

In the mid-1930's the Whitchurch Warehousing Company modified the narrow boat 'Tangmere' and hired this out for holidays. The enterprise was relatively short-lived.

It was the vision of G F Wain of Waverton that led the way for inland waterway cruising in the mid-1930s. His company was Inland Cruising Association Ltd, based at Rowton Bridge. They commissioned a fleet of motor cruisers, between 1934 and 1937, designed for hire purposes that were described as: *comfortable and easily handled by the most inexperienced.* Their early fleet comprised nine boats: 'Barbara', 'Stanford', 'Beryl', 'Bobby', 'Freda', 'Betty', 'Audrey', 'Valerie' and 'Jazz'. Taylor's Boatyard constructed some of these early cruisers, whilst others were built in the Midlands and in Birkenhead. In the post-war period, ICA also constructed their own cruisers at their Waverton yard; eventually operating 25 boats at the time of their closure in 1974.

They also offered a 'Camping Craft': *well built of mahogany, dimensions 12ft x 5ft x 1ft draft offering a Fore well with comfortable seating for two persons, steering wheel, etc.* There was also an *After well for camping equipment.* This was powered by a Ford engine and was fitted with a reversing propeller. All this could be had for three guineas per week in the high season. Their brochure went on to say: *These cruises can be undertaken by the novice to motor boating as well as the expert, or by the family man with responsibility of youngsters in perfect safety - in fact, anyone to whom a happy, care-free holiday is the first consideration, with the added attraction of economy.* The 1930's hire charge for the larger boat (28ft x 6ft 10in) was £9 5s 0d per week.

LTC Rolt
It was, perhaps, LTC Rolt's book 'Narrow Boat', first published in 1944, pleading for *something that is a part of the soul of England,* as H J Massingham writes in his foreword, that brings to mind what many canal enthusiasts recognise as bringing awareness of the inland waterways to the general public.

Rolt was born in Chester but had moved south. In the late 1920s one of his relatives had acquired a disused horse-drawn Shropshire Union (later Peate's) fly boat called 'Cressy', converted to a cruiser at Frankton with a Ford Model T engine installed. Rolt, an engineer, travelled on its maiden voyage then bought the boat ten years later, had her hull repaired and decorated her in traditional style. He met a few of the Number Ones (owner/captains) and soon learnt from a boatman that, "If no one went no faster than what I do there'd be a sight less trouble in this world". Rolt felt that boatmen had a *natural intelligence not acquired from Council schools and newspapers* and remarked on the *inborn gypsy love of colour and polished metal* although he had perhaps not realised that most boatmen were not descended from gypsies. One of the interesting conversations he held with boatmen was about the extinct use of 'animals' - two donkeys to pull each boat, and was told of a legendary boatman who, when the animals were tired, would put them in the boat and haul it himself. (Author's note: this is not as difficult as it may seem, the author having bow-hauled a narrowboat 20 miles in a day by himself.)

He noted that the terms port and starboard were not used but that "Hold In" (towards the towpath) and "Hold Out" were used. Rolt found the cratches and stands supporting the gang planks on working boats were *picked out with bright geometrical patterns of colour* and described the traditional roses and castles paintings on the narrowboats, the painted dipper and 'Buckby' water cans decorated with flowers and bearing the owner's name. (Usually they carry the boat name.) He saw day boats being used - short distance square-bilged boats taken by the boatmen to a wharf where they left it and took another back. Day boats, open or joey boats had flat bows and sterns where the rudder could be fixed at either end to save winding (turning the boat around).

'Animals' Tony Lewery

Brochure Cover
David Wain OBE

Rolt cruised from Banbury to Middlewich then headed southwest on the Middlewich Branch and then east along the old Chester Canal to Nantwich. He would have gone to Llangollen, he says, but for the outbreak of war. He noted considerable traffic of Thomas Clayton horse-boats working between Birmingham and Ellesmere Port, and an occasional 'Josher' (named after Joshua Fellows who started Fellows, Morton & Clayton), as well as a few Cowburn or Cowper motor-boats travelling from Wolverhampton north via the Middlewich Branch. Then he headed south along the Birmingham & Liverpool Junction Canal, cut *straight as a Roman road* where *for the first and only time on our travels we found ourselves wishing that Cressy was capable of a little more speed.* He had found the joys of the older winding waterways which had taken the boredom out of boatmen's lives for 150 years and he acquired some of the boatman's philosophy *never so struck by the absurdity of expending such prodigality of power and effort, rush and nervous strain, for the sole sake of saving an hour or so of time which was seldom or never utilised to any creative purpose.*

Rolt's nostalgia was not always borne out by tales from working boatmen such as Edward Ward, recorded in Jean Stone's 'Voices from the Waterways' who often had to work from dawn to dusk and beyond to secure their next job, while 'lock-wheeling' to ensure the next lock was ready for them in order to save every vital ten minutes. "Every minute counted, you couldn't afford to waste time", he stated.

Rolt, with Robert Aickman, formed the Inland Waterways Association in 1946 to promote the waterways for both pleasure and commercial traffic. The Association has flourished and resulted in the restoration and repair of much of the canal system.

Post-war
In the immediate post-War period, Deans, a firm of builders from Waverton entered the hire boat business. Their first offerings were modified bridging pontoons. For canal use the deck was replaced with a box cabin suitably partitioned for an Elsan toilet. Being flat bottomed they ideal for canal cruising. Inland Cruising Association also used some of these converted pontoons. Deans expanded their fleet with clinker-built hulls constructed by Taylor's. They fitted the cabins themselves. R Wyatt opened a hire business at Stone in 1948. The Association of Pleasure Craft Operators was founded in 1953.

British Transport Waterways had a stand at the Boat Show in 1955 and commissioned their first hire cruiser in 1956 at Chester, while publishing their first cruising booklets. They replaced the difficult toll system at locks with an easier annual licence in 1957.

In the 1960s two more Taylor boats were put out for hire. This time by Roger Brown at Christleton Bridge. These were the 'Merlin' and the 'Jenny Wren'.

During the 70s and 80s Jim Marshall, then later Rick Turnock and Di Parker, ran horsedrawn narrowboat cruises from Tower Wharf with their horses, George, Louise, Johnny and Snowy. Not only did these attract thousands of visitors to the area, but they were also frequented by local schools. The tale of one such trip was fictionalised by the prize-winning children's author Berlie Docherty, and, entitled 'Snowy', ended up on the school curriculum.

Today, there is a wide variety of boats of all shapes and sizes using the canal system, from dinghies to canoes, from converted traditional narrowboats to new steel ones built for hire cruising or private owners, and from hotel boats to cruising restaurants, such as that at the Mill Hotel in Chester.

Snowy hauling narrowboat 'Betelgeuse'
c1985
Ric Turnock & Di Parker

NOTABLE PLANTS Roger Stephens

The canal system is an important wildlife corridor with a wealth of habitat for wildflowers, birds, insects and animals. Even under the city walls, moorhens and mallards nest in spring, while swans and their young regularly crop the grass from the edge of the towpath.

The canal also supports many water plants. A survey of 1875-77 found a number of interesting plants in Chester:

Ranunculus peltatus*   Pond water-crowfoot   near baths
                                            (now demolished by Water Tower)
Plantago media   Hoary plantain   basin
Ceratophyllum demersum*   Rigid Hornwort   basin
Acorus calamus*   Sweet-flag   basin
Sagittaria sagittifolia   Arrowhead   basin
Iris pseudacorus   Yellow flag   stone bridge
                                            (Cheyney Road bridge)

**Rigid
Hornwort**

Yellow Flag

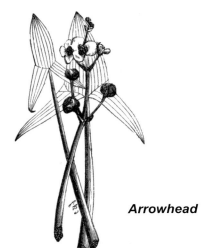

Arrowhead

219

In 1988, the late Norman Povey surveyed the canal and basin and failed to find the species marked * overleaf. However, he found several new plants:

Ceterach officinarum	Rustyback
Asplenium trichomanes	Maidenhair spleenwort
Onobrychis viciifolia	Sainfoin
Impatiens capensis	Orange balsam
Butomus umbellatus	Flowering-rush
Pentaglottis sempervirens	Green alkanet

Other notable plants include *Impatiens glandulifera* Indian balsam, which has spread along the banks of many English waterways and can be found growing under the city walls; the enormous leaves of *Rumex hydrolapathum* Water dock; and the nettle lookalike *Lycopus europaeus* Gipsywort, whose leaves if rubbed on the skin can create a false tan (supposed to make the skin look like that of a swarthy gipsy). Maidenhair spleenwort (listed above) is found in the crevices of walls where you can also find the tiny lilac-flowered *Cymbalaria muralis* Ivy-leaved toadflax.

Sweet-flag

Gipsywort

220

GUIDE TO EXPLORING THE CHESTER CANAL   Ray Buss
FROM THE DEE TO NANTWICH
A guide to one of the oldest canals in the country

This guide is written primarily for walkers, but can also be used by boaters (who should start near the dry dock in the canal basin, page 232) and cyclists. It covers the whole 19.4 miles of the Chester Canal, split up into shorter sections:

1. Chester to Christleton
    a. The Cross to Hoole Lane (which overlaps slightly with the next section) - 2.5 miles
    b. Cow Lane Bridge, Frodsham Street, to Christleton - 2 miles

2. Christleton to Tiverton (Beeston Iron Lock) - 9 miles
3. Tiverton to Nantwich - 8 miles

The first section is within the City of Chester and, although not very long, covers some of the most historic and interesting sections of the canal, where there is a lot to see. The second is largely in the countryside and covers a flat portion of the canal, where there are not as many points of interest, although it is still a very pleasant walk, especially on a bright day. The last part is again through countryside, but here there is more to see, with another 5 locks and some pretty scenery as the canal wanders alongside the River Gowy and then on to its final destination at Nantwich.

Accessibility ♿
Since the towpath alongside the canal is flat and there are slopes giving relatively easy access to the canal at many of the bridges, especially those close to Chester, much of this walk is likely to be suitable for wheelchair users, pushchairs and those with impaired mobility. Where there are steps on the main route of the walk, alternatives are suggested if available. However, there are some areas where access may be more difficult, such as on the steep slope alongside the Northgate Locks and over the 'roving bridge' at Tower Wharf.

From Chester to Christleton the surface of the towpath is hard, mostly of asphalt. Elsewhere, the surface varies from asphalt, through cobbles to mud, depending on the section concerned. Under some of the bridges, the surface is of raised bricks (originally to ensure a good foothold for the towing horses) and these may cause some difficulties, as may the cobbled sections (recently added as a feature and to slow down cyclists).

Starting Points *(maps on pages 223 and 239)*

Section 1(a) - Chester – The Cross, at the crossroads of Bridge Street, Eastgate Street, Northgate Street and Watergate Street *page 224*

Section 1(b) - Cow Lane Bridge, Chester, by the Gorse Stacks Car Park at the top of Frodsham Street *page 242*.

Section 2 – Christleton, behind The Trooper public house on the A41 *page 252*

Section 3 – Tiverton, on the A49 near The Lock Café and Beeston Market *page 264*

How to get there
Chester is well served by public transport and all the other starting and finishing points are accessible by bus; check with the operators for times before travelling.

Those travelling by car to Chester could make good use of the Park and Ride facility on the A41 at Christleton. This car park is just over the main road from the Chester Canal, which passes to the rear of the Trooper public house. So catch the bus into the city and walk back.

The guide ends close to Nantwich Canal Centre, Chester Road, Nantwich, where there is a car park. Buses pass regularly along this road running between Nantwich and Chester; check with the operators for times before travelling.

WALK 1a STARTS HERE

Chester – The Cross
At first sight, it may seem strange to start this walk some way from the canal, but to appreciate its history you really need to have an idea of what Chester was like in the middle of the 18th century. At that time, all that remained of the Cross itself was a square base, the rest of it left buried under the steps of the Church after being knocked down by Parliamentarians in the Civil War. Standing at the Cross were sedan chairs - the taxis of the city - used by Georgian ladies to avoid the mud and muck on the city streets. While waiting for a fare, the men who carried the chairs chatted and whittled vent pegs for beer barrels from bundles of sticks, strewing the footpath with their debris. In 1800, a chair could be hired *To or from the Ellesmere Canal Wharf, from or to any part of the City, for 1s 6d.*

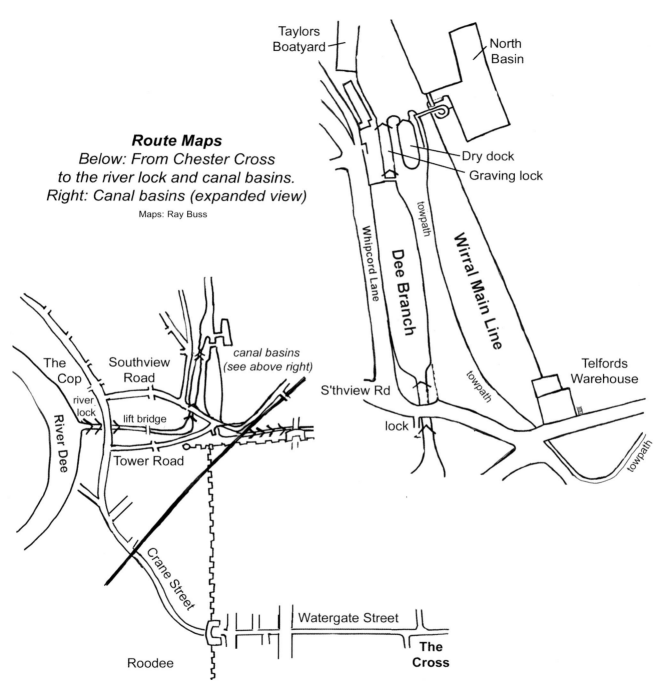

Route Maps
*Below: From Chester Cross
to the river lock and canal basins.
Right: Canal basins (expanded view)*

Maps: Ray Buss

Taylors Boatyard

North Basin

Dry dock

Graving lock

Whipcord Lane

towpath

Dee Branch

Wirral Main Line

towpath

Telfords Warehouse

towpath

canal basins (see above right)

The Cop

Southview Road

S'thview Rd

lock

river lock

lift bridge

River Dee

Tower Road

Crane Street

Roodee

Watergate Street

The Cross

Looking towards the Cross in Georgian times; street markets were common. Old engraving

If you were standing by The Cross at that time, you would have been at the heart of a city that was by far the largest and most important industrial centre for miles around. At least fifty different manufacturing trades operated here, and the city was also the main trading and leisure centre for Cheshire and North Wales. So transport links were critical to the success of the city, one of the most important of these being the Port of Chester, which stretched along the River Dee and its estuary for some 12 miles.

With the increased competition for shipping from Liverpool towards the end of the 18th century and the advent of canals elsewhere in England linking other key industrial centres, such as the Potteries, demand rose for a canal linking Chester to other English towns. With the Trent & Mersey Canal being cut through Middlewich, it was suggested that a canal link the two. The city's leaders met to discuss these proposals and those meetings were attended not only by local dignitaries, but also by distinguished advisers such as James Brindley, who had built the

Bridgewater Canal only a few years before. They were held in the Pentice, which was a lean-to town hall constructed against the south wall of St Peter's Church at the Cross (see illustration, page 13). The Pentice was demolished in 1803.

As the early chapters of this book describe, the process of turning this demand for a canal into reality was far from simple and there were many problems along the way. The canal today is not as envisaged by the first designers or engineers, but is the product of a whole series of events and changes over more than 100 years, eventually linking with other English and Welsh canals. This walk will pick up some aspects of these various changes along the way; for the full story, readers will need to refer to the rest of the book.

Walk down Watergate Street on the left hand side. What are now shops at ground level along this street were once vaults, cellars and warehouses, holding imported goods from foreign lands as well as cheeses and other commodities from Cheshire awaiting export. On the first floor row above, there were shops as well as the houses of the Georgian gentry. There was also an Assembly Room where the rich would have meetings and balls, especially in the winter season. By the end of the 18th century, new larger assembly rooms were built on Bridgegate and Eastgate streets.

Just on the right before the crossroads with the main road stand the Guildhall (formerly Trinity Church) and the Old Custom House Building. The church's earlier spire was used by sailors to navigate the Dee Estuary with its treacherous moving sands, before the river was canalised in the early 18th century. The Chester Guilds, formed in medieval times, included all the tradesmen, craftsmen and merchants of the city - from their ranks the aldermen and councillors were chosen - who, in turn, elected the mayor and officials. The Guilds also tried, and failed, to build a new port (the New Haven) on the Wirral shore of the Dee, but this soon silted up.

Cross Nicholas Street – now the Inner Ring Road. Rich Georgian houses once stretched along both sides of this road but the eastern side was demolished for road widening in the 1960s. Fortunately, the houses on the west side are now listed buildings.

Passing the Tudor 'Stanley Palace', you eventually reach the Watergate. The original gate here was demolished in 1778 and

Old Custom House Building
Gordon Emery

the new arch designed by J Turner, who was one of the canal shareholders and also built the 'Bridge of Sighs' which is seen later.

Chester Electric Lighting Station
Gordon Emery

Continue down Crane Street past the Racecourse (the Roodee) and under the railway bridge. Among the many merchants having yards along Crane Street were John Chamberlaine, one of the main sponsors of the Chester Canal, and Samuel Weston, one of its first surveyors. Weston once lived in the Georgian 'Paradise Row' on the site of the present 'Express' Hotel. To your right is the frontage of the Victorian 'Chester Electric Lighting Station' now converted to apartments but once Chester's electric supply which, in 1913, was supplemented by an innovative hydro-electric station on the Dee.

Beyond the traffic lights, on your left, are the older buildings of Crane Wharf, stretching down to the river. Follow the cobbled track to the riverside and turn right. Continue along the riverside until you reach the imitation lift bridge, then turn right up the slope back to the main road. Turn left and stop for a moment on the bridge over the canal lock. When the Chester Canal was first built, it entered straight onto the river a little further downstream, just opposite where Southview Road is today. There was no lock and so the first section of the canal was a tidal basin. About 25 years later, it was decided to build a lock here to protect the basin from the tides, so the old channel onto the river was filled in.

Originally, the main road crossed the canal lock to the tidal River Dee over a 'swing bridge'. This had to be removed when the road was upgraded in the 1960s and an extension to the lock was constructed to enable boats to get under the road. When using the lock, timing is crucial since if the tide is too high the boats will get caught under the bridge, with disastrous results. If the tide is too low, any boats going out on to the River Dee and going upstream will not be able to pass over the weir that runs between Chester and Handbridge. This unique single lock with two sets of gates at one end stretches to 140 feet, twice the length of a normal canal lock. It is a 'broad' lock, as are all the locks on the Chester Canal, which was designed to take wide-beamed barges, sometimes known as 'flats', with a beam of 14 feet.

Old Chester Quay. *Note the shipbuilding in the distance.*

Although still dependent on the tides, the lock was once well used and a lock-keeper was employed to look after it. There was a lock-keeper's cabin alongside it but one of the last lock-keepers, George Evans, drowned here tragically one evening in 1920 while chasing one of the rats he thought was invading the cabin. Nowadays, the lock is used only occasionally, and passage has to be booked with British Waterways in advance, so the chances of your spotting a boat here are slim. Beside the lock, there used to be a boatbuilding yard, one of many in the area, operated by William Roberts, a pioneer builder of launches for use on the River Dee.

Carry on and go left into The Cop, a small park alongside the river. Walk along the path up the bank to look out over the River Dee again. Although the River Dee was a major route to the Irish Sea for many centuries, flooding and shifting sandbanks were always a problem for the boatmen and their passengers. There was a major flood in the first half of the 18th century and this led to the construction of a defensive bank, known as 'The Cop', which you are now standing on. The River Dee itself was canalised from Queensferry to here in 1737 in an attempt to attract more ships to the city by preventing the river from shifting its course.

At the far end of The Cop, there is a stone wharf, which is all that remains today of the old Cheese Warehouse that used to occupy this site. As the River Dee bends left towards the sea here, it is joined by a small stream, Finchett's Gutter, also known as Bache Brook, which runs down from Hoole. Above the inlet pipe are some granite blocks, marked to show the datum

A narrowboat entering the river lock from the Dee
Photo: Tuesday Night Club

line for the River Dee dated 1853.

Go back to the road, cross it using the pedestrian crossing, then return to the bridge over the canal. Turn left down the slope alongside the canal. From here, you can get another good view of the lock and its unusual combination of gates. Just beyond the end of the lock is a 'lift bridge': a modern addition built as part of the new housing development. This is the only 'lift bridge' on the Chester Canal, although there are plenty to be found on other parts of the Shropshire Union, such as the Llangollen Canal. On the other side of the canal is 'The Boat' a building whose architecture evokes the boatbuilding history of the area. This was built for the Scouts when their old hut was demolished.

Behind it, you can see the top of the Water Tower, built in 1322 to guard against attacks on the city from the river, which lapped against the walls here. Later, the tower was used to monitor shipping in and out of Chester.

On 4th May 1772, the quarry near the Water Tower was the site for the sod cutting ceremony that marked the start of the Chester Canal. There were great celebrations that day, with bands playing and flags flying as the Mayor and a grand procession marched to here from the Pentice (see Celebrations, page 32).

This was not surprising since the process of getting authority from Parliament to build the canal had been far from straightforward. There was opposition from the owners of the Trent & Mersey Canal, who did not want competitors to take their business. In the end, the subscribers to the Chester Canal had to agree a compromise that would not allow them to link with the Trent & Mersey at Middlewich (see 1772 Act, page 26).

Walk alongside the canal to the 'lift bridge'. Where you are standing, there was once a large basin, extending almost to the edge of what is now Southview Road, the road to your left. It was surrounded by a variety of warehouses and other industrial buildings, including a boatyard, all of which have now disappeared. Gradually, the basin became filled up through a natural process of silting, aided by a variety of other factors, such as laid up

The new 'lift bridge', 'The Boat' and the Water Tower
Photo: Ray Buss.

boats. Archaeological excavations of this area prior to its redevelopment in 1996 uncovered the remains of 'Earl', a flat built at Frodsham in 1802 for use on the Ellesmere and Chester Canal, one of over 30 boats buried here. It is believed that the basin was also used as a dumping ground for stone from the demolition of the old Market Hall on Northgate Street.

Flats in the Dee or Lower Basin, 1935   West Yorkshire Archive Service, Wakefield ref. c299

229

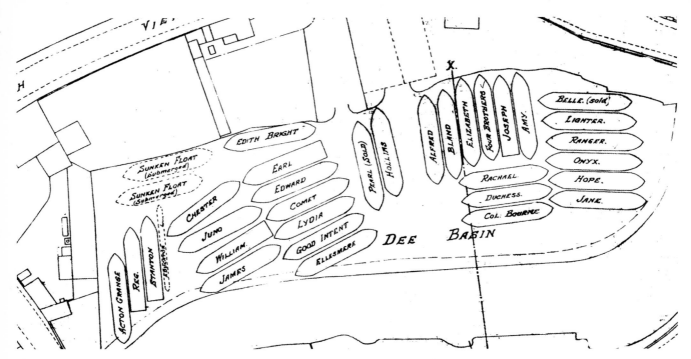

Plan of Sunken and laid up boats in the Dee or Lower Basin, 1952 Boat Museum Trust

The neat row of old houses on the far side of Tower Road beyond 'The Boat' was the first block of Council Houses built in Chester. As the foundation stone at the eastern corner of the row states, they were constructed in 1904 in accordance with the Housing of the Working Classes Act.

Carry on alongside the canal to where the canal bends left. When the canal was first built in 1774, it connected with the River Dee a little further downstream with a tidal section, including a basin, leading to 5 locks going up in a staircase to just below the City Walls. The present link to the river is later and was built in 1795 when the Chester Canal joined up with the Wirral Line of the Ellesmere Canal. Two of the locks in the staircase were taken out and replaced by two new locks on the Dee Branch of the canal, separate from the main line. The first of these locks, Bridge Lock, is just under the bridge to your left and leads into a small section of the canal known as Williams Moorings, where a number of private boats are kept.

On the far bank of the bend, there was one of the many sets of stables in the area. Little remains of those buildings today, except for a few bricks.

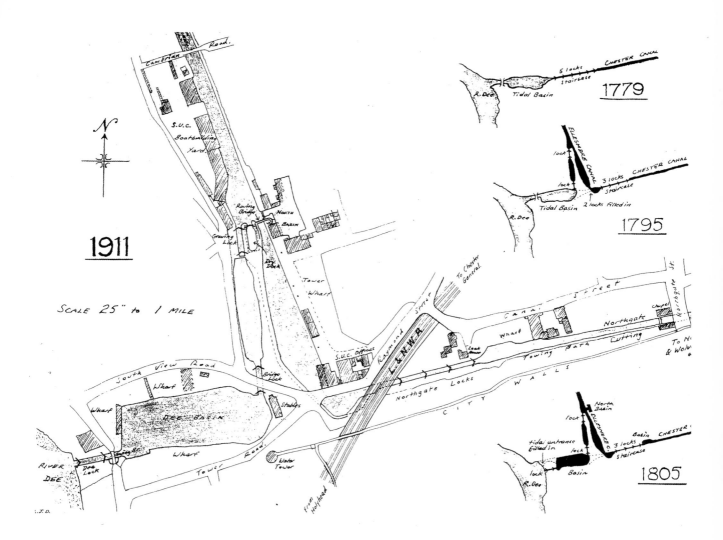

Basin changes before the Dee or Lower Basin was filled in   Map by Roger Dean

Go up the steps. Cross Southview Road into Whipcord Lane and walk along the footpath next to the canal railings. *[Those with wheelchairs, pushchairs or bikes should retrace their steps to the lift bridge, turn right and go towards the fish and chip shop. Turn right onto Southview Road and walk up it past the junction with Whipcord Lane to the end of Tower Road. Cross Tower Road here and go down the sloping track opposite. Turn left at the bottom onto the canal towpath and carry on under the bridge towards the Dry Dock - omit the next two walk directions.]*

The flat 'Willow' on the River Dee Branch of the Wirral Line
Geoff Taylor Collection

From here, you get your first view of the Wirral Line of the canal, which is at a higher level than the Dee Branch, and also of the boats in Williams Moorings. Currently, these are all narrowboats, which have a beam of just under 7 feet so that they can use the narrow locks found on much of the canal system.

At the end of the railings is a high brick wall. About 20 feet past the advertising hoarding go right through the opening in the wall and up the steps to the area alongside the next lock. This lock is the Graving Lock, since it could be used to 'grave' boats; i.e. take them out of the water to clean the bottoms. This would have involved the insertion of wooden planks in the slots in the sides of the lock, and these are still kept in a brick structure up against the wall on to the road. As the lock was drained, the boat would have come to rest on the planks and work could be done on the hull. This could not have been for major jobs, since it would have obstructed the passage of other boats, so perhaps it was only used for short jobs lasting no more than a day or so. Longer jobs would have been done in the Dry Dock alongside. The Graving Lock used to be covered by a sliding shed, to protect the workmen. The holes for the tracks on which this shed ran are still clearly visible either side of the lock.

The white painted building to the north of the lock is generally known as the stable block, but this was probably not its prime function, which was more likely to have been workshops and offices for the boatyard nearby. In the 1970s and 80s, it did have a use as stables since it was

Boat passing along the Dee Branch of the Wirral Line. *Note the graving lock sliding roof in the distance.*
Geoff Taylor Collection

the base for a horse-drawn trip boat that used to work in the area. [See Leisure.] In the corner at the south of the lock is a small brick building which is the sanitary station for boaters who need to empty their toilets, since the discharge of sewage direct into the canal has been banned for many years.

Cross over the bridge at the bottom of the lock to the buildings alongside and stop at railings in front of the steps down into the Dry Dock. Alongside the lock is the Dry Dock, which is still quite often used today, especially for the essential task of 'blacking' the bottoms of boats. It was built to take flats, and still takes the wide river launches each winter but is normally occupied by just a couple of narrowboats at a time. Its location is ideal in that it can be easily filled from the top level and emptied into the bottom pound rather than having to resort to the use of pumps. Originally, this whole area, including the extensive boatyards

233

behind the Dry Dock was a major centre for boatbuilding and boat repairs, especially of wooden boats. [See Boatbuilding, page 83)]

Continue on past the end of the Dry Dock and turn left up the slope onto the 'roving bridge' over the canal and stop. This is one of many bridges over the canal: most carry roads, railways or footpaths, but here the towpath changes from the west side to the east side of the canal, and this 'roving bridge', allowed the horses to cross over to the other side without being unhitched from the boats they were pulling. On the outside wall of the spiral exit to the bridge is a commemorative plaque to L T C Rolt, a famous author and one of the founders of the Inland Waterways Association. [See Leisure, page 212]

Working boats 1880   Geoff Taylor Collection

Stand on the bridge and look north. At this point, you are actually on the Wirral Line of the Ellesmere Canal, not the original Chester Canal. From here this line of the canal goes north towards the Mersey and the Manchester Ship Canal, which it joins at Ellesmere Port. The range of buildings on the left is Taylor's Boatyard. This complex of boatbuilding and maintaining facilities, including the Dry Dock and Graving Lock were originally built for the Shropshire Union Railways and Canal Company, which not only owned the canal but also operated a fleet of boats carrying cargoes up and down the system. Quite suddenly, in 1921, the company decided to pull out of carrying and boatbuilding and therefore had no need of the boatyard here. Half of it was taken over by J H Taylor, who had previously had one of the yards on the Dee Basin. [See Boatbuilding]

On the right hand side of the canal is the newly restored North Basin, which was re-opened in 2000. In its heyday, it would have been surrounded by warehouses and was a major transhipment point for cargoes travelling up and down the canal to Ellesmere Port. The towpath crosses the entrance to the North Basin here over a swing bridge, which needs to be turned through 90° to allow boats in and out.

Retrace your path back over the bridge to the Dry Dock and carry on along the towpath in front of you. Here the canal becomes very wide to cope with the many boats that would gather here waiting to be loaded and unloaded. This scene is repeated as the historic boats gather here each Easter on their way to a boat gathering at the Boat Museum, Ellesmere Port.

Historic boats 2003   Photo: Ray Buss

Ahead of you on the other side of the canal, just in front of the bridge, stand a number of old buildings, none of which were here when the Chester Canal was first built. They date from some 20 years later, when the link was made with the Wirral Line of the Ellesmere Canal and a healthy trade developed from the River Mersey at Ellesmere Port to Chester and beyond.

Projecting out over the canal is a warehouse designed to allow boats to be loaded or unloaded under cover. It was built in the 1790s by the canal company's engineer of the time, Thomas Telford, and is now a popular pub and restaurant called, not surprisingly, Telford's Warehouse!

The L-shaped building beyond the pub, now known as Raymond House, housed both the offices of the Ellesmere and Chester Canal Company and the 'Ellesmere Canal Tavern' or 'Canal Packet House', which served passengers waiting to use the Chester to Liverpool Packet Boats. These boats operated very successfully between Chester and Ellesmere Port,

Crane inside 'Telford's Warehouse'
Photo: Mike Penney

where passengers transferred to a ferry across the Mersey to Liverpool. The heyday of these boats was the early 19th century and they were so popular that the landlord of the hotel had to take a second establishment, the 'Coach and Horses' on Northgate Street. By the 1850s, railways had taken all the business away and the buildings here became the head offices of the Shropshire Union Railways and Canal Company (see page 72), formed in 1845 by the amalgamation of several canal companies.

Carry on along the towpath and under the road bridge, stopping just as you get to the other side. Low on the wall beside the towpath is a steel ring with a hook on it. In the era of horse-drawn boats this would have been used to guide the towropes and adjust the pulling angle so that boats coming out of the locks could turn more easily under the bridge.

Just the other side of this wall, in the small parkland area adjacent to the city walls, used to be Chester's first Public Baths, opened in 1849, with both a swimming pool and washing facilities for people and clothes.

Carry on round the bend of the canal and under the large railway bridge. Here the main railway line to North Wales crosses the canal. It was originally built to carry four tracks for this busy route to Holyhead and the ferry to Ireland. Although canals were the main transport system at the start of the 19th century, by the time this bridge was built in 1846, they were beginning to be superseded by railways. Canals, railways and roads often run alongside each other, since they all tend to follow the contours in the land.

The railway bridge has obliterated nearly all signs of the bottom two locks of the original 5-lock staircase that was built to bring the canal down from just under the city walls to the level of the River

Ring and hook
Gordon Emery

Dee, although there is a hint of the beginnings of the edge of a lock chamber in the sloping stone edge that can be seen just past the bridge on the opposite side of the canal.

Walk on under the bridge and up to the staircase of three Northgate Locks. Originally called the Water Tower Locks and carved out of solid rock, these impressive locks lift the canal up 33 feet from the basin below to the main line of the canal. They are a testimony to the engineering skills of the original team that built them well over 200 years ago. At the turn of the 19th century they would have been a hive of activity, with many working boats coming and going. Even today, in the busy summer months, you will often see pleasure boats going up or down, sometimes on their own and sometimes in pairs. You might even see boats passing in the middle as one goes up and another comes down! Working these locks may have been straightforward to the old boating families, but they can pose quite a challenge to the novice hire-boater and British Waterways have

Northgate Locks (originally named Water Tower Lock)
Waterways Trust

installed notices at the top and bottom to explain how it should be done! On one side of the top lock is the Lock Cottage, which is built in a style typical of Thomas Telford, and on the other side is a stone plaque commemorating the start of the Chester Canal in 1772. The plaque depicts the seal of the Chester Canal Company, which has Beeston Castle in the middle with the skyline of Chester on the horizon and a canal on the right hand side running between them.

Just beyond the top of the locks, on the opposite side to the towpath, there used to be a wharf and a turning point for boats, while near the locks there was a cotton factory, possibly linked to a rope works. One of the rope makers was John Pemberton, a mayor of Chester, who wanted to watch his men working on the rope walk and had the semi-circular tower, Pemberton's Parlour, built into the city walls here for that purpose. Further along the walls is a rectangular tower, Morgan's Mount, named after Captain Morgan who had a gun emplacement here in the Civil War.

Just beyond the top lock is a steel plate in the towpath. This covers a set of horse steps, once used if the horse fell in, but now inoperable due to the side strut of the covering plate.

Looking down at the Lower Basin in the mid-19th century, before the railway was built.
Note the baths (left) and the lean-to boat-shed against the road wall opposite Telford's Warehouse.

Narrowboat 'Swan' and a steamer in the Lower Basin 1916.

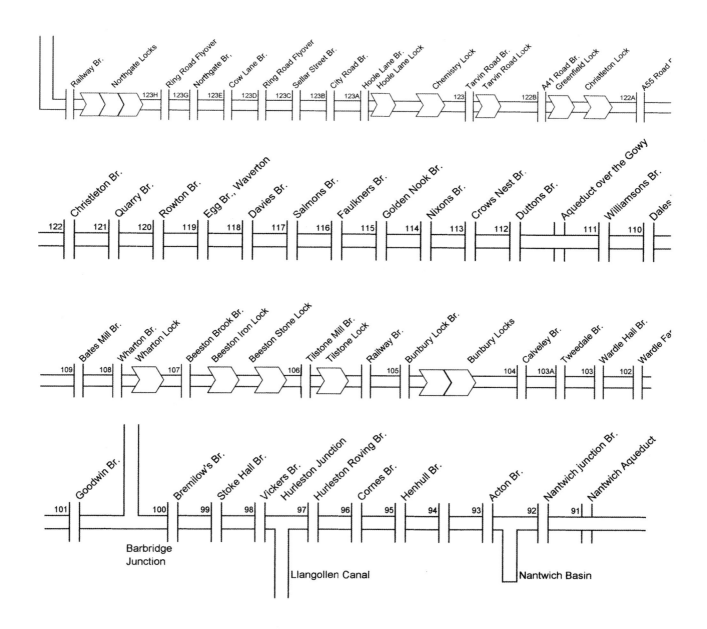

Strip maps showing the Chester Canal
From the Wirral Line junction in Chester (top left) to Nantwich Basin (bottom right).
Map: Ray Buss

Walk up to the top of the locks and look along the canal. From here, there is a dramatic view along the massive rock cutting that takes the canal under the City Walls. The original plan for the construction of the Chester Canal envisaged that this section would have to be a tunnel but, when the work here started, the remains of an old ditch, possibly of Roman origin, were found. This made the excavation worker easier and a cutting was made instead, although it was still necessary to cut out large sections of the bedrock here. This rock is typical of the sandstone in the area, being largely Chester Pebble Beds. It is a designated RIGS (Regionally Important Geological/Geomorphological Sites) important for the cross bedding of sandstone showing dunes structures, which prove Chester was once much nearer the equator.

Cupola belltower
Gordon Emery

High up on the left hand bank above the canal can be seen the roof and green copper cupola of the old Blue Coat School. There are two bridges crossing the canal here, the large one carrying Northgate Street into the City. The present Northgate dates from 1810, but the old one used to house the City Gaol (see page 44). The small bridge was specially built in 1793 so that the prisoners could access the chapel in the Bluecoat Hospital. It became known as 'The Bridge of Sighs' since it is said that condemned prisoners from the Gaol crossed it to receive the last rites in the chapel before being executed. This slender stone structure can still be seen just to the west of the large bridge although it has lost its high railings that were necessary to prevent prisoners leaping off in a bid to escape death.

Go under the Northgate Street bridge. Above you is one of the best sections of Roman Roman fortress wall surviving in Britain, now bulging outwards.

Rope marks
Photo: Ray Buss

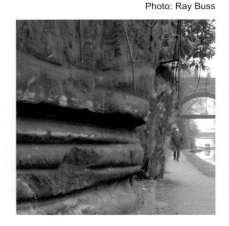

Walk to the bend in the canal before the large round tower in the city walls. As you walk along this section, you may catch sight of some steel rings in the rock. Given their position and height, these were clearly not used for the mooring of boats. The exact use is not known, but the most probable explanation is that they were used for the tethering of horses. It is known from the records that large numbers of boats used to gather in this area waiting to discharge or take on cargo and so there must have been quite a large transient community under the walls in the heyday of the canal in the mid-19th century.

Also along this section, you can see lines of holes in the rock face, 'pudlocks,' which were to take the wooden joists, 'put-ups', used to support a platform for the men working on quarrying the stone or perhaps for the roof of small lean-to structures. There is more evidence of the horse-drawn canal traffic along here, with marks from the towing ropes cut into the rock on the bend in the canal.

Stop below the large round tower. Originally known as the Phoenix Tower or Newton Tower, this is now known as King Charles' Tower because, from here, King Charles I watched his troops fighting in the suburbs after their defeat at the Battle of Rowton Moor. On the opposite bank of the canal, just to the left of the row of small houses, is part of the stone wall of what used to be a large basin for boats.

To this day, visitors to Chester walk around the city walls. In 1872, Henry James, the American writer looked down and saw "burly watermen in smocks and breeches".

The presence of the canal encouraged the development of a number of industries alongside it from here to the outskirts of Chester. On the opposite bank, where a small development of retirement flats now stands, there used to be a steam saw mill. Also in this area was one of the major boat building yards for the Chester Canal, known as King's Quay.

Walk on to the bend in the canal. Here was a small arm of the canal running off the main channel into a large shed (see map overleaf). A bridge carried the towpath over the arm and, although the arm itself has long since been filled in, part of the brick wall for the bridge can still be seen on the bank leading up from the towpath. The large brick building close to the wall is of more recent construction.

Carry on past the modern brick building and walk under Cow Lane Bridge. Although the present bridge is modern, one was built when the canal first opened since it linked the city to an important area known as Gorse Stacks - where gorse was stacked before being burnt as firewood by the city bakers.

WALK 1a ENDS HERE. *To return to the Cross, turn right up the pub slope and go along Frodsham Street then right along Foregate Street and Eastgate Street.*

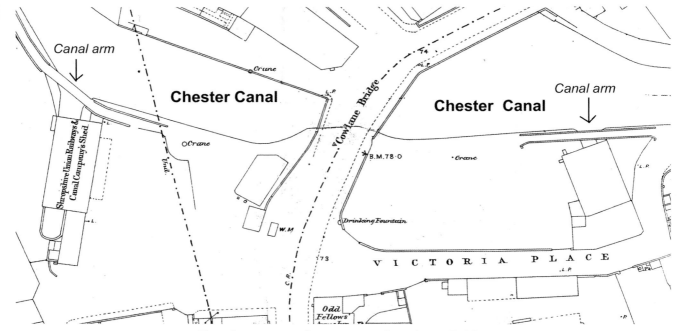

Two former canal arms near Cow Lane Bridge

WALK 1b STARTS HERE

Cow Lane Bridge is aptly named, for the cattle market was just over the canal and livestock was frequently driven across it, sometimes escaping into nearby shops! The cattle market had previously been on Northgate Street but was moved here early in the 19th century following complaints from residents about the smell and noise.

The original Chester Canal Company's yard was here. As well as being used for cargo, it was from here, in 1775, that passenger boats began operating to Beeston and, when the canal was extended in 1779, onwards to Nantwich Basin. There was a regular timetable and variable fares were charged depending on the distance travelled: the trip from Chester to Beeston costing 6d (see Passenger Carrying, page 105).

Just beyond the bridge, there was a timber yard on the site of what is now a public house; the yard used to receive timber from Sweden shipped in from Ellesmere Port down the Wirral Line of the canal. A little further along on this side of the canal, there was another small arm of the canal running off the main channel into a wharf, with a bridge carrying the towpath over the arm.

Narrowboat 'Sandbach' at Cow Lane Wharf Grosvenor Museum

On the opposite side of the canal, there were further timber yards and tile and brick yards - one of them just by the winding hole where, coincidentally, there is currently a retail shop selling tiles! Milton Street, the road just beyond this was once called 'Botany Bay'; some say that this was because it was the haunt of criminals and other less desirable characters! The large building which currently occupies most of the site here is now a Bingo Hall, but was built as a very grand cinema, the Gaumont Palace, with a mock-Tudor façade onto Brook Street and a fine dining room.

Other industries along this section of canal included two chemical works and a steam saw mill, so there would no doubt have been many boaters and, in the area. All of these required sustenance and a number of public houses were built in this area. One of these was the Grosvenor Arms, now converted into a private house on the end of Queen Street and painted pale green. Another was the Crown Vaults opposite what is now the Mill Hotel. By contrast, the

A view from Cow Lane Bridge, early 20th century Grosvenor Museum
Note the bridge over the former canal arm.

local churches did what they could to serve the boaters' spiritual needs and there was, at one time, a floating Bethel Chapel on the canal here (see Living aboard, page 246 & Welfare and Worship, page 167).

Alongside the canal here there are wooden posts, which, although modern, have a gnarled look about them. This is in keeping with what would have originally been here, since the records show that the first posts were reused timbers from an old iceboat.

Walk along the towpath and under the concrete fly-over that carries the inner ring-road.
Wherever they were built, canals encouraged the development of industry and Chester was no exception. From here to the outskirts of the city there grew up a range of mills, factories

and warehouses, all of which relied to some degree on the canal for their business. They stretched all along the canal, one of the largest being Griffiths Mill, which stood on the right of the canal where the modern flats are now, just before the flyover.

A little further on is the Mill Hotel. Originally, there was a Roman cement mill on this site. Much later, Wiseman's Cestrian Corn Mill, was built here in 1830, utilising 32 iron stanchions to hold up its five floors. It was subsequently taken over by Griffiths Mill as a warehouse, when the fortunes of Wiseman & Co declined. After Griffiths also closed, the building had various

Griffiths Mill (now demolished)
Grosvenor Museum

uses, including as a furniture warehouse, before it was converted to a hotel, which first opened in 1987 and has been extended twice, first to the east and then over the canal, with its own private footbridge. The canal is seen as a positive feature by the hotel owners, who are supporters of the Chester Canal Heritage Trust, and operate a restaurant boat, 'L'Eau-T Cuisine', from here both lunchtime and evenings. This is a wide-beamed boat reminiscent of the flats that would have operated on these waters in days gone by, but this one carries the very latest technology, including a hydraulic drive system that allows the boat to be driven from both ends, thereby removing the need for it to turn round at the end of its journeys up and down the cut!

The Mill Hotel. Formerly Wiseman's Cestrian Corn Mill, then Griffiths Mill warehouse. Photo: Ray Buss

Rope marks on Union Bridge
Photo: Ray Buss

Walk under Union Bridge.

This bridge was not one of the original bridges since, at that time, there was no need for a link across the canal here. But as industry developed in this area, the need for a bridge grew and this one was built around 1820 to link Egerton Street with Sellar Street. If you look carefully at the corners of the supporting columns of the bridge, the marks of towropes can still clearly be seen. The bridge also still has its cobbled towpath designed to give the horses a good foothold. On Sellar Street is a pub called the Union Vaults, named after the Shropshire Union Canal.

The new housing development on the right, designed to give the feel of an industrial townscape was also the site of other businesses, including Albion Mill, another owned by Wiseman & Co. As the corn milling industry declined, other businesses took their place. One was established here in 1950 by Colin Witter, making towbars for cars, but outgrew the premises and moved to Shotton. The Witter family

'The Option'
(also see page 213)
Colin Witter

have had a long-standing interest in the waterways and in 2003 they travelled from Twickenham to here in the *Option*, a 17 foot open-top river launch, repeating a journey first done 100 years previously by Colin's father, Preston Witter, in the same boat.

Go under the next bridge, which carries City Road across the canal. This bridge is far larger than Union Bridge and its age is clear from the inscription on the iron work over the road alongside: *Jo Moore & Co, Iron Foundry, Chester 1863.* This road was an essential part of the infrastructure linking the city with its grand General Station, built in 1847-8 to a Francis

The canal and associated industries, c1950
Chester History and Heritage

Thompson design and meriting a Grade II* listing. It was a good job that the bridge was big and strong, for by the end of that century, it was also carrying trams into the city centre.

Just beyond the bridge are a number of buildings that reflect Chester's strong industrial and commercial heritage. On the corner of Russell Street lies the Old Harker's Arms, now a popular pub and restaurant. In the 19th century it was a boot and shoe factory and for many years, it was Harker's Warehouse, trading in rope and cotton and using the canal for both receiving and delivering goods as well as serving as a chandlery for the boats themselves.

Further along on the right is a large building, the tower of which declares that this is the Steam Mill, although this is a relatively modern name for this building, which was originally built by Frost's the millers in 1834. In 1817, Francis Aylmer Frost had commenced operations at the Dee Mills in Chester. When these premises were completely destroyed by fire two years later, his firm of F A and J Frost acquired a disused cotton mill in Steam Mill Street and in 1854 the firm's name changed to F A Frost & Sons. In 1910, when they then transferred their milling operations to Ellesmere Port, the building was taken over by Miln's Seeds and the name on the tower changed. On the other side of Steam Mill Street there was another steam mill, built in the 1780s, shortly after the Chester Canal opened in 1779. Some of the buildings on this original site still remain.

Further still along the canal, but on the opposite bank, lies the site of Chester's old Lead Works. Now a prestige housing development, the old Shot Tower still remains, although slightly hidden by the apartment blocks. Built in 1800 by Walkers Maltby & Co, its original role was to make lead shot for use in the Napoleonic Wars with lead mined in North Wales. Walkers, Parker & Co. bought the firm in 1889 and the tower continued in use till 1986. It is now the only remaining example of a shot tower in Britain.

'Boughton Gold Rush'
Chester History & Heritage

In 1927, this part of the canal was the site of the 'Boughton Gold Rush' sparked off by a rumour that there were 200 gold sovereigns hidden in a mattress that had been thrown into the canal here. When the canal had to be drained for some repair work, scores of people flocked to the site and were to be seen scrabbling around in the mud searching for the lost gold, but nothing was ever found!

WALK 1a ENDS HERE. *To return to the city centre go back along the canal or climb the steps here, turn right on to Hoole Lane and turn right again at the traffic lights to return along Boughton or catch a bus.*

Water storage tower
Gordon Emery

TO CONTINUE WALK 1b.

Walk under Hoole Lane Bridge to Hoole Lane Lock. This is the first of five single locks that take the canal up from Chester to Christleton. We are reaching the limit of the old industrial area of Chester, one of the last buildings being the Waterworks, with its enormous water storage tower rising up in front of you.

On the far bank of the canal lies a small chapel with a pretty spire that has been converted into houses. This used to be St Paul's Mission, linked to St Paul's Church on Boughton and may well have been provided specifically for the boatmen and their families. Just beyond the chapel there are neat rows of terraced cottages that face the canal, called Water Tower View and Tollemache Street, named after a family strongly associated with Beeston, 10 miles further along the canal.

Walk on past the Waterworks to Chemistry Lock. The lock here was once called Spitalfields Lock, but is now named after this area of Chester, which in the first half of 19th century the was the site of Major and Turner's factory producing naphtha – no doubt a very smelly process in those days! The factory was destroyed by fire in the 1850s and the company transferred production to a new site in Queensferry.

Boat waiting to enter
Hoole Lane Lock near
the old mission church
Photo: Ray Buss

The cottage alongside the lock here would have originally been for the lock-keeper, but is now a private house, although the owners still have to rely on the towpath for access to their home. One of the reasons for this is that the main Chester-London railway line runs just the other side of the house. The spill weir that carries water from above the lock to the canal below runs virtually under the house, which could pose problems for the owners if it ever got blocked by weed!

Chemistry Lock and the Waterworks Tower Photo: Tuesday Night Club

Walk on past the terraced houses running down to the canal and go under the road bridge just after the Bridge Inn to Tarvin Road Lock. The surroundings of the canal here have changed from the dense mix of houses and industrial buildings in the inner city to a more rural aspect. When the canal was first built this would have been open countryside, but here too businesses gathered around the canal. In the area just below the lock there used to be another mill, originally for grinding corn but later working as a feldspar mill. The building that backs onto the canal was part of the mill and still has a hoist at the top of its three storey gable end.

Today, the surroundings of Tarvin Road Lock and its lock cottage have regained their picturesque feel and this is enhanced by a rather quaint round building just to the south of the lock. This was used by the 'lengthsman', the man employed to maintain a length of canal, to store the grease and oil needed for lubricating the lock-winding gear, along with the tools he would need to cut the grass on the towpath and carry out day-to-day repairs. There are a number of these along the canal and would no doubt have been well used as the canals had to be kept open day in, day out throughout the year. Just alongside the canal here are the grounds of Chester Boughton Hall Cricket Club.

Tarvin Road Lock Cottage Photo: Tuesday Night Club

Walk on along the towpath under the large road bridge and up to Greenfield Lock. This stretch of canal is even more rural, despite the presence of suburban houses whose gardens back onto the canal. The large bridge here is almost like a tunnel since it is for a major trunk road, the A41, which today carries far more traffic than ever could have been imagined when the canal was built. The old lock cottage here is also now a private house. From Greenfield Lock you will get the first glimpse of rural Cheshire on the far side of the canal. Here the main railway line runs in a deep cutting between the canal and the fields beyond. When this cutting was built in the 1840s, the canal had to be diverted away from the railway and the line of this temporary diversion can still be seen as a reed bed just to the right of the towpath. Near the next lock at Christleton there are some traces of the old stonework from the diverted path of the canal.

Continue along the canal towpath to Christleton Lock. This is a very straight section of canal up to the last lock on the flight of five lifting the canal up from the City of Chester to the Cheshire plain. The large flyover just beyond the top of the lock carries the main A55 linking the motorway network with North Wales and is one of the last reminders of fast-moving modern life before the canal moves on into a more tranquil world, much of which is little different to how it would have been 200 years ago.

Walk under the flyover and through bridge 122, Christleton Bridge. All the bridges that you will have passed on the way out of Chester have been numbered down in a series from 123L to 123B [The numbering system starts with the first bridge at the south end of the Shropshire Union Canal at Autherley Junction]. Christleton Bridge bears the number 122 and is the first of the old brick bridges that would have been built as part of the original construction of the canal. The village of Christleton is just a short walk to the north of the canal and is an old settlement, mentioned in the Domesday Book. The present Church in the village dates back to the 16th century, but was substantially rebuilt in 1739 and then again in 1876, although this was evidently a Christian settlement from even earlier, as its name implies. There are also a number of old houses, including the Old Hall, built around 1603, from which the Ince family moved in the early 18th century to the newly built Christleton Hall, now the College of Law. Close by this bridge is a well-known public house, the Old Trooper.
THIS IS THE END OF WALK 1b.   WALK 2 STARTS HERE.

Walk along the backs of a row of houses to bridge 121. The high building near the end of this row of houses used to be Butler's Mill, which was still working up until the 1970s. Towards the end of its life it was producing mainly animal feeds, but in earlier times it also ground flour for its own bakery. Grain for the mill was brought here along the canal from Ellesmere Port in Mersey flats [see Cargo Carrying Flats and Barges, page 133]. The converted building has has retained some its original features. The wooden gantry overhanging the canal contained a hoist to lift the grain from the barges, originally using horse power but gas driven in its later years. The bridge here is know as Quarry Bridge, named after the old sandstone quarry to be found just to the north of the canal here. Stone from here was used for many buildings in the area, including St Peter's Church, Waverton, a couple of miles further along the canal.

Continue to the large brick building on the right - the 'Cheshire Cat' pub, hotel and restaurant. The countryside here is now largely rural, with just a few houses, and you are likely to see ducks and swans. If you are lucky, may even catch sight of a kingfisher. The pub now know as the 'Cheshire Cat' used to be Christleton Lodge, a large Victorian mansion, which has been tastefully restored with the outhouses being used for guest bedrooms.

Christleton Mill, now converted into apartments Photo: Tuesday Night Club

Opposite the pub is a small boatyard with a slipway. Its relatively modest appearance belies the significance of this area as being the base for the first ever fleet of holiday boats for hire on Britain's canals. Mr G F Wain and a group of his friends established the company in 1935 in the area on the other side of Rowton Bridge and it operated successfully until petrol rationing in the Second World War forced its temporary closure. It reopened in 1946 and was kept running by the Wain family as Inland Hire Cruisers Ltd up until 1972. After the war, there was another hire boat company, Dean's Pleasure Boats, which operated the boatyard you can see today and which, for a time, specialised in boats built from converted pontoons. (See Leisure, page 212) The yard is now used as the base for a number of privately owned boats.

Carry on under bridge 120. Another old brick structure, this is Rowton Bridge. It was just to the south of here that the Battle of Rowton Moor was fought during the Civil War, resulting in a defeat of the Royalists. From the top of the bridge, you can see a small broken down building across the main road. This was the field hospital for the troops in the battle and is now a listed building (illustration overleaf).

Walk on to bridge 119. Again, this section of the canal is largely rural in character, with fields of grazing cattle, some of which may come down to drink at the water's edge. These incursions

Civil War field hospital
Photo: Mike Penney

by livestock, coupled with the wash from passing boats, caused considerable erosion here in recent years, which effectively widened the canal. Work by British Waterways has now repaired the banks with a mixture of steel piling and a new 'soft' defence system, which uses wooden posts and plastic mesh behind which plants soon get established in the mud and do a good job of stabilising the bank. It is a relatively new technique and it remains to be seen how durable it is, but it is certainly softer than the use of steel piling and probably better for wildlife too. Normal order has therefore been restored - at least for a while!

The bridge at the end of this section is known as Egg Bridge. The present structure dates from 1937 when the old bridge was replaced so that it could carry heavier traffic. Apparently, the original name for the bridge comes from the egg shape described by the arch and its reflection in the water. When it had to be demolished, it was tested to destruction to give the engineers an indication of the strength of the design! This information was presumably used to set weight limits for other bridges along the route, most of which are now restricted to 7.5 tonne or 10 tonne loads.

The presence of the canal in this area gave rise to a number of businesses. There was a coal wharf just to the west of Egg Bridge, with a tile and cement depot on the opposite side of the canal. To the north of the bridge there was a rubber works.

To the east of the bridge was Victoria Mill, which ground flour from grain brought along the canal from Liverpool in Mersey flats. The old mill has now been converted into apartments, with a modern, but sympathetic, development of town houses linked to it.

Continue on along the towpath under three bridges, 118, 117 and 116. On the opposite side of the canal is a line of modern houses and bungalows, with gardens that run down to the water. These are some of the more recent dwellings in the newer part of Waverton, developed since the mid-19th century. Once past these houses, the canal is now in open countryside and sweeps in a long bend to the north of the old village of Waverton, with its church tower standing out clearly across the fields amid the trees.

Egg Bridge and Waverton Mill Photo: Ray Buss

This is another ancient settlement, mentioned in the Domesday Book and with strong links to the Eaton Estate of the Grosvenor family; the dukes of Westminster. An unflattering description in the History of the County Palatine and City of Chester 1882, says that Waverton *Occupies a flat and very uninteresting part of the hundred!* St Peter's Church was first mentioned in 1093, but the present building is from the 17th century; built of local red sandstone, the roof is dated 1635.

The three bridges that cross the canal on this section are named after the landowners when the canal was built. Like others along this stretch of canal, they were built by Weston and Lawton for the Chester Canal Company in about 1775 and were provided to give the farmers access to their land: bridges such as this are known as 'accommodation bridges'. The first one you come to is Davies's Bridge (No 118). Then comes Salmon's Bridge. Alongside was a bone works, which would have probably supplied bones to the larger works at Tattenhall (see below) as well as manufacturing its own glue and other by-products, such as bone-meal for use as a fertiliser. The third bridge is Faulkner's Bridge, named after Thomas Faulkner, who owned land both sides of the canal. On 6th June 1776, he wrote formally to complain about water leaking from the canal and making the tracks to the north of the canal impassable for his cattle.

Along this stretch, the banks of the canal on the towpath side have also been repaired and reinforced using the new system of wooden posts and plastic mesh described earlier. Around here, you should catch your first sight of the Peckforton Hills in the distance and the famous Beeston Castle perched on top of its rocky outcrop; a view of the castle was the main feature on the Chester Canal Company seal.

Carry on through open country under three more bridges, 115, 114 and 113. The countryside here is fairly flat and open, with not a great deal to see. Here the canal and the road come close together in an area once known as Gypsies Field, since it was a popular stopping point for the travelling community.

About here, the opposite bank of the canal becomes lined with moored boats. The local farmer has diversified from his agricultural interests to take advantage of the commercial opportunities offered by the growing interest in the leisure use of canals. This must bring a good return, since these boat moorings stretch for some 1.5 miles, and the vessels come in all shapes, sizes and ages! Although passing these boats at the regulatory idling speed can be tedious for boaters, spotting the variety of colours and the personal touches given to both boats and moorings by the proud owners helps relieve the boredom.

The towpath here can be rather muddy and the banks are choked with reeds in many places, but it is quite a haven for wildlife and hundreds of swallows can be seen feeding here on hot summer days. By the time the next bridge is reached, Nixons Bridge, the line of boats has stopped and the bank to the south of the canal becomes a steep embankment, beyond which runs the Chester to Crewe railway line. This bridge nearly collapsed in the winter of 2004-05 and sections of it had to be fairly extensively rebuilt.

Less than half a mile further on, lies Crows Nest Bridge, number 113. To the east of the bridge is a builders' merchant and a telecommunications mast with a multitude of aerials. This was once the site of a brick works, built around 1860, producing field drainpipes as well as bricks.

On the other side of the bridge, was a large bone works, which started in 1857 as a slaughterhouse some 150 yards east of the bridge. By 1890, the bone treatment plant had been added extending the works towards the road and a 100ft high chimney built to carry the smoke away from the boilers that were used to treat the bones. It was big business, with over 70 men being employed and bones being brought in from all over the area by rail. By all accounts, the smell could be pretty horrendous! The canal was used to bring in coal for the boilers and to carry out the glues, gelatine, fats and bone meal that the works produced.

By the 1950s, trade declined and the works had closed by the 1980s. Although the bone works has gone, the area here is still semi-industrial, with a small but thriving boatyard, agricultural machinery suppliers and even a skating and boarding rink inside one of the old sheds!

Boatyard and other industry at Crows Nest Bridge. *Early canal minutes referred to it as 'Crownest'.*
Photo: Ray Buss

With the canal and the growing industry came the need for services and, in 1854, the Aldersey Arms Hotel was built about 100 yards south of the bridge. First owned by the Alderseys of Chester, it was taken over in 1863 by Mr William Jones, who developed the business so that by 1891 it had five stables with twenty stalls for horses from the canal and those of the travellers staying at the inn. In 1910, Mr Jones even bought the brickworks and his family continued to run the hotel into the 1980s. Sadly, in recent years the hotel has fallen into decline and has been shut for some time. Further down the road and left along Newton Lane (about 20 minutes walk from the canal) are the premises of Cheshire Farms ice cream, which could be worth a visit on a hot day!

Carry on along the canal for about a mile, under bridge 112 to a sweeping dog-leg bend in the canal that bends first left and then right. This can be a fairly bleak section of the canal, since there is little to stop the prevailing wind as it comes in from the west across the Cheshire plain. The bridge is Dutton's Bridge, no doubt another one named after the local landowner. As the canal bends left, it follows the line of an embankment with trees on either side, including a large group of larches on the west side. This structure carries the canal in an aqueduct over the River Gowy. This river rises near Peckforton and flows towards the River Mersey at Stanlow, near Ellesmere Port, where it is pumped under the Manchester Ship Canal before finally discharging into the Mersey. The river water runs in a small culvert under the canal, which no doubt gave this place one of its names - 'Brook Hole' - although it is also know as 'Brockholes'. Above the river is a pedestrian tunnel, which you may care to investigate if you have time. It can be reached down a steep path running from the towpath alongside the fence; this path forms part of the Eddisbury Way, which runs from Frodsham to Higher Burwardsley.

Brook Hole *- the pedestrian tunnel under the canal and over the River Gowy.*
Photo: Ray Buss

As the canal bends right to resume its course towards Beeston, there is a weir on the outside of the bend, which allows excess water to run over and down into the river. Since water from the River Gowy was once used to feed the canal further up, near Tilstone Lock, this water is effectively just returning to its origin.

Walk on under three more bridges (111, 110 and 109). The country here is starting to become more hilly as Beeston gets closer and the canal therefore meanders slightly along the contours of the land. The two bridges here are Williamsons Bridge (No 111) and Dales Bridge (No 110) and the valley of the River Gowy can be seen below the canal on the right. This is an area rich in wildlife, and barn owls are a common sight here, encouraged by the owl boxes installed along the river valley by the Broxton Barn Owl Group.

The last of the three bridges in this section is Bate's Mill Bridge. The Mill, which was at one time called Horton's Mill, lies just to the south of the canal and relied on water from the River Gowy to power the water mill that ground the corn. The mill is still there although it has now been converted to a private house. The water wheel still works but now provides electricity for the house and the sound of it turning can still be clearly heard from the road.

On the far side of the bridge is the Shady Oak, a well-known pub. It was a regular stopping off point for the boaters of old, when the pub was often known as the 'Old Shady'. Pleasure boaters of today still find it a welcome stop, being the only canal-side pub between Christleton and Barbridge. It is also a good starting point for the walk up to Beeston Castle, which presides over the Cheshire plain from its craggy vantage point just to the south of the canal.

Walk towards the next bridge (108) and the lock. This is Wharton's Bridge and just beyond it is Wharton Lock. This is the first lock for some 8 miles and marks the beginning of another climb for the canal over the next 2.5 miles, this time up to a level that will take it to Nantwich.

In the 18th and 19th centuries, there was a water mill here alongside the River Gowy – Beeston Lower Mill. Census returns from 1841 and 1851 show that the miller was Hugh Warton (*sic*), so the lock and bridge may have been named after his family. Evidence of the mill and the mill pond can still be seen near where the River Gowy is crossed by the Sandstone Trail, a long distance footpath which runs from Frodsham to Whitchurch. It crosses the canal here, with one of its mileposts positioned alongside the lock and this section is also the footpath up to Beeston Castle.

Wharton Lock and Beeston Castle
Photo: Ray Buss

The path goes through a bridge under the railway, which would have been built as an accommodation bridge for the mill and for the lock cottage that used to be here. It was destroyed by a German bomb in the Second World War and was never rebuilt, although there is a small brick structure alongside the lock, which might have been part of it. Around the lock there are the remains of a number of large wooden posts, to which the old boatmen would have hitched their ropes as they worked their boats through the lock.

The view of Beeston Hill from alongside this lock is impressive and it is easy to see why Ranulf, sixth Earl of Chester, built the castle here in 1225. Having just returned from the Crusades and seen numerous castles on his travels, he constructed it to help in his guerrilla warfare with the Welsh. Earlier, there had been an Iron Age rampart on the site and there is also some evidence of occupation in both the Stone and Bronze ages. In 1237 it was seized by Henry III and was held at different times by both sides in the Civil War before being finally demolished in 1646. The village of Beeston which lies at the foot of the hill was mentioned in the Domesday Book as *Buistane.*

Continue along the towpath to bridge 107. The canal here enters another picturesque section as it follows the contours of the land just above the River Gowy, and its wooded banks are a haven for wildlife, including kingfishers. As the canal straightens out for its run to the next

View of BEESTON CASTLE, &c. in Cheshire.

Grosvenor Museum

lock, it is joined by the railway on the other side of the river as they both make for the same gap through the rolling countryside. To the south of the railway line is a house and the embankments of a reservoir, which was built as a strategic oil reserve. Today, the grassy banks of the structure are home to a herd of farmed deer, whose antlers can sometimes be seen silhouetted against the skyline. The river, running here at the bottom of the bank just to the south of the canal is known locally as Beeston Brook and this gives its name to the next bridge - Beeston Brook Bridge.

For a considerable period at the end of the 18th century, this was the end of the canal from Chester since the lock just beyond the bridge had collapsed and defied all attempts to repair it. Hence, a wharf and associated buildings were built here to deal with the limited amount of traffic still using the canal during that period, including passengers travelling to and from the market here at Beeston.

Stop just before the bridge. On the opposite bank of the canal are the remnants of the old terminus. It is now a small boatyard, from which a small fleet of hire boats is operated by the owner Chas Hardern, who also runs a boat repair and maintenance service. The white-painted building from which he works used to be a stable block for the canal horses and the old hay loft above is a shop which sells an amazing range of canal books and giftware.

On the towpath side, there is a hole in the bank which looks as if it is the result of erosion. It is actually the site of another set of horse steps, provided by the builders of the canal so that any horses that fell in the water could climb back out.

Chas Hardern's Boatyard at Beeston
Photo: Ray Buss

SECTION 2 ENDS HERE

SECTION 3 STARTS HERE

Carry on under the bridge to the lock about 50 metres beyond it. This is Beeston Iron Lock, and the date clearly displayed on the entrance wall to the lock chamber is 1828, nearly 50 years after the canal first opened. The unstable ground conditions around here, known as 'shifting sands' were notoriously problematic for the first builders of the canal. For instance, on 5 November 1787, it was reported that *the Walls of Beeston Brook Lock* had *given way due to Sand being washed out.* These problems resulted in the closure of the lock and, although some trade continued with goods being carried round the lock, an Act of Parliament in 1796 stated that *the said Canal Navigation is now, and has been for a very long Space of Time, in a very ruinous Condition.*

When it was first built, the lock here was a double one, and was just to the north of the present site. Various attempts to repair it were made in 1797 and again in 1820. By 1827, the great engineer, Thomas Telford, had come on the scene and completed a major project, rebuilding the whole Beeston section on a new course to the south of the original line.(See map, page 288.) The double lock was replaced with two single locks, the lower one being this Iron Lock, formed of iron plates to prevent further damage by the shifting sand. As you will see from the warning notices around the lock, the problems continue in some small measure to this day, since the walls have moved in and boaters are now advised to navigate the lock singly rather than in pairs as they can do elsewhere along the Chester Canal.

Two views of Beeston Iron Lock
Photos: Ray Buss

Walk on along the towpath to the next lock.
Beeston Stone Lock is the upper of the two locks constructed by Telford and is, as its name implies, built of stone. Here there is a pretty lock-keeper's cottage and another of the small round buildings used by the 'lengthsman'. At one time, there used to be a water tap here for boaters needing to fill up with water.

Behind the lock cottage is a small hill with a sandy bank, which is now home to a large warren of rabbits. The ease with which they have a created their homes clearly shows how soft the ground is about here, but they have kept clear of the 'shifting sands' at Iron Lock which would be too unstable even for a rabbit warren.

Just beyond the top gate of the lock, the towpath crosses a stone pavement which covers the channel carrying water from the top level of the canal round the lock and down into the bottom 'pound'. This 'by-wash' runs through a culvert, which you can see if you look over the low brick wall running out from the lengthsman's hut. These features are a critical feature of the engineering of the waterways system since they ensure that the water level is adequate in all sections of the canal, regardless of whether the locks are being operated.

Above: **Stone Lock Cottage and weir**
Below: **Lengthsman's hut**
Photos: Ray Buss

263

Carry on along the towpath to bridge 106, Tilstone Mill Bridge. This stretch of the canal is another pretty section with wooded banks on the opposite side and the young River Gowy running along in the valley just to the right of the towpath. It makes ideal conditions for a whole host of wildlife, including kingfishers, and foxes, as well as the ubiquitous rabbits. In the spring and summer twilight, the trees swarm with pipistrelle bats searching for food.

As the canal curves right in its run up to the bridge, the opposite bank gets higher and there are houses on top of it that enjoy wonderful views of the canal and the castles at Beeston and Peckforton. To the south of the canal on the other side of the Gowy, are some small artificial lakes used by anglers; the area round here is a popular nesting site for mute swans, and you might need to take care as you pass since they can be pretty aggressive if they are guarding eggs on the nest or their young cygnets.

The approach to the bridge here and the lock just beyond it is one of the prettiest on the whole canal and no doubt features in many holiday photo albums as well as in guidebooks. As you approach, you are likely to hear and see water spurting out of a small hole just under the bridge. This is the outflow from the 'by-wash', which allows water to flow down from the canal above the lock to the level below.

The building just to the right of the bridge is Tilstone Mill, which is now a private house, but used to be a water mill and carries the date 1838 over its front door. Water to power the mill was brought to the Mill Pond on the other side of the road from two different courses of the

Tilstone Bridge and Lock in the distance
Photo: Tuesday Night Club

River Gowy system, one running alongside the next section of the canal and the other by diverting it from its normal channel just up the valley to the right. After being used to work the mill, the water returned to the river which runs along just below the level of the towpath.

Walk under the bridge and up to Tilstone Lock. The picturesque setting for this lock, with cottages overlooking it and trees all around belies its chequered history. This was another of the many original structures of the canal that did not prove strong enough and in June 1783 the whole of one side fell down. This disaster was so critical that the owners of the canal sold one of their boats, the flat *Peploe,* to raise the £80 needed for its reconstruction, which was completed by March 1784. Here there is also another of the unusual round 'lengthsman's huts'.

Carry on along the canal to the next bridge. Just to the right of the towpath here is a hollow, which would have contained the long, narrow millpond for Tilstone Mill but which has clearly been dry for many years. It has become overgrown and includes a good number of alders and crack willows, well named for their habit of bending and cracking but then regenerating where the collapsed branches re-root into the soil on which they have landed. This is another spot where you might see a kingfisher flying low along the canal or even sitting on the branch of a tree on the opposite bank.

As the canal bends left and right here, it again comes close to one of the streams that form the Gowy river system. All canals need a constant supply of water to keep them up to the right level and ensure that the locks can operate without draining the summit level. The provision of such water was one of the key challenges for the builders of the Chester Canal and, in 1778, a reservoir was constructed about a mile and a half to the southwest up on Bunbury Heath. The engineer was instructed to build it large enough to hold 1384 locks of water, which had to be channelled past Bunbury Mill Pool before entering the canal somewhere along this stretch. Only four years later, it was partially drained by an angry landowner as retribution for the failure of the company to pay its debts to them.

The railway line also gets nearer until it eventually crosses the canal and the river at the next bridge. One or two boats might be moored up just before this bridge since, hidden behind the railway embankment and the bridge lies a stretch of towpath that is now part of the base for a boat hire company, Anglo Welsh Narrowboats. If you pass on one of the change-over days in the boating season, then this will be a hive of activity as boats are returned and then cleaned and prepared for their next guests. If boats are also waiting to go up the locks and others are coming down, then there may well be an air of some confusion around who is doing what, but in the boating world this is generally accepted as one of the features of canal travel, the slow pace that encourages patience!

Carry on past the moored boats, go under Bunbury Lock Bridge, No 103, and up to Bunbury Locks just beyond. The hire-boat company also have the use of the buildings alongside the locks, which used to belong to the Shropshire Union Railways and Canal Company, as the sign on the gable end of the large building by the bridge still clearly shows. In the cargo-carrying years of the canal, this would have been a busy place, since it was one of the bases for maintaining the boats and looking after the horses. It would have also been where the fast or 'fly' boats changed horses to enable them to keep up their high speed carriage of important and perishable cargoes. Hence the magnificent block of stables to the south of the top lock, which used to have 22 stalls. This building retains many of its original features externally, even though the interior has been cleared and is used as part of the hire boat operation by Anglo-Welsh. Most of the stable doors are still in place, many with their original door furniture and cobbled areas outside. Rather less in keeping is the roller shutter door which has been inserted into the eastern gable end; this and the concrete slipway leading up to it was created when the building was being used by a boat building company in the 1960s. This was established in 1962 by a local man, Mr Cartmell, who built cruisers and hired them out before he left the area in 1967. In 1969, Dart Line took over the site, both as a hire-boat base and for making steel narrowboats.

The two locks here are the last ones on the Chester Canal before its terminus at Nantwich and, just like the first three locks on the main canal at Northgate, they are also built as a staircase. But these at Bunbury are on a rather smaller scale (rising 15ft 7in, by comparison with the 33ft' at Northgate) and their rural setting gives them a much friendlier feel than their imposing cousins in Chester. In the busy boating season, they are a magnet for sightseers, who come to watch the boats coming and going and marvel at both the engineering and the manoeuvres of the boats. Boatmen had a rather different view of sightseers, they called them 'gongoozlers' - those that look and do no work.

At the bottom of the locks, there is a small basin, which is currently used by the hire company as part of its maintenance operation, including the repainting of the boats in wet weather under a plastic tunnel. To the north of the top lock is the old lock-keeper's cottage, now a private house. Behind the basin, there are some small cottages, and records suggest that one of them served as a beerhouse in the 1850s. There was also a bone mill operating in this area around that time and no doubt all these businesses relied to a considerable degree on the presence of the canal to support their trade.

Horse treads
Photo: Ray Buss

The main village of Bunbury, which has Saxon origins and was mentioned in the Domesday Book, lies about a mile to the south of the locks on top of the hill. It is an interesting and attractive place, well worth visiting if you have time. The outstanding feature is the church of St Boniface, the present building was erected by Sir Hugh Calveley in 1386 but its roots go back even further, probably before the Norman Conquest. The village also has pretty thatched cottages, some small shops and a couple of excellent pubs. On the road up to the village is Bunbury Mill, which has been on this site from at least the 13th century and was restored as a working mill in 1977; this too is well worth a visit. Amazingly, or so it might seem now, the mill once imported corncake from America via Liverpool and the canal, then by cart up the hill, to produce animal feed.

Stables
Photo: Ray Buss

Walk on along the canal for about one and a half miles to the next bridge 104. The first section of canal here is fairly narrow and there are some permanent moorings for boats running for about 200 yards from the top of the locks. This can sometimes cause further confusion for boaters who are not familiar with this part of the canal, especially if there are more than one or two boats waiting to go down, since the queue then has to form up alongside the moored boats. Thankfully, incidents of 'canal rage' are relatively rare, although disapproving words may occasionally be exchanged!

On the opposite side of the canal are the remains of what used to be a brick works, now in a fairly ruinous state, although the vaults of the brick kilns can still be seen amongst the undergrowth. Once the moored boats are passed, then the canal opens out and there is another 'winding hole', where the long boats can turn in safety. After

Bunbury Lock Bridge *The warehouse beyond still proudly bears the name of the Shropshire Union Rly & Canal Co, Carriers. It is now the office and shop for Anglo Welsh*   Photo: Ray Buss

this, the canal enters open country again and there are fields on both sides. As the next bridge at Calveley approaches, the railway line also comes back closer to the canal, just to the north this time.

At Calveley Bridge, follow the towpath as it leaves the south side of the canal and crosses over to the other bank. After crossing the bridge, turn right past the barriers and walk down the gravel track towards the moored boats. Since Chester, the towpath has been on the south of the canal, but here it changes sides across this 'roving bridge' and keeps to the north all the way to Nantwich. Often, this change of side is governed by topography, with the towpath normally being on the side of the canal that has been banked to create the water channel. This may be the reason here too, although it is difficult to see, but the switch of bank also brings the towpath to what would have been an important site for the working boats, and there are still some signs of this left.

Along here, there were a number of cheese warehouses, which would have made use of the canal for transporting their Cheshire Cheese and, with the coming of the railways, this area became an important interchange between the canal boats and the trains right up until the

268

1960s. There also used to be a station and the platforms can still be seen if you look over the fence onto the railway line, which is just to the north of this area. In the area that is now covered by grass and cinder tracks, there were railway sidings running up to the warehouses. Among the remaining buildings is an old wharf, still with its roof overhanging the canal which would have helped keep the cargoes dry as they were loaded and unloaded. There is also a slipway, which can be used to get small boats on trailers into and out of the canal.

Calveley Village gets its name from the Calveley family that built Bunbury Church and who were given land around here by Richard I towards the end of the 12th century. The old family home, Calveley Hall lay a mile or so to the northwest of the village and was later the home of the Davenport family, but it was demolished in the 1950s.

Walk along to the Old Wharf building. Since being abandoned as a wharf, this building has had a number of uses, including at one time being the base for a hire-boat company. Today, it is owned by British Waterways and has been extended to provide services for pleasure boaters, including a water point, showers, and a toilet and disposal facilities for waste. This change of use has retained some of the old features, including the stone edgings to the wharf, held together with huge metal staples. The wooden supports for the overhanging roof are also original, still clearly displaying the rope marks where the boats would have tied up. Some of the other buildings here are used by British Waterways maintenance teams as workshops and for storing spares and equipment.

Continue along the towpath and under bridges 103A and 103. Both sides of the canal here are used as permanent mooring sites for boats, for which the owners pay an annual fee to British Waterways. Therefore, the beginning of this section of the towpath is shared with the boaters and some of the old warehouse buildings are also alongside, so it does not immediately appear to be

Calveley Old Wharf
Photo: Ray Buss

a public thoroughfare. But it soon opens out and, after running past some unfenced gardens, gets into the country again. The two bridges along this section are Tweedale Bridge and Wardle Hall Bridge.

After a fairly wide section, the canal narrows and has high banks on both sides of a cutting about a mile long, which has lost the rural charm of many other parts of the canal. To the north of the canal lies the busy A51 main road from Chester to Nantwich. This was known as Watfield Pavement and is thought by some to have been a Roman road; certainly a bronze Roman coin was discovered when Wardle Hall Bridge was rebuilt in 1978. It was later a medieval packhorse route and in 1729 formed part of the first stage coach route in the country. Back in 1775 when the canal was being cut, the 'Chronicle of 24th July reported that: *A few days ago, as the workmen were cutting the Chester Canal on Wardle Green; about 27 inches below the surface in a bed of marl [clay], they found a spur of surprising dimensions; its length was 13 inches, its thickness was 4 inches: the rowel was 13 inches round, and the gags 3 inches long. It is supposed to have lain there since the year 1643, when a skirmish happened at the time the parliament troops besieged Nantwich; it is now in the possession of Joseph Harding of Buckley.*

To the south of the canal, there is a capped landfill site, complete with methane vents, and then a huge complex of warehouses and industrial buildings, the ones closest to the canal being owned by NWF, major suppliers to the agricultural industry in the area. During working hours, huge articulated lorries can often be seen crossing the canal here; with the demise of cargo-carrying on the canals, it is ironic that the lorry drivers sometimes stop to wave at the passing boats and even take photographs!

The industrialisation of this area to the south has no current links to the neighbouring waterway but earlier users of the site, including two brickfields, may well have made use of the canal. In the Second World War it was an airfield, largely used for flight training. It operated between March 1942 and October 1946 with a range of aircraft, including Miles Masters, Ansons, Harvards and Hurricanes.

Carry on to Wardle Farm Bridge, number 102. Here the canal bends sharply left under the bridge and then straightens up again by turning right after it goes under the main A51 road. For boaters, this bridge is known today as one of the places where meeting another boat coming the other way can be a bit daunting, especially without brakes and only limited manoeuvrability! For the canal builders of the 18th century, this bridge was notable as being another structure that was not up to the job. In 1794 it was declared to be dangerous but the committee decided they did not have the money to repair it, what little they had being saved to attempt to repair the lock at Beeston. Thankfully, the structure today is a relatively modern one that is well able to take the very considerable loads imposed on it by the heavy traffic above.

Continue under bridge 101 and on to Barbridge Junction. The canal emerges into more rural country here despite the proximity of the main road, from which Goodwin Bridge (no 101) carries a small road to the houses on the north of the canal and to the buildings at Barbridge Junction, where the canal link from Middlewich joins the Chester Canal from the northeast.

The bridge over the Middlewich Branch at Barbridge   Photo: Ray Buss

In terms of the development of the canal network, this junction is highly significant, since here, in 1833, the Chester Canal was joined up, at long last, to the Trent and Mersey Canal at Middlewich and could access the prosperous salt and pottery traffic that it carried. Even then, there was fierce rivalry between the canal companies and hefty tolls to pay at the other end of the 'Middlewich Cut', which were not finally lifted until 1888, well over 100 years after a canal from Chester to Middlewich was first proposed.

In the 1830s, the canal also linked with Telford's Birmingham & Liverpool Canal at Nantwich and, by 1846, the Shropshire Union Canal Company had been formed. So the junction at Barbridge became one of the busiest on the whole system with many boats coming and going, transhipping cargoes. Even today, it is a busy meeting point for pleasure boats. Although many of the buildings and other structures that were here in the canal's heyday have now gone, some are left and there are traces of others. Probably the most magnificent of all is the winged bridge over the end of the Middlewich Cut.

Barbridge Junction 1957, *just before the old buildings over the canal were demolished.*
Edwin Shearing

Walk over this bridge and stop for a moment by the buildings on the other side. Here is a large house which is typical of the style built by Telford along his canals as residences for lock-keepers and managers; this one is especially grand since it was occupied by the Canal Inspector. On the opposite side of the small road to the house there is a little brick building: this is all that remains of the complex that once spanned the canal. These buildings, which included a roof and covered walkway right over the canal, were demolished in 1958 but for many years were used for the storage and transhipment of goods, such as cheese and other agricultural commodities.

Walk a little further along the canal to a short narrow section, with a single storey building on the opposite bank of the canal. This other building looks fairly anonymous now, and its origins are not known, but it was probably used as the toll office. If you look closely at the edges of the canal banks here, you will see that this narrow channel was originally a lock, and the spaces where the lock gates would have fitted can still be clearly seen. While most locks were built to raise or lower the level of the canal, they also had other uses. This one would have served as a 'gauging lock' in which the working boats would be measured to ascertain what weight of cargo they were carrying and, therefore, determine either what toll they should pay for using the canal or what payment the carrier should receive for his load. This would have been done by bringing the boat into the lock, where it would be held while the amount of freeboard was measured, from which the weight carried could be calculated. At a busy junction such as Barbridge, this would have been a very important activity, especially in the days when the canal owning and carrying companies were in intense competition and fortunes could be made or lost in this young business.

The village of Barbridge no doubt derived benefit too from all this activity in its midst, not the least of which being the public houses, especially the Jolly Tar immediately opposite the junction. Although its architectural style may not make it as attractive as other canal side pubs it has a distinguished history of serving the boating community and is still popular with boaters today.

Carry on along the towpath past some moored boats to the next bridge, number 100. This section of canal is built up on a small embankment and is higher than the main road just to the south. In the 19th century, this area was home to both a flour mill and an iron foundry. There are now permanent moorings for boats as well as others for visitors, catering both for those who want to base their boats here and for those stopping for the night on one of the popular canal routes, such as the Four Counties Ring and the trip to Llangollen. On the opposite bank is another popular canal-side pub with its own moorings for patrons. The inn here used to be called the Kings Arms but today is called the Barbridge Inn. Another name change has occurred just beyond the pub: Bremilow's Bridge was once called Stoke Hall Bridge.

Continue past the next two bridges, 99 and 98. After bending left past some pretty cottages with gardens running up to the water's edge, the canal widens again and its character begins to change, more reminiscent of the Shropshire Union Main Line than the old Chester Canal. Bridge 99, Stoke Hall Bridge, appears to be sagging a little in the middle and may be due for some restoration work soon!

Just beyond the bridge the towpath crosses a 20 yard long concrete weir designed to take floodwater from the canal down into the river valley just below. At the end of the weir, there is the winding gear for a sluice gate, similar to that for the paddle on a lock, which can be used to adjust the water level in the canal. As the canal sweeps right again, you may catch sight of the chimneys of a big old house through the trees on the hill on the opposite bank. This is a reminder of how prosperous a farming area this has been for many centuries. Just beyond the house that you can see is another large farm, the home of the ice cream manufacturer Snugbury's, which might be worth a visit on a hot day by taking the footpath from the next bridge, Vickers Bridge. The farm buildings just to the north of the bridge here have recently been converted into houses.

As you walk under the bridge and past the moored boats, you will see some square buildings on the hill just beyond, which are part of the water reservoir at Hurleston.

Carry on under the large pipe over the canal and round the bend in the canal to Hurleston Junction. The canal here is wide and can be windswept at times. This rather bleak appearance is not helped by the complex of buildings and shiny metal pipes which can be seen on the opposite bank. Some trees have been planted on a small bank to try and hide them from view but they stand out clearly in what is otherwise a very rural setting. These are all part of the infrastructure for the large Hurleston Reservoir, the retaining wall of which is supported by the large grass bank on the opposite side of the canal. The location of this reservoir so close to the canal is no accident, since it is fed by water brought down from the River Dee by the Llangollen Canal, which joins the Chester Canal at this junction. It provides drinking water to the residents of both Crewe and Nantwich.

Stop for a moment opposite the junction with the Llangollen Canal just before the next bridge, number 97. Looking west up the Llangollen Canal, you will immediately see the first of the four locks that are sited here and which begin the canal's climb to Llangollen *via* Wrenbury, Whitchurch, Whixall and Ellesmere, crossing the River Dee on the wonderful Pontcysyllte Aqueduct. This is a 'narrow' canal since the locks are built to take only 7 feet wide narrowboats.

This canal was built by the Ellesmere Canal Company, which was set up in the 1790s to link Ellesmere in Shropshire to the Mersey at Netherpool/Whitby, now known as Ellesmere Port. It considered several routes, but in the end decided to link up with the Chester Canal both here and at Chester, where it built the section of canal known as the Wirral Line, which runs up to Ellesmere Port and which was completed in 1795. The link here was later, not being completed till 1805. Historically, this was of great significance and represented a major upturn in the fortunes of the owners of the Chester Canal Company, which would probably not otherwise have survived. It also meant that any problems over water supply were solved by the flow of water brought down from the Welsh hills. By 1813 the partnership had been so successful that the two companies merged to create the Ellesmere and Chester Canal Company.

This was another important junction in the canal era and there was once a typical Telford's lock-keeper's cottage here. It was built just behind where you are standing now with a view up the locks rather than alongside the locks themselves. This presumably meant that the lock-keeper was in a better position to see and control the traffic coming from different directions.

Looking down from the top of Hurleston Locks – the start of the Llangollen Canal.
Photo: Ray Buss

Walk on along the towpath and under the next three bridges, 97, 96 and 95. The first of these bridges is Hurleston Bridge and is only just beyond the junction. The second, Cornes Bridge, is a fairly unattractive structure built with concrete beams and beyond it the canal continues its wide sweep through the countryside. Just before a pipe bridge, the canal widens even more into a winding hole for boats to turn, and where a number of boats have been left to rot over the years. There is still one there today and it presents a very sorry sight with it sunken hull and rotting superstructure showing among the reeds.

Beyond the pipe bridge, the canal widens even more and there are some moorings for boats. At the end of this stretch the canal narrows again quite quickly as it goes under the third bridge, Henhull Bridge, which carries the main A51 road to Nantwich.

Carry on to the next bridge, no 93, Acton Bridge. Having run straight for some time, the canal twists and turns again on this stretch as it follows the contours of the hillside. One of the old bridges, Blue Stone Bridge (No 94), has collapsed completely and its site is marked only by a narrowing of the canal.

The bridge at Acton is still there and from it a footpath runs up to the village of Acton, which was a very important Christian centre in the Kingdom of Mercia, during Saxon times. The present church, which can be clearly seen from the canal, has some Saxon carvings and a Norman font. In the churchyard there is a sundial and close by there are almshouses dating from the 17th century.

On a clear day, looking over the hedge to the left of the towpath you should be able to see the church tower and buildings of Nantwich Town. The fields in this area are where the Battle of Nantwich took place on 25th January 1644. This victory over the Royalists ended a six week siege of Nantwich and is regarded as the turning point in the Civil War.

Walk on to Nantwich Junction Bridge, bridge 92 and stop just before it. This is the last section of the Chester Canal, which was completed in 1774 and finished at Basin End. Although no longer the terminus of the canal, it is still an important centre in a number of ways. On the opposite bank of the canal itself are the moorings for members of the Nantwich and Border Counties Yacht Club. In the main basin just to the right, there are lots more boats and also a thriving boat building, repairing and chandlery business, as well as a brokerage company for those thinking of buying their own narrowboat! It is well worth a visit.

'Taylor-built' boats at Nantwich 1968
Geoff Taylor Collection

Of course, in the days of the working boats, Nantwich Basin would have been busy in other ways. The main building, which currently houses Nantwich Canal Centre shop, used to be a cheese warehouse. The basin also dealt with boatloads of limestone, and in 1880 the local paper carried an account of the _annual operation of running off the water at the Canal Basin, Acton, so as to remove the limestone which falls into the canal in course of unloading the boats, and also to dredge the mud which accumulates in the bed of the basin. The water is let off by means of a sluice communicating with the river,_

and the chance of netting and catching eels and other fish attracts a large number of persons besides those actually engaged in the work. At the end of the outlet culverts an eel cage is placed, and as the stream lowers these find their way into the trap. The fish thus captured are the perquisites of the workmen, but there are generally a number of outsiders who wade into the mud waist high, on the chance of capturing some of the eels. Two men were particularly active in this work on Monday afternoon. Besides eels several bream and other coarse fish were taken. The work of dredging also brings to light a large number of eels, and before eight o'clock on Tuesday morning the canal workmen scooped out of the mud no fewer than 21, some of them being very fine.

Turning back to the bridge here, notice how narrow the canal channel is by comparison with all the others you have seen. This is because Nantwich Junction Bridge is the first bridge on a much newer canal. The Chester Canal which you have been following till now was designed in 1772 to carry 14ft wide Mersey Flats, and the bridges therefore had to be wide enough to take them. The next section of what is now the Shropshire Union Canal - built as the Birmingham and Liverpool Junction Canal between Nantwich Basin and Birmingham - was not completed till 1835, and was built to carry only narrow-boats, 7ft wide, by then the industry standard.

A narrowboat passing through 'narrow' Bridge 92
Photo: Ray Buss

Basin End Nantwich. *This old cheese warehouse is now used as a chandlery.* Photo: Ray Buss

Under this bridge there is a stop-gate that can be swung across to close the canal and stop the water if necessary. This could have been in the event of any disputes between the owners of the two canals but was more likely to prevent the loss of water should there be a collapse in the embankment beyond!

From here, you can cross the bridge and walk down the path to Nantwich Basin - the original terminus of the Chester Canal, before returning here and continuing along the canal towpath to the Nantwich Aqueduct. By the time the Birmingham and Liverpool Junction Canal was built, more than 50 years after the Chester Canal, civil engineering had developed to such a degree that no longer was it necessary for canals to follow the contours of the land as far as possible. The complementary techniques of building up embankments and excavating cuttings meant that the newer canals could follow much straighter routes than their predecessors. One of the masters of this new technology was Thomas Telford, who was the main designer for the Birmingham & Liverpool Canal.

But it was not only the lie of the land that could dictate the route of a canal. Here at Nantwich, the owners of Dorfold Park, just to the west, objected to the intended route, so the engineers Telford and Cubitt had to build the half mile Nantwich embankment to avoid the park. The result is a magnificent piece of engineering, with its centrepiece the wonderful single-arched cast-iron aqueduct, spanning Chester Road: an English Heritage listed Grade 1 structure.

But even this new section of the canal was not without its problems since parts of the embankment collapsed a few times just after it was first built and had to be strengthened. To this day it has to be carefully checked on a regular basis and repairs carried out from time to time. **Since the canal never did quite reach Nantwich, the walk must end here, just to the southwest of the town. Leave the towpath just before the aqueduct by walking down the side steps that have recently been built and lead down to Welsh Row, the main road into Nantwich Town Centre.**

WALK 2 ENDS HERE

Nantwich Aqueduct undergoing repairs
Waterways Trust

The Chester Canal is over 230 years old and is still a busy waterway, enjoyed by many thousands of boaters, walkers, cyclists and anglers every year, to say nothing of all the people who live and work along its banks. This is a remarkable achievement for a project that started as the vision of just a few Chester businessmen in the 1770s and suffered great adversities during its early years. If it were not for the perseverance of those involved and some fortuitous alliances that were formed with other canal companies in the late 18th and early 19th centuries, then the Chester Canal today could be just another of the disused waterways of England and Wales. The aim of this guide and its associated history has been to tell the story of that achievement for the interest of all those today who travel along or it live by it.

We hope that you have enjoyed it.

POSTSCRIPT: SURVEYORS AND ENGINEERS Stewart Shuttleworth

Chester Canal

The "quiet canal" reveals little of the human stories behind its construction. The Chester Canal and its associated waterways demonstrate a microcosm of the national picture at the time when civil engineering was taking off in Britain. People with the appropriate experience and competence were in great demand. Several famous names emerged with associated networks of colleagues. Learning by pupillage became practice. Established local professionals found new openings on local canal projects. 'Fast track' promotion was possible for people with the right skills, in the right place and possessing some 'nous'. The same people might have repeated involvements with one canal company or switch across to neighbouring companies. The more influential engineers had freedom to engage in projects subsidiary to their resident projects.

The early chapters relate the role of that icon of the canal age, *James Brindley* (1716-72) in the conception of the Chester Canal. Brindley started his career as a Staffordshire millwright

James Brindley's letter of release to the Chester Canal proprietors
(Also see page 29)
Cheshire RO Z/TAV/55

and rose monumentally to become the canal engineer of his time. His story is well documented and shining through is a paradox between an apparently unassuming, semi-literate countryman and a fantastically creative engineer. His epitaph (see page 33) and the style of the typical Chester Canal bridge, built by Weston and Lawton, his former employees, pay tribute to him locally.

Samuel Weston (1768-1804) had given evidence in Parliament on the company's behalf as described earlier and was appointed as their first engineer in 1772 with **John Lawton** as his assistant.(Lawton had died by January 1774) Weston was a Cheshire man who had been a staffholder and leveller for Brindley on the Bridgewater Canal and had been a contractor for a four mile section of the Leeds and Liverpool Canal. He left the Chester Company in 1774, after taking the *Dead levell from Wardle Green to Beeston Mill* and surveying a proposed branch to Gresford and *levelling in Shropshire*. His departure may have been related to the partial collapse of the Gowy aqueduct. However, in November 1777, it was Weston who took a complete inventory of the canal. At a later stage he carried out a survey of the whole of Chester City for a map published by Hunter, in 1789. Later in his career, Weston worked on projects near Oxford including the canal and a turnpike road. Locally he was also contractor for the Ellesmere Canal Company's Wirral Line together with his son, **John Weston** from 1793-6.

Two overlookers were employed *upon Trial on Business of the Canal* in March, 1774. The first, **William Cawley**, was paid extra until Mr Morris took over as engineer. He later worked under Mr Moon, the clerk and later surveyor, as an assistant for £60pa. He was discharged in 1780 but re-emerges in the 1790s as part of the survey team for the Wirral Line. The second, a **Mr Heald**, was still working for the company in January 1775, when he was warned to obey Morris's orders! He was discharged with three months' salary in June the same year.

One gets the impression that the Chester Canal Company had extraordinary troubles in managing their engineering staff, as minutes mentioning both Morris and Clowes also show.

Thomas Morris had, at an earlier stage, acted as a staffholder for Weston in the original survey of the Chester Canal and then surveyed Eaton Brook with him. Morris, too, had worked with Brindley on the Bridgewater in the 1760's. Early references suggest he was first employed as a carpenter. Later, it is thought, he had responsibility for the canal to the west of Altrincham. He must have left to work elsewhere for, in 1774, he was sent for from Ireland by the Chester Company to replace Weston. His terms were accepted in March 1774. His first task as the new engineer was to *set out the Canal immediately from Brockholes Land to Beeston Brook House*. He was warned, in October, *to take his instructions from the Committee for the Breadth &c of*

The Subscribers to the Intended Canal from Chester to Middlewich
to Samuel Weston Dr

		£. s. d.
April 23. 1770 Expences for Myself and horse 3 Days attending ye meeting		0. 11. 2
25 Set out from Astmoor to Middlewich to take the Survey		
To Victuals and Drink at Northwich for Men		0. 2. 6
Do at Middlewich		1. 7. 8
Do at Minshall		1. 19. 10
Do at Beiston brook house		0. 10. 11
Do at Barbridge		0. 4. 0
Do at the Highway Side		0. 5. 0
Do at the Black Bear in Chester		1. 11. 8
Do at Tarporley		3. 11. 9
Do at the Bear in Chester		3. 10. 4
To Cash paid 2 men for telling the Land Owners Names from Boughton to Waverton		0. 2. 4
To Do to 4 men for do to Tiverton		0. 4. 0
Do to 4 Men for do to Lea Green bridge		0. 4. 0
Do to 2 men for do to Middlewich		0. 3. 0
To Victuals and Drink at Mrs Oultons in Middlewich		0. 2. 8
To Cash paid Thos Hehual for 5 days Chaining		0. 6. 0
Do to Joseph Leathwood for staff holding from 23 Ap to 2o of June being 31 days at 1/6 ⅌ day		2. 7. 6
To Cash paid Thos Morris for staff holding 31 days at 2/6 ⅌		3. 7. 6
For Myself Levelling and taking the plan and finishing it 38 Days at 10. 6 ⅌ Day		19. 19. 0
To Cash paid Mr Poole for Vellum books and paper		1. 6. 0
		£ 41. 18. 6
To Mr Morris's bill for Gauging the Water at ye Summit		4. 7. 0
		£ 46. 5. 6

Weston's expenses
(Also see page 31)
Cheshire RO Z/TAV/55

all Bridges to be built on the Canal. In November, he was asked to survey Barbridge Valley and see if he could find a better way of crossing it; then, in June 1775, he was to *Survey the Summitt immediately*. He was discharged in August 1777, with £75 as compensation for his salary. The reason was not recorded but it was probably the company's financial state rather than his work, as in March of that year he had been admitted to the (Smeatonian) Society of Civil Engineers. Then, in 1805, his son listed repairs needed to the canal.

Josiah Clowes (1735-94) was asked, in September 1776, to give his opinion on the Brockholes Valley. He may have done this, but he refused to carry out a survey for a new line for part of the canal in 1777; so Mr Moon, the company clerk, surveyed with Morris. The committee must have had some intimation of Josiah Clowes' working pattern because, when they finally employed him, in April 1778, as *General Surveyor and Overlooker of the Works,* the minutes record that the *said Joseph Clowes is to be constantly resident in the Neighbourhood of the Works + at no time to absent himself from the Overlooking & Management of the same without the leave of the Committee first obtained in writing.* In June he was to *go through the whole works + see what defects there were.* However, despite his orders, by August, Clowes had been threatened with stopped wages for absenteeism and, at the end of October, referred to as *the Engineer*, he was dismissed for not attending the works agreeable to his contract. Despite these difficulties on the Chester Canal, he went on to work on the Stroudwater Navigation and was appointed engineer for the Thames and Severn Canal Company. He was responsible for the construction of some of the longest canal tunnels in England.

John Moon had become surveyor by default. After his survey with Morris in 1777, he surveyed Wardle Green to Middlewich, and Bunbury Lock to Nantwich later the same year. In 1778, after Clowes' dismissal, Moon had to lay out the intended reservoir at Bunbury Heath, with embankments of 22 feet and 16 feet to store 1384 locks of water. (The proposed 22 feet height was later reduced to 16 feet.) Water had to *be carried clear of Bunbury Mill Pool, not to communicate therewith* (see overleaf). The reservoir would have been made redundant by the Hurleston Reservoir fed via the Ellesmere Company's Welsh line.

It was Jessop as contractor in partnership with James Pinkerton who cut the line from Beeston to Nantwich, starting in 1778, and finished the canal as it was to stand.

William Jessop (1745-1814) was to become the leading canal engineer of the canal mania period (1789-96). He was the principal engineer for the Ellesmere Canal Company between 1791 and 1801 with Thomas Telford as assistant.

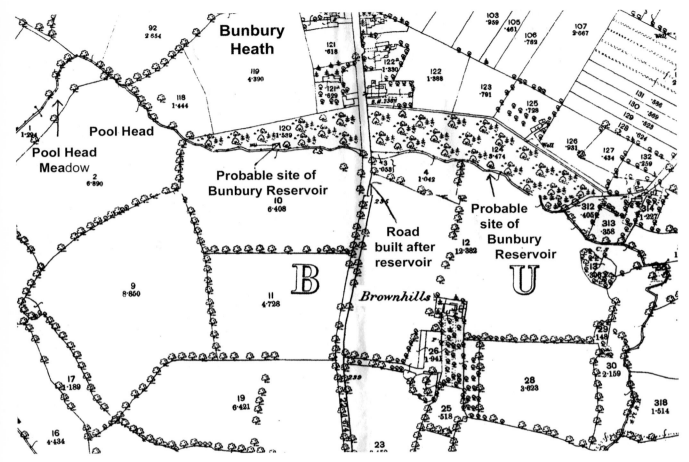

Bunbury Reservoir

Lost for 200 years, the probable reservoir site was rediscovered using research for this book. Company minutes revealed that the reservoir, surveyed by John Moon, had to be built with embankments and would have contained about a thousand locks of water (say 15 million gallons). The owner of the land, John Fern of Brownhills, partially drained the reservoir when his rent was not paid. A search of the area of Bunbury Heath revealed three possible site, one to the north was too small, one to the south had no embankments and still retained its medieval field names by 1839. Whereas the 'plantation' on the 1839 tithe map was a modern name, is directly north of Brownhills, had a clear embankment at the east end, and had two field names, Pool Head and Pool Head Meadow at its western end. The Tarporley-Whitchurch Turnpike was built in 1828 cutting the reservoir, by then probably a plantation. The western part of the now mature woodland has deep drainage channels still visible whilst an embankment can still be found in the publicly accessible part of the wood at the eastern end.

James Pinkerton (c1736-1784) was the oldest brother of a two generation family who were the first and only nationwide canal contractors. James and his brother, John (d1813) were the family firm's leaders. After 1780, John appears to have become the chief contractor in the family. Another brother, Robert (fl 1775-1796) was also involved. Three of James' sons were involved in the next generation of the firm, James Jr. (c1766-c1840), Francis (fl1785-1810) and George (fl1785-1805). They were linked with Jessop for 20 years starting from 1774, when Jessop chose Pinkerton as contractor on the Selby Canal. The relationship had difficulties on the Dudley Canal in 1785 where Pinkerton had a contract. Both he and Jessop signed a bond of fulfillment. Pinkerton was not able to fulfil and had to pay back £2000 but Jessop was released from the bond.

Joseph Turner (c.1729-1807) appears to have carried out engineering work, presumably on a contractual basis. He was said to be the leading architect in Cheshire and North Wales. Amongst his many works in Chester were the Bridgegate, the Watergate and the rebuild of the Inner Pentice. In North Wales his works included the new bridge at Bontuchel near Ruthin, and Ruthin Gaol. On the canal he may have built the Water Tower (Northgate) Locks, he built an arched bridge on Dee Lane (Canal Street) in 1780, and, in 1793, the Bridge of Sighs. Around the same time a newspaper advert announced a large auction of imported wood from his yard.

Ellesmere Canal

John Duncombe (d.1810) from Oswestry was appointed engineer, in 1796, to determine the line of the junction with the Ellesmere Canal. The following year, Duncombe moved to the Ellesmere Canal Company as their surveyor. Later he became best known for his association with Telford.

The Chester Company authorised **John Fletcher** (1756-1835) as their surveyor to work alongside John Duncombe on the link with the Ellesmere Canal from Whitchurch. Fletcher went on to work as a contractor for the Ellesmere Company on the Hordley - Weston Lullingfields section in 1795 and the Whitchurch Branch in 1796, then the Church Bridge, Norbury Section in 1801 Together with his partner John Simpson, contracts grossed over £40,000.

The eldest son of a husbandman (agricultural labourer or smallholder), John first became a schoolmaster In Chester, but went on to buy the failing Chester Chronicle. A libel suite landed him in prison for six months but he rose again to become mayor of the city. He was said to enjoy a considerable reputation amongst contemporaries, and to have *encouraged all kinds of enthusiasts, inventors and projectors.* His friend, Telford, described him as an *able mathematician and mechanic* when crediting his observation on mills, and it was Fletcher writing as *Projector* in his own paper on 29th May 1779 who promoted *a new communication by water from Chester to Liverpool... not subject to the present necessity of a tedious, expensive and dangerous passage around the West Point of Wirrall.* Twenty years later, it was Fletcher that registered the first packet boat from Chester to Ellesmere Port. He also owned a timber yard and several flats on the Chester Canal and the Mersey.

As well as building the new road from Wrexham to Llangollen, Fletcher *set out the racecourse* and built the first grandstand on it, funded by subscription. He was employed as a surveyor by the Post Office for *a great number of years.*

In order to progress the notion of a grand waterways route between the Severn and the Mersey a group of promoters worked between 1789 and 1791 with Duncombe and Joseph and **William Turner** (c1795-c1820). The latter was an architect from Whitchurch and Joseph's cousin. He surveyed the Whitchurch Branch (ie. the proposed Eastern Canal, see Ellesmere Canal, page 53) and **Arthur Davies** was also involved. A rivalry ensued between Turner and Telford after Turner unsuccessfully competed for the post with the glorious title of *General Agent, Engineer, Architect and Overlooker of the Works* in 1793. The rivalry was strengthened by Turner becoming a member of the Committee until 1795 when he still remained as a shareholder. Revenge was sweet in 1810 when he successfully altered Telford's plans for Whitchurch basin. However, in 1815 he was declared bankrupt.

The Wirral Line was *surveyed, designed and mapped* by Joseph Turner, Morris, Cawley and **John Chamberlaine** and went to quarter sessions at Chester in 1792.

Chamberlaine's inclusion as part of this team is interesting in that it demonstrates another prolonged and varied involvement in the development of local waterways. He was a key person in the early stages of the Chester Canal. A local businessman, he had properties in Watergate Street and later bought the old jousting croft to build Queen Street, alongside the newly-built canal. He had various other interests including coal merchandising and gravel extraction. In 1769 he had been *elected a councilman* and made the city aware of the threat posed to local business by the Trent and Mersey Canal.

He was involved in the early survey with Weston and Allen and gave evidence in Parliament. In 1774. Although he asked for 100 guineas for every year he had been helping the company they only paid him 100 guineas in all, perhaps because the treasurer was feeling the pinch,

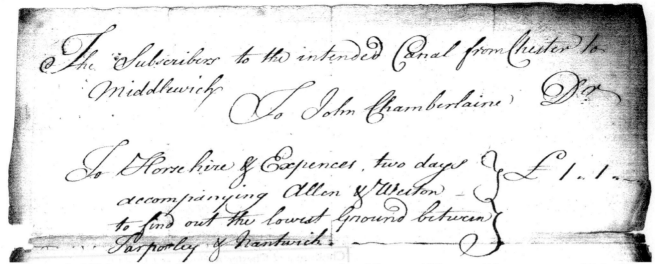

An early bill from John Chamberlaine accompanying Allen and Weston *(Also see pages 27 & 29)*

Cheshire RO Z/TAV/55

but this was still a considerable amount for the time, indicating the level of his contribution. His interests in the canal may, however, have been to the detriment of his other businesses as he was often severely in arrears for his warehouses, causing him to be the subject of council minutes.

Thomas Telford's (1757-1834) appointment in 1793 was part time as he continued to hold his post as Surveyor for Public Works for Shropshire. Jessop had created the canal company's post because he could not supervise construction in the middle of the canal mania. Like Brindley, Telford became one of the icons of his time. His origins were Scottish and he trained as a stonemason. The relative roles of Jessop and Telford in their various joint projects and in particular Pontcysyllte Aqueduct are disputed to the extent of a conspiracy theory surrounding the disappearance of Jessop's papers. It is telling of our culture that one individual is sought as the source of inspiration for an achievement like Pontcysyllte, even though Telford himself referred to it as *your aqueduct* in letters to Matthew Davidson, the resident engineer. The aqueduct was also a source of grievance for William Turner whose masonry scheme was rejected in favour of Telford's *stream in the sky*.

Jessop left in 1801 and Telford worked with ***Thomas Denson*** (d.1811), the resident engineer. Denson was Duncombe's clerk from the early days of the Ellesmere and replaced him as Engineer in 1803 until his death. He assisted Telford in his role as Shropshire's County Surveyor.

287

Telford later rebuilt Beeston Locks and laid out the Middlewich Branch with **William A Provis** (1792-1832). Provis worked extensively with Telford, initially doing surveys and drawings, and later as a resident engineer, as recorded on deposited plans. He also drew designs for the dock works at Ellesmere Port.

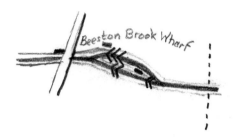

Birmingham and Liverpool Junction Canal

The line was surveyed by **D Houghton**, land surveyor, and Provis under Telford's direction. **William Cubitt** (1785-1861) took over as engineer in 1833. Cubitt was a Norfolk man with a varied career. His father was a windmiller and Cubitt devised the 'patent sails' allowing the mill shutters to be controlled by a single striking rod. He invented the prison treadmill and built and managed a gasworks. He had previous canal experience with the Oxford and the Worcester and Birmingham companies. Telford had suggested improvements at Ellesmere Port which were carried out, after his death, by Cubitt with Provis as his contractor.

SOURCES

Primary

CRO = Chester & Cheshire Archives TNA = The National Archives SA = Shropshire Archives

Proclamations Book Z/MP1 p33 CRO
A Three Week Tour of Lancashire, Cheshire and North Wales by G H Steele 1808 CRO
Assembly Book 4 Z/AB4 CRO
Letters from J Brindley, subscribers names, accounts, minutes of 2 meetings, invoices from Sam Weston & others Z/TAV/55 CRO
City Treasurers Accounts Z/TAD/10 CRO
Chester Canal Minutes RAIL 816 TNA
Chester & Ellesmere Canal Minutes RAIL 826 TNA
Ellesmere Canal Minutes RAIL 827 microfilm TNA
Birmingham & Liverpool Junction Minute Books RAIL 808 TNA
Shropshire Union Minutes RAIL 623 TNA
Plans of the Intended Navigable Canal & field book with list of landowners Z/QRP1-3 CRO
Chester Canal Act 12 Geo III c.75
Field Plans c1774 British Waterways Museum, Stoke Bruerne.
'Adams Weekly Courant'/ 'Chester Courant' microfilm at CRO
Journal of the House of Commons: T&M Canal 1766
Journal of the House of Commons: Chester Canal 1770-2
Deeds of John Chamberlaine ZCR669 14-21 CRO, ZCHD/9/57 CRO, CR37 1-8 CRO
Map of Chester by Sam Weston. Pub Hunter 1789 PM18/4 CRO
Joseph Turner, settle disputes, improvement for Pentice, arch, Exchange, Eastgate, freedom gratis, Watergate etc ZAB4 CRO
Map of proposed canal Chester-Mersey pub. Hunter PM11/10 CRO
Map of Chester Canal, Gentleman's Magazine PM11/1 CRO
Chester Guide & Directory. P Broster 1781 (1st Ed) & 1782(2nd Ed)
1796 Act of Parliament Z/CLA 10 CRO
Register of Boats 1795 QDN/4/1 CRO
Extract of register of boats, in waterway order. 1795 QDN/4/2 CRO
Register of Canal Boats, Nantwich 1877 LUN/ 4452/1 CRO
Register of Canal Boats, Chester 1877 DH/1/1-6 CRO
Several deposited maps of the Ellesmere Canal, B&LC etc QDP1, 2, 3,5, 9, 10, 14, 15, 17, 21, 64, 77, 78, 90, 148, 222, 235, 305, 475. CRO
Several maps of Eastern Canal, Western Canal, Extensions & Deviations of the Ellesmere Canal, Ellesmere & Chester Canal to Middlewich, Birmingham & Liverpool Junction Canal etc DP 287, 288B, 290, 292, 295a, 296, 298, 304, 304a, 304b, 304c, 305. SA
Postcards Ellesmere Canal PC/E/8/1. SA
Postcards Whitchurch Canal PC/W/14/3. SA
Map of Cheshire (showing old course of canal at Beeston) 1831. Pub A Bryant CRO
Narrow Boat by LTC Rolt (first pub. 1944)
Cheese Boat 'Peel' RAIL 1019/8 TNA

Snowy by Berlie Doherty and Keith Bowen. Pub Collins (1992)
Journal of Inspector of Canal Boats, Chester 1924-55 ZDH/3/3 CRO
Journal of the Inspector of Canal Boats, Nantwich LRN/103 CRO
Cheshire Observer CRO
Chester Chronicle CRO
Chester Courant CRO
Records of W J Yarwood & Sons Ltd, shipbuilders of Northwich DDX 289 CRO
City of Chester Minute Books, 1933-4. Chester History & Heritage

Secondary
Available at Chester Library

Chester Canal Projects by Edwin A Shearing. Pub Journal of the Railway & Canal Historical Society Vol XXVIII Nos 3 & 4
Canals of the West Midlands, The, Vol 5 by Charles Hadfield. First Pub David & Charles 1966
Illustrated History of Canal & River Navigations, The, by Edward Paget Tomlinson. Pub Sheffield Academic Press
The Shroppie, A portrait of the Shropshire Union Canal by Thomas Pellow and Paul Bowen. Pub The Landscape Press 1988 (2nd edition 1994)
Canal to Llangollen by Thomas Pellow and Paul Bowen. Pub The Landscape Press 1985
Voices from the Waterways by Jean Stone. Pub Sutton Publishing 1997
Richard Whitworth, Journal vol XXVII no 4 1982 p426
Chester Guide, The, by Gordon Emery. Pub Gordon Emery 2003
Curious Chester by Gordon Emery. Pub Gordon Emery 1999
Ellesmere Port 1795-1960 by T W Roberts. Pub Gisborne, New Zealand 1995
Britain's Canal & River Craft by Edward Paget-Tomlinson. 1979, Paperback edition 1993.
Charles Hadfield, Passenger Boats on the Chester Canal, 1775-1806, by Charles Hadfield in Railway & Canal Historical Society Journal in March 1998 (Reprinted from May 1956).
British Canals: An Illustrated History by Charles Hadfield (David & Charles, Newton Abbot, Devon, 4th ed. 1973)
The Canal Age by Charles Hadfield Pub David & Charles 1968
The Hundred of Wirral by Philip Sulley Pub Birkenhead 1889
The Ellesmere and Llangollen Canal by Edward Wilson 1975
Claytons of Oldbury, by Alan Faulkner. Robert Wilson Publications.
FMC: A Short History of Fellows Morton and Clayton Limited by Alan Faulkner. Robert Wilson Publications.
The Shropshire Union Narrowboats, in Waterways World (September 1995) by Alan Faulkner.
J Crichton & Co. Shipbuilders by John Dixon & Geoff Pickard 2002
The Ellesmere and Llangollen Canal, An Historical Background by E A Wilson MA, Pub Phillimore & Co Ltd 1975
Bunbury, The History of a Cheshire Village Ed: Frank A Latham Pub: Local History Group 1989
The King's England, Cheshire by Arthur Mee Pub Hodder and Stoughton 1968
Tattenhall, The History of a Cheshire Village Ed Frank A Latham Pub Local History Group 1977 Photos Derek Pierce and others
A History of Cheshire; Volume 9, Cheshire 1660 – 1780: restoration to Industrial Revolution by J Howard Hodson Pub Cheshire Community Council Publications Trust Ltd 1978
Waterways World Guides 1981 and 2004 editions
Cruising on the Shropshire Union Canal, British Waterways Inland Cruising Booklet c1957

2000 Years of Building - Chester's Architectural Legacy Ed Stephen Langtree and Alan Comyns Pub The Chester Civic Trust - 2001

Chronicle of Chester by Herbert Hughes Pub Macdonald and Jane's 1975

Biographical Dictionary of Engineers, A Ed A W Skempton Pub Thomas Telford 2002

William Jessop, Engineer by C Hadfield & A W Skempton 1979

The great days of the canals by Anthony Burton Pub David & Charles 1989

Available in Chester and Cheshire Record Office

Early steam tugs on the Birmingham & Liverpool Junction Canal by Terry Kavanagh, Waterways Journal Vol 2.

The Life and Times of Jack Woolley, Fly-Boatman by Terry Kavanagh, in Waterways Journal Vol 5.

Flats and Flatmen of the Rivers Mersey and Irwell by Terry Kavanagh, in Waterways Journal Vol 6.

Early Mersey Passenger Steamers up to 1840 by Terry Kavanagh in A Nautical Miscellany, ed John Shepherd, published by the Liverpool Nautical Research Society, 1998.

Mersey Sailing Ferry Boats, by Terry Kavanagh in LNRS Bulletin, Vol 40, no. 1 (Summer 1996). :

Shropshire Union Flats and Flatmen by Terry Kavanagh in Waterways Journal Vol. 7

Available in the Boat Museum Archive, Ellesmere Port.

Terry Kavanagh's articles 'Steam on the Shroppie', RE:PORT No. 80 (August 1987); 'The Millers Tale', RE:PORT No. 88 (May 1989); and 'The Leeds and Liverpool Canal Tugs', RE:PORT No. 117 (July 1995).

Alan Faulkner, 'Steam on the Shroppie' and Dr E. A. Shearing, 'More Steam on the Shroppie', both in RE:PORT No. 81 (January 1988).

**A horsedrawn flat (probably 'Jeanie')
at Christleton Bridge c1920s**

King Charles' Tower
Grosvenor Museum

INDEX

Artistic licence: This engraving of the Dee Basin shows Chester Cathedral standing above the city walls rather than the Infirmary which was actually there.

OTHER CONTACTS

FRIENDS OF 'TOWY' *for the preservation of Narrowboat 'Towy'*
www.freewebs.com/Towy

THE SATURN RESTORATION PROJECT *to save a Shropshire Union Fly Boat*
Membership Secretary, Shropshire Union Fly-Boat Restoration Society Ltd., Three Bridges, Grindley Brook, WHITCHURCH SY13 4QH

OTHER BOOKS from Gordon Emery

Hidden Highways of Cheshire by RJA Dutton £9.99 *Cheshire's landscape unfolds as John Dutton takes you on a fascinating tour of ancient highways hidden by time and the changing use of the countryside. Find salters' ways and medieval lanes with a guide that is second to none.*

Curious Chester by Gordon Emery £15.95 *If you thought you knew Chester then you need to read this book - 2000 years of Chester's history.*

Chester Inside Out by Gordon Emery £7.95 *The ideal companion to Curious Chester. See the alleys and hidden places in the city. With four walks.*

Miller of Dee by Roy Wilding £9.99 *A well-researched guide to the many mills of Chester through the centuries.*

Death in Chester by Roy Wilding £11.95 *From gladiators to the Black Death, from Roman to Victorian gravestones, with a few hangings and ghosts thrown in for good measure.*

The Chester Guide by Gordon Emery £4.95 *If you're visiting Chester or just want a quick run down on its history, this smaller Chester guide is for you.*

Curious Clwyd, volumes 1 & 2 by Gordon Emery £11.95 each *A pictorial album of oddities in northeast Wales.*

Family Walks on the North Wales Coast by Gordon Emery £2.95 (half price) *Although ten years old all these 16 walks (1-5 miles with shorter alternatives) are still available by car or public transport.*

Available from bookshops or by post (add £1 p&p) from:
Gordon Emery, 27 Gladstone Road, CHESTER, CH1 4BZ
Send SAE for full list.